IMAGES
of America

NEW BERLIN AND THE BUFFALO VALLEY

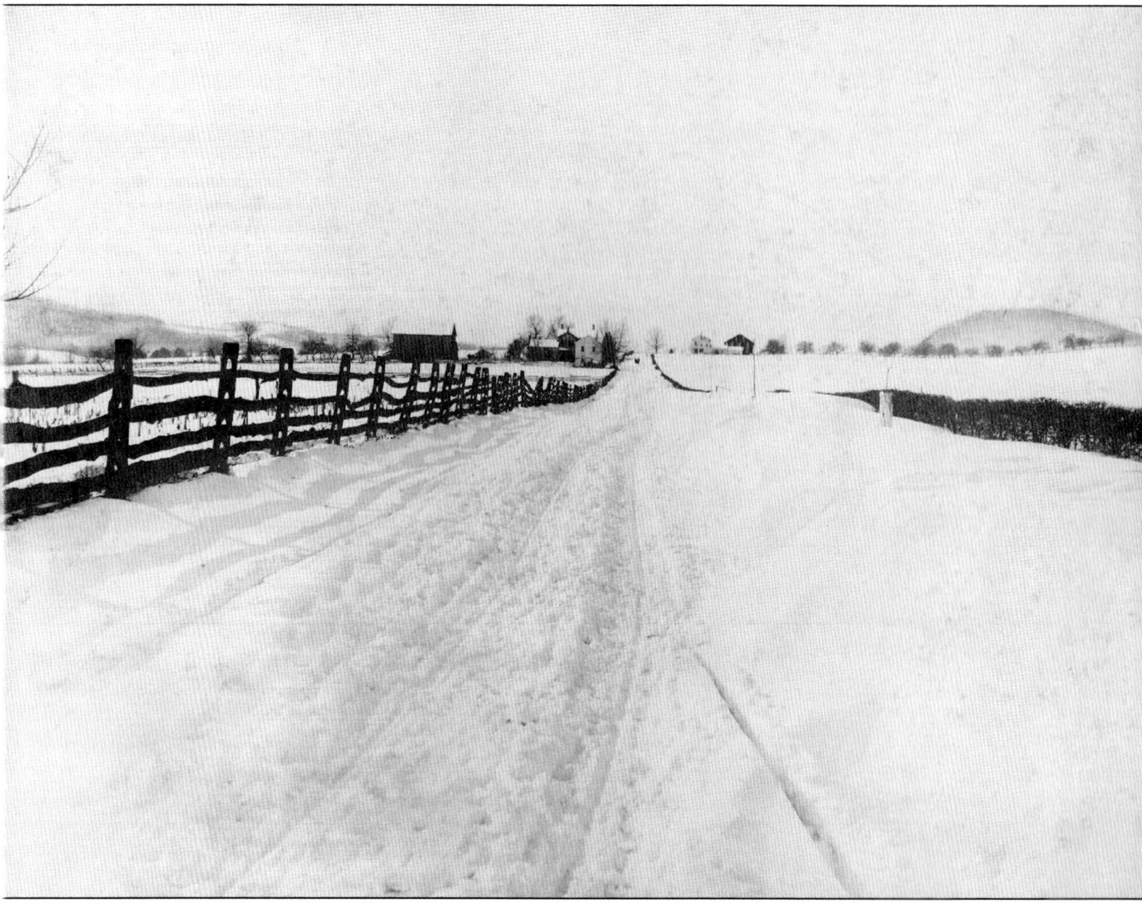

Jack's Mountain was photographed in 1904, looking west from New Berlin. The farm on the left, or south, side of Route 304 was then Homer Smith's and, until the late 1900s, Robert and Alice Hummel's residence. On the right, north, side was one of the original Christopher Seebold III farms that, until recently, remained in the Blaine Seebold family. Route 304 bends northward to Dice. (New Berlin Heritage Association.)

On the Cover: The Union Seminary opened for instruction in New Berlin in 1856. It was renamed Central Pennsylvania College in 1887 and became affiliated with Albright College in Reading until 1902. Teacher Ida Bowman and her Central Pennsylvania College students are seen in a cabinet photograph in 1897. From 1902 to 1911, a new school without religious affiliation operated under the name, again, of Union Seminary. (NBHA.)

IMAGES
of America

NEW BERLIN AND THE BUFFALO VALLEY

Jeannette Lasansky

ARCADIA
PUBLISHING

ISBN 978-0-7385-9838-3

Published by Arcadia Publishing
Charleston, South Carolina

Printed in the United States of America

Library of Congress Control Number: 2012947936

For all general information, please contact Arcadia Publishing:
Telephone 843-853-2070
Fax 843-853-0044
E-mail sales@arcadiapublishing.com
For customer service and orders:
Toll-Free 1-888-313-2665

Visit us on the Internet at www.arcadiapublishing.com

Contents

ACKNOWLEDGMENTS

Teamwork has made *New Berlin and the Buffalo Valley* possible. In particular, I would like to thank the following: Diane Lengle and Joan Maurer, who have provided invaluable assistance in my working with the New Berlin Heritage Association collection; Donald Snyder, who gathered Mazeppa images; David Goehring, for sharing railroad information; and Jack L. Fisher, who researched one-room schools, early land patentees, and more. Lois Huffines helped search the courthouse collection, and Alan Richard scanned all of the images for this Arcadia project.

We are also indebted to those who have worked on aspects of New Berlin's heritage, in particular: Raymond Allen, Vincent Barsch, Louis Eaton, Robert DeVett, Gary Hackenberg, Mellie Leiby, Gloria Maize, Harry Maurer, Joan Maurer, Mark Michael, Robert Miller, Marie Purnell Musser, James Ritter, Ray Smith, Winifred Smith, David Solomon, Charles M. Snyder, Paul Souders, Ruth Spangler, Margaret Strome, and Logan Swanger.

Thanks also go to the Union County Historical Society and the New Berlin Heritage Association, along with Fred Blyler, John Bower, Kathryn Dieffenderfer, Vicki Garinger, Beth Johnson Hackenberg, Sharon Herald, Mike and Carol Manbeck, Billy Mattern, Jeffrey Mensch, Evelyn and Donald Miller, Ronald Nornhold, Robert Page, Joseph Prah, Eleanor Rawitz, Judy Everett Reed, Janice and Donald Snyder, Gary and Ruth-Alice Spangler, and Cherry Will, who shared images.

My introductory text was reviewed by Patricia Longley. Betsy Robertson was the book's final copy editor. Shawn McLaughlin, Union County's director of planning, contemplated Union County's future.

I thank Nada Gray, cochair of Union County's 1813–2013 Committee. She suggested Arcadia as our publisher as she headed this, her second, bicentennial celebration. The first was in 1976. For financial support and encouragement, thanks also go to Union County's present commissioners, Preston Boop, John Mathias, and John Showers, who have recognized the value of these efforts, as have Union County commissioners since the early 1970s.

Please join us as we celebrate Union County's bicentennial. We enter into the county's 21st year with a better understanding of those who have gone before and the times in which they lived. Birthdays such as this are a great excuse to pause.

Images that appear in this volume courtesy of the Union County Historical Society are designated with the abbreviation UCHS and are followed by a collection number. Images that appear courtesy of the New Berlin Heritage Association are noted as NBHA.

INTRODUCTION

Northumberland County, the mother of many counties, was a large landmass of 15,000 square miles. From 1792 to 1813, it included parts of present-day Bradford, Centre, Clearfield, Clinton, Lycoming, Mifflin, and Schuylkill Counties as well as the whole of present-day Sullivan, Susquehanna, Wyoming, Lackawanna, Luzerne, Snyder, and Union Counties.

In 1813, roughly 649 square miles and 15,000 residents would constitute newly formed Union County, bounded by the Susquehanna River on the east and mountain ridges trending northeast on its southern and northern borders, with a short western flank nearly three miles long. Centre and Mifflin Counties were to Union's west; Clinton and Lycoming Counties were to Union's north; Perry was to its southern side; and Columbia (later, Montour as well) and what remained of Northumberland County were on its eastern flank across the Susquehanna.

As was the pattern elsewhere in Pennsylvania, an increasing population and demographic shifts dictated the need for closer government in areas of significant settlement growth. While the county seat location for Union County was still being determined, its first court session was held in Mifflinburg in February 1814. By May 1815, Longstown (or Longa Stettle, later called New Berlin), named for George Long and centrally located in the newly formed Union County, was designated the official county seat. In 1787, Long had bought 226 acres along Penns Creek for about $1,200 from George Albright, the original patent holder and another Lancastrian. Long purchased an additional 65 acres from patent holder John Ord Jr. In 1792, town lots were surveyed, with the first sales being made on January 18, 1793, to Adam Snyder of Berks County, with John Mitchell of Buffalo Township being the first householder. Later that year, there were 10 families residing in Longstown.

As soon as its brick courthouse was completed, New Berlin became the official center of Union County government as well as of commerce, culture, and education—both secular and sectarian. New Berlin would serve as a gateway to the southern part of Union County, comprising the townships of Centre, Jackson, Franklin, Middle Creek, Penns, Washington, Chapman, Perry, Beaver, and West Beaver. It also served the north-central or adjacent parts of Union County: Union, Limestone, Buffalo, and West Buffalo Townships, most occupying an area known as "the Buffalo Valley." When Union County was split in 1855, its southern portion of nearly 332 square miles, below Penns Creek, became Snyder County. The county seat for Snyder became Middleburg, almost due south of New Berlin, and the new Union County seat moved to Lewisburg, northeast and on the Susquehanna River.

New Berlin and the Buffalo Valley will focus on how the initially bustling town of New Berlin settled into more leisurely 20th-century activities and contained a population that hovered between 820 and 900 people from the 1970s until the present day. Photographs and text will feature the farmlands and rural industry nearest to New Berlin: Dry Valley, Dice, and White Springs. Then, areas farther into the Buffalo Valley—hamlets like Vicksburg, Buffalo Crossroads, Mazeppa, and

Cowan—will be highlighted. Lastly, the book will touch upon dense woodlands near Forest Hill and Spruce Run with nearby Red Bank and Rand.

Areas that appear pastoral and perhaps sleepy today were centers of religious fervor in 1772, when the German Baptist Brethren or Dunkards in Battletown/Barberstown (Dice/White Springs) arrived; when "the silk stocking congregation" of Presbyterians at Buffalo Crossroads gathered in a grove starting in 1773; and when the United Evangelical Church, established in New Berlin in 1807, was followed by its affiliated Union Seminary (1856–1883) and Central Pennsylvania College (1887–1902). Also, from the 1830s throughout the 19th century, plain-sect Amish from Lancaster settled in Limestone and Buffalo Townships. The period of local religious fervor mirrored national movements of the late-1770s to the Civil War.

In the beginning, New Berlin had 44 log residences and businesses and one frame structure. Stone and brick construction was soon to follow. In 1813, there were 59 taxable residents, or 45 households—either landowners or tenants not including children or wives. There also were free African Americans living in the white households of John Lashalls, John Louden, and William Wilson. As late as 1824, two African American men were sold as slaves by New Berlin's John Brobst.

The region was well positioned for continued growth. When Penns Creek was running high in the spring, it provided water access by arks to the Susquehanna and Baltimore and, starting in the 1830s, to a nearby canal network that extended to Philadelphia. A wooden covered bridge connected the area to the south, while a road near Lick or Switzer Run skirted the western edge of New Berlin Mountain and led into the heart of Buffalo Valley. Nearby was Haines (now County Line) Road, an important link between Berks and Centre Counties.

By October 1815, New Berlin's preeminent building—a two-story brick courthouse—was finished. Two years later, a stone jail and wall located at the corner of Market and Plum Streets were constructed by Frederick Hipple of Centre Township. Also erected was a stone building that stands at 135 Front Street, the former home of tanner Abraham Shrock, while a brick "state house," adjacent to the courthouse, provided county offices and jury rooms. The Emmanuel Reformed Church on Vine Street was the third imposing brick building, erected in 1821 on the land of Christopher Seebold II, an ark builder and operator, tavern owner, contractor, and miller. A gristmill—perhaps the most essential business in establishing any community—had been built in Longstown as early as 1780, while others, such as Seebold's on Switzer's Run, were close at hand.

New Berlin became a church-dominated town, displaying separate spires for Presbyterians, Lutheran, Reformed, Methodist, and United Evangelical congregations. It was a town populated by attorneys, government officials, and jurists, as well as active printing establishments that met general as well as church printing needs starting in the mid-19th century. There were the customary shops for any good-sized population center: carpenters, turners, and joiners to meet households' needs; coopers to build arks and barrels; blacksmiths, wheelwrights, gunsmiths, and tinsmiths; potters, weavers, and tailors; tanners and saddlers; and physicians. Grist and saw millers, too, were found in the county seat.

The settled and prosperous community represented by these buildings in the early 19th century was a far cry from the living conditions 60 years earlier. In 1755, during the French and Indian War, there were about 25 families living in the area from White Springs to Dice, and from Longman's Town to the Winfield area—what was called Buffalo Valley. When the British and Americans under Gen. Edward Braddock were defeated near Fort Duquesne in Western Pennsylvania by the French and their Indian allies, the Indians entered Buffalo Valley, probably via Penns Creek (Karondinha/Kaarondinhoh) or the Warriors' Path that went from Franktown near Hollidaysburg east through Woodward, White Springs, Winfield, and Sunbury. Early European settlers, many of the LeRoys or Kings, the Leiningers, the Brylingers, and Licks, were killed or captured at that time. The Indians took 15 horses, 15 scalps, and 10 prisoners. When peace was restored in the early 1760s, the Beattys, Bickels, Boveards, Emericks, Foughts, Hoys, Hunters, Klinesmiths, Overmeyers, Shivelys, Smiths, Sutherlands, and Youngs were among the new names in Buffalo Valley.

The Treaty of Fort Stanwix in 1768 with the Iroquois and the "New Purchase" concluded this period of unrest. It gave Commonwealth proprietors Thomas and Richard Penn six special Proprietary Manors and awarded land to the officers of the Pontiac War. The majority of tracts were allotted to settlers via a lottery held on April 3, 1769. Applications with one's name and a description of the land desired were placed in a trunk and drawn, then numbered in the order of the drawing. Settlers got a warrant, had land surveyed, and then patents were issued. A total of 2,782 applications were made on the first day. This was an era of extensive land surveying, and Samuel Maclay, a farmer, legislator, and surveyor who lived near the Dreisbach Church in Buffalo Valley's Limestone Township, played an especially active role.

By 1769, John Lee had built a stone house (still standing) in Winfield; John Beatty was in New Berlin; John Wilson was at the mouth of Turtle Creek; Jacob Grozean was at the present Grove's Mill; and Barney Parsons was near Spruce Run. Lee's house was the site of the area's last Indian massacre, on August 13, 1782, near the end of the American Revolution. Many settlers were already clearing land. The need for local government became apparent, so, on March 21, 1772, the county of Northumberland was created from the northern parts of Berks, Bedford, Cumberland, Lancaster, and Northampton Counties. The new county seat was named Sunbury, after William Penn's childhood home, and was within reach of the territory's settlers. Other counties would break off from this mother county over time.

During the decades leading up to 1855, New Berlin prospered and was Union County's major cultural hub, as reflected in the dominance of the fine brick houses built in the first half of the 19th century. Some of these structures had attached businesses, such as what became Dr. Samuel Wilson's, at 300 Market Street. There were several large hotels, since destroyed by fires. Fine long guns, high-case clocks, and painted sets of chairs and rockers were in demand, and area craftsmen obliged. Stave barrel makers, wooden pump makers, and wheelwrights plied their trades along or near Penns Creek. Schools were built to educate the local youth through the eighth grade.

Patents important to this study were Thomas Cavet's, thought to be the land originally granted by the Penns in February 1755 to Sebastian Leyninger (Leininger), who was killed nine months later by Indians, or the area that was known as Battletown (later, Dice). Also, land granted to Thomas Craig in 1767, its patent then issued to Reuben Haines in 1772, and subsequently purchased by Robert Barber, was called Barberton (later, White Springs). The 619-acre tract on which the Dreisbach Church was built, called "Isabella," was awarded to Capt. William Plunkett, father of Elizabeth Maclay. That parcel was sold to Martin and Anna Eva Dreisbach in 1775. Nearby, the town of Vicksburg would be established on another "officer tract" called "Kernton," awarded to Capt. Jacob Kern, who had served under Col. Bonquet in the French and Indian War.

Buffalo Crossroads (earlier called McCreights or Sleeptown) was a village situated on two original tracts. The north side, 330.5 acres owned by Henry Sees, was later named Beaver Farm, and the south and east sides, 249.5 acres owned by Edward Bonsall, were later named Beavers' Retreat. Beaver Run crossed both tracts. Boyer Town (also called Union and Unionville, later Mazeppa) was the southwestern tip of a tract awarded to Col. John Kelly, while Guldy's Mill (also called Farmersville, later Cowan) was awarded to Francis Forster, who sold it in 1779 to Jeremiah Parker. Forest Hill was originally granted to Thomas Rees in 1773, and the 56.5-acre tract was later named Rees Addition. Red Bank is located on a tract originally granted to Aaron Levy in 1775 and named Aaron's Staff.

Barbertown, or White Springs, was where the Dunkards, later called United Church of the Brethren, were established in the 1770s by Christian Shively, among others. Physical evidence of this, one of the county's earliest permanent settlements, was preserved until recently: a large hewn log barn and a frame house with sliding interior doors that allowed for large group worship. Near Vicksburg, the Groffdale Mennonite meetinghouse, along with family enterprises such as produce markets, a buggy-making shop, and greenhouses, are evidence of a plain-sect group that prospers more than 200 years later.

Buffalo Crossroads, Mazeppa, and Cowan—with general stores, gristmills, distilleries, sawmills, lumber camps, wheelwright and blacksmith shops, and local schools—exhibit cultural signposts of the past. These places are today home to churches that represent the strong ties of Pennsylvania German descendants to Lutheran and Reformed traditions. Active and fertile farms surround these communities still, though the farmers' Buffalo Valley Grange No. 520 is no longer active in Buffalo Crossroads. Housing clusters retain identities like Red Bank, Rand, and Pleasant Grove. But Forest Hill, with its church, general store, and gas station, remains the major gateway to area recreation facilities. These center on Halfway Run and the Raymond B. Winter State Park, with its CCC-built dam, bridges, and recreational buildings. Nearly 90 years from its founding, this recreational region still provides a welcome refuge from the heat of summer months and a place for winter sports like ice-skating, snow-shoeing, and its annual SnowFest.

One-room schools dotted—and still form part of—the cultural landscape of the Buffalo Valley. Some have place-names like Lick or Switzer (as in a creek) or Vicksburg (a hamlet) or Pontius (as in the surname of the adjacent family that had donated the school grounds). Well into the 1950s, these one-room schools were attended by children in farm families, from first through eighth grades, and from within a two-mile radius. Some schools began as private subscription endeavors, as in White Springs, or were established by vote under Pennsylvania's first public education law of 1834. Those that still stand have had varied uses since closing: as active schools for plain-sect Groffdale Mennonites, who adhere to notions of education that were practiced in an earlier time; as homes, like the Strawbridge School on the eastern edge of Buffalo Township; or as storage facilities for farmers. Some fell into neglect and were subsequently razed. The Red Bank School was kept and used for township meetings by West Buffalo Township and is still publicly owned and maintained.

Starting in the mid-to-late 18th century, people living, working, and celebrating—both communal and personal—were captured in photographs. The daguerreotype, a "modern photograph" of the mid-1800s, was produced by itinerants like Mr. Carscaddon, staying at New Berlin's Kleckner's Hotel. As the 19th century progressed toward the 20th, New Berlin photographer Charles Venus produced cardboard-mounted "cabinet" photographs of town parades. By 1915, Mifflinburg's young amateur photographer and enthusiast Grover Bierly took glass-plate images of prominent buildings; some became real-photo postcards. Urs H. Eisenhower (b. 1858), from Millmont, photographed at least one New Berlin parade and went to Vicksburg and Buffalo Crossroads, where he made real-photo postcards for farm families at 50¢ a dozen. Eisenhower also recorded notable activities that caught his eye, such as the paving of the Old Turnpike (present West Route 45), while area streetscapes, homes, and churches as well as school group portraits were the inclination of Stephen B. Horton (b. 1882). Horton was a boarder at the West Milton Hotel from 1907 to 1911 and a Uneeda Biscuit salesman who traveled the roads of rural Union County. In the 1950s, aerial views of Vicksburg and Mazeppa were taken by companies and disseminated as real-photo postcards.

A great variety of trades and events were photographed as "still lifes." Such moments include Reish distillery workers in Cowan, flour millers in Forest Hill and Mazeppa, the first train ride of the New Berlin/Winfield line, turn-of-the century lumber camps, water pipeline workers, and occasional train wrecks—all documented through photographs. In some cases, names, dates, and places are noted on the photographs' reverse sides. In the 1950s, photography was still primarily a black-and-white medium, but the eye behind the lens was often a family member or friend. The photographs became more private, candid, and closely held.

People remark that, after 1855, Lewisburg and Mifflinburg prospered at the expense of New Berlin. Indeed, urbanization was felt elsewhere in the county rather than in New Berlin and parts of the Buffalo Valley, since modern transportation supplanted Penns Creek arks, the train to New Berlin was short-lived, and Union County's major paved roadway, Route 15, would not be a significant factor as it was for the county's six river towns. As a consequence, New Berlin and the Buffalo Valley would remain relatively unspoiled, peaceful, and filled with reminders of values past, to be thoroughly enjoyed by small businesses and new families today.

One

New Berlin

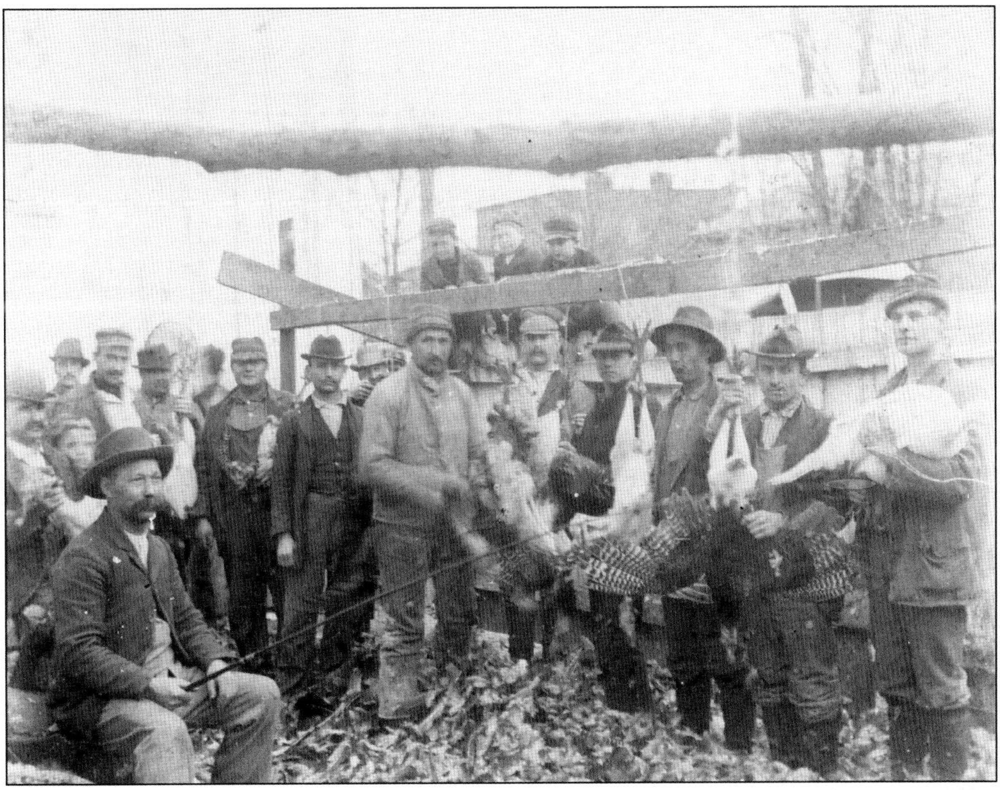

Before Christmas 1905, turkeys are being plucked at the rear of John W. Hoch & Enos Oldt's store at the northeast corner of Front and Vine Streets. Hoch & Oldt's became Calvin Wetzel's, then Joseph Seebold's, and finally Showers' Store. Among those shown here are Enos Oldt (left foreground) and "Banty" Wetzell, Everett Benner, Charles and Bob Spaid, Henry Wittes, Luther Walker, Wesley Shamay, and Henry Solomon. (UCHS, 2011.42.16.)

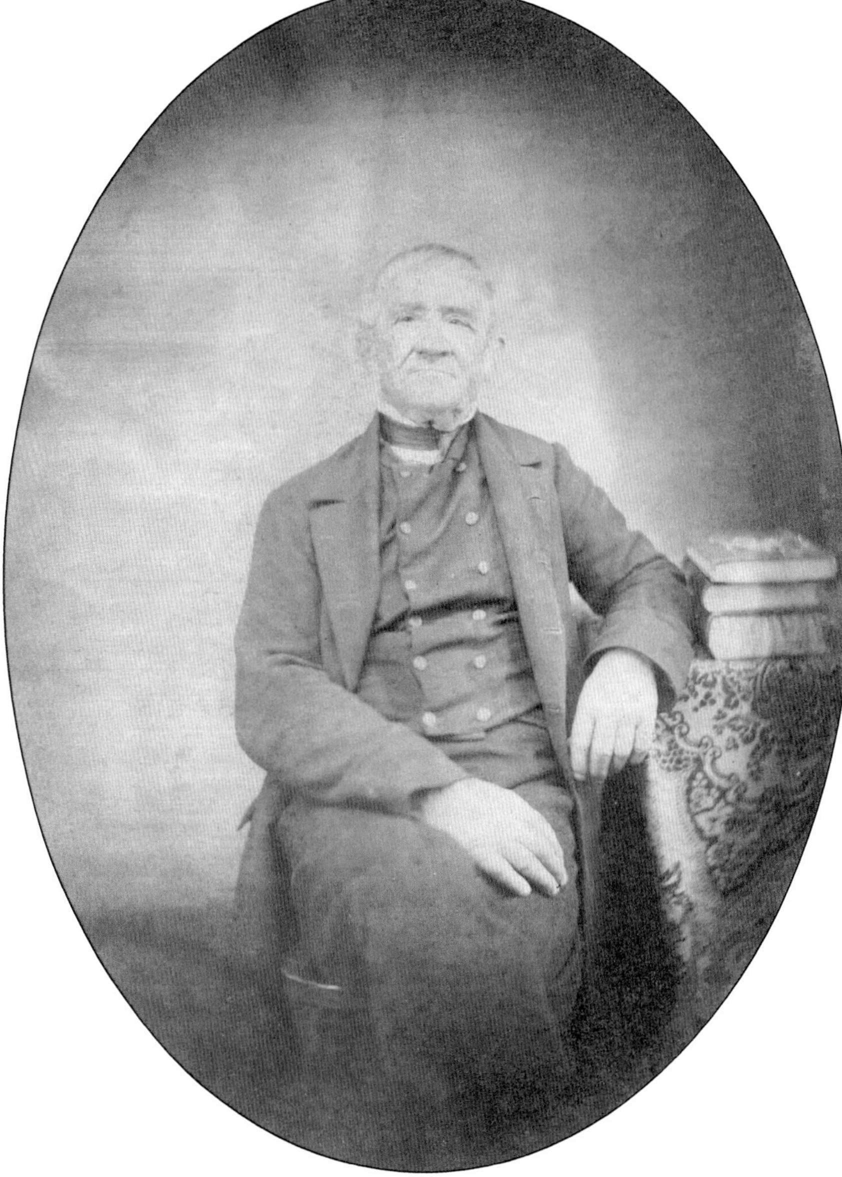

Christopher Seebold II (1763–1839), a Revolutionary War veteran, moved to Longstown in 1795 and was one of 16 male residents. He was granted a five-acre tract that would include the plot on which the first Union County courthouse would stand. Seebold gave $200 toward its construction. One of Seebold's trades was navigating a boat on Penns Creek, carrying produce down the Susquehanna to Baltimore. On return trips, he brought merchandise to New Berlin, using horses to pull his boat upstream. An inventor, Seebold sought a patent for an improvement on the washing machine in 1816. In 1813, he became justice of the peace when Union County was formed; in 1817, he was the local secretary of William Findlay's Democratic-Republican for Governor Committee, and in 1820, he was elected Union County treasurer—the fourth man to hold that office. Seebold also built the Union Hotel in 1818 on the corner of Vine and Market Streets and the German Reformed and Lutheran Church in 1825. He is buried in the New Berlin Cemetery. (Ruth-Alice Seebold Spangler.)

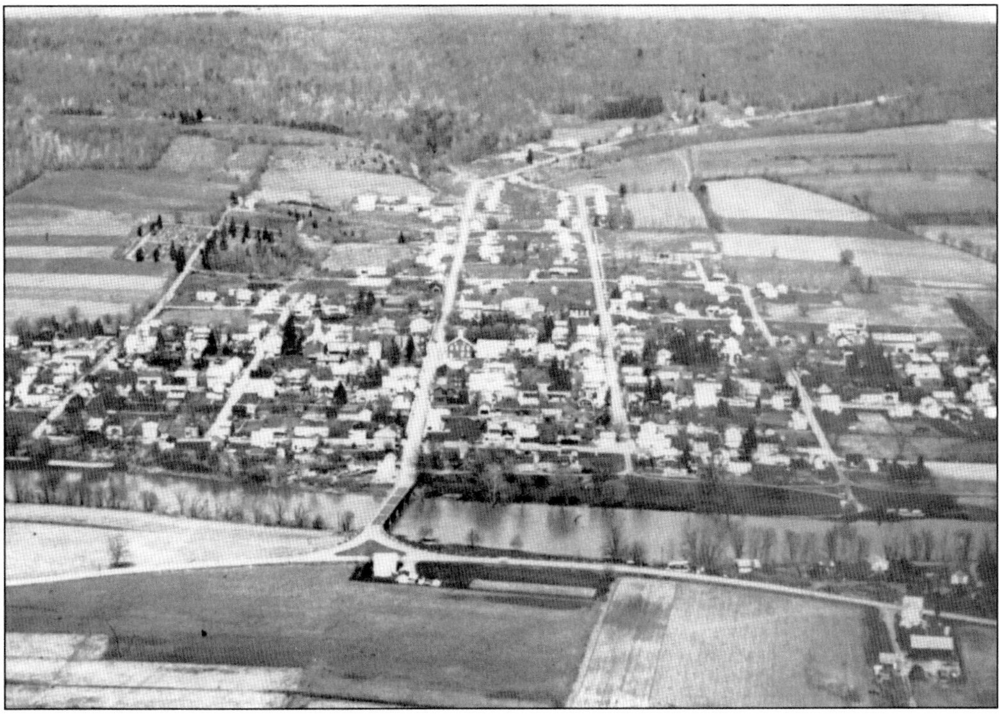

Today, New Berlin (named Longstown in 1792) lies nestled at the base of New Berlin (also known as Shamokin Mountain) and stretches alongside Penns Creek, as it has done since its early settlement period in the 18th century. The above photograph, taken in 1965, displays the proximity of the town and the creek. Penns Creek's waterpower was harnessed by a manmade milldam and used by a gristmill and a sawmill, placed on the north and south banks, respectively. New Berlin's Water Street was located on a high bank so that the creek flooding rarely affected its residents, and this in turn allowed the borough to prosper unimpeded for decades. A covered bridge connected New Berlin to rich farmlands on Penns Creek's south side, such as those shown in the real-photo postcard below. This southern half of Union County was called Snyder County after the split in 1855. (NBHA.)

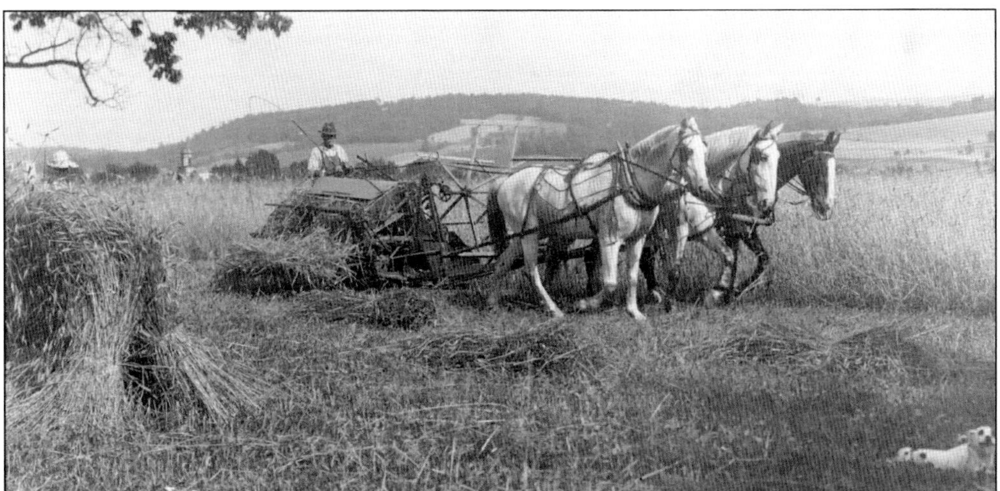

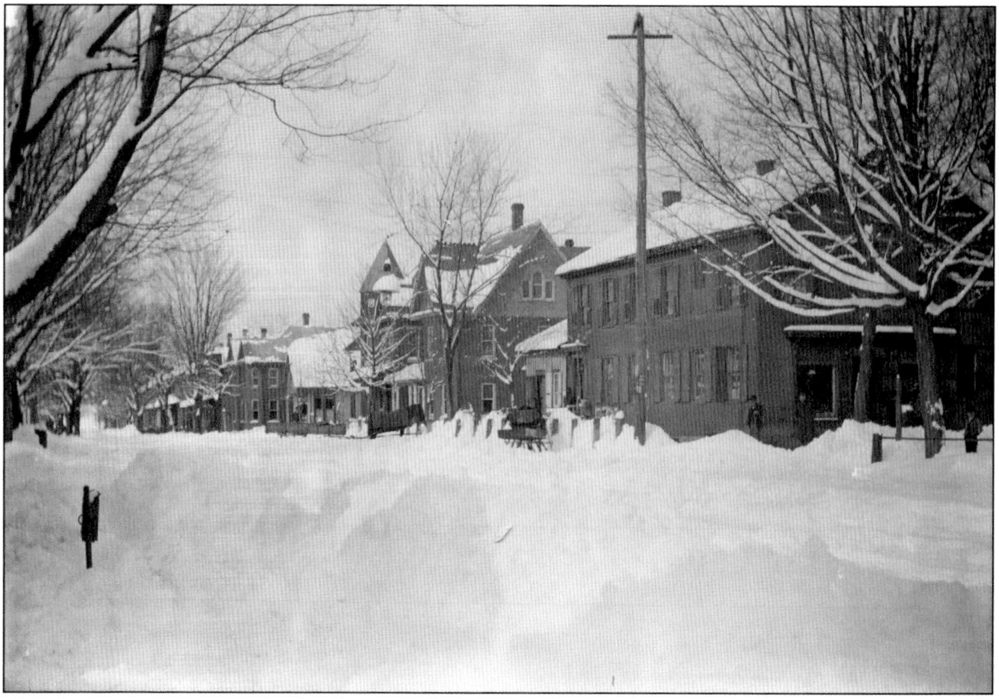

Weather events in New Berlin have included record snowfalls, as in the real-photo postcard of Front Street (above) and a tornado that brought devastation to the Crystal Springs farm of Christopher Seebold V (1861–1936) on June 17, 1920 (below). Son Clarence Seebold (1897–1985) would reminisce how he and his brother Blaine (1902–1977) stood in the kitchen and held the kitchen door shut with all their might while the tornado passed through their property. The high winds flattened the barn. (NBHA.)

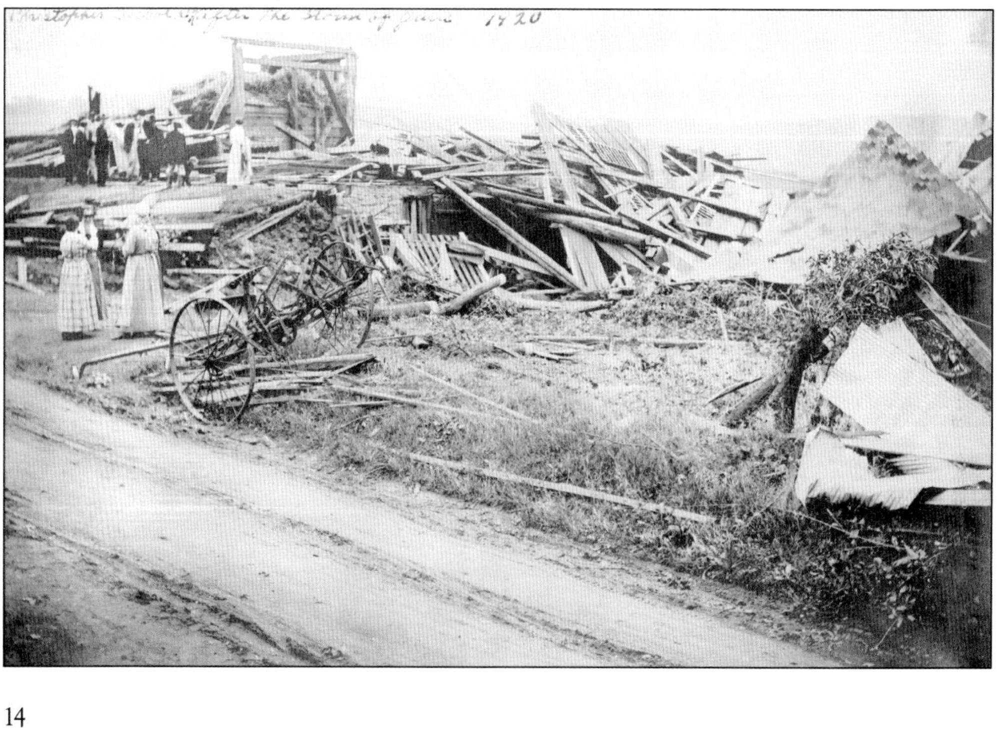

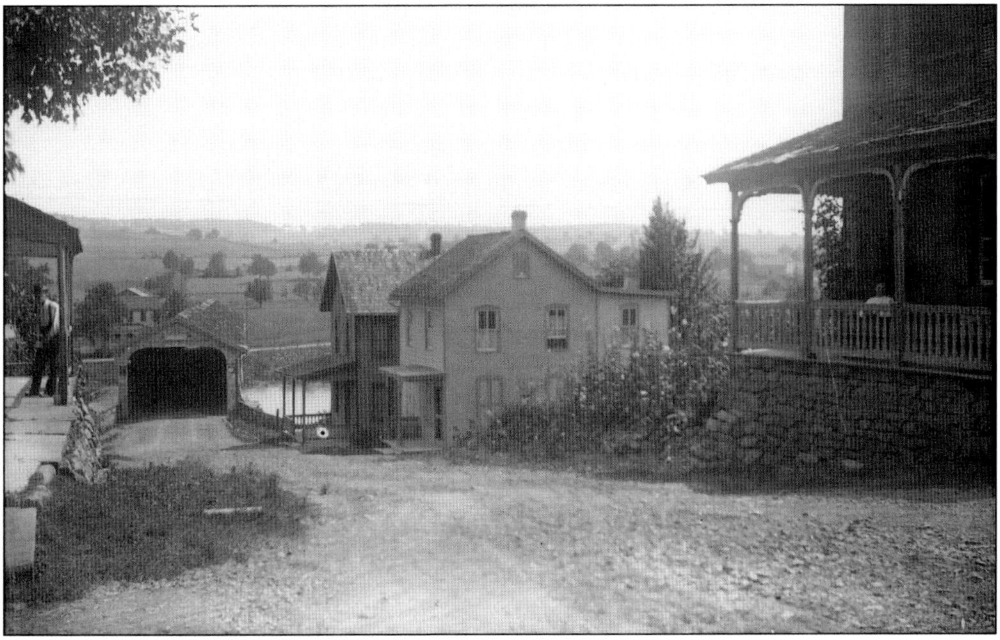

The covered bridge at New Berlin was erected prior to 1820 and spanned Penns Creek. On the New Berlin side (above), the road from the bridge rose quickly up a slope, past Water Street, and into the heart of town at Market and Vine Streets. A sign on the bridge reads "1878," which may have been the date for major repairs or restoration. When the covered bridge was being taken down, its wood sheathing was removed and the bridge's Burr arch-truss system was exposed (below). Theodore Burr of Torrington, Connecticut, built some of his earliest and largest bridges in this area of Pennsylvania's Susquehanna River watershed. The covered bridge was replaced with a steel bridge that, in turn, was replaced in 2007 by a wider span. (NBHA.)

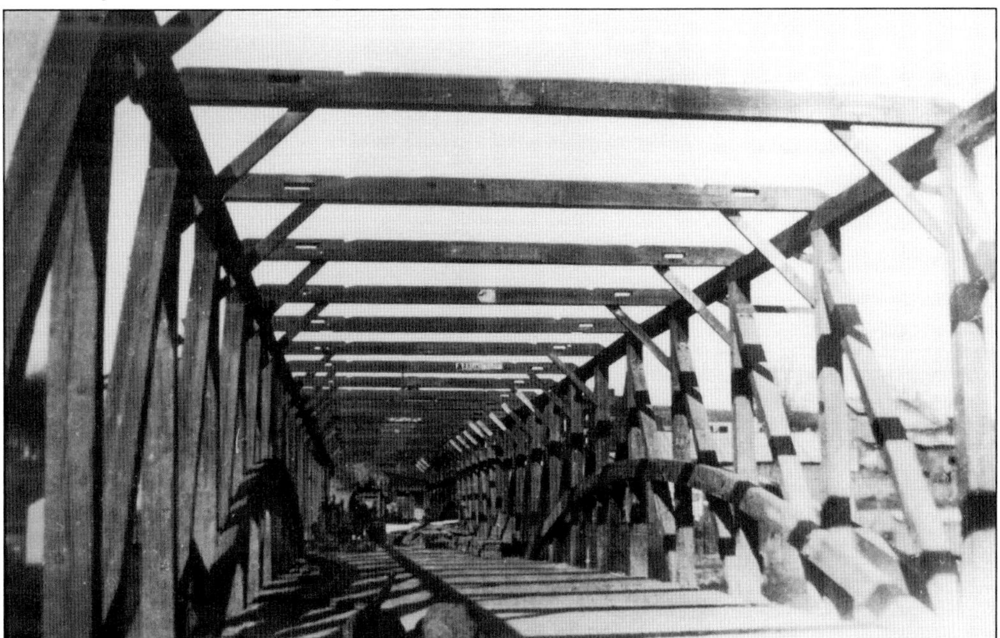

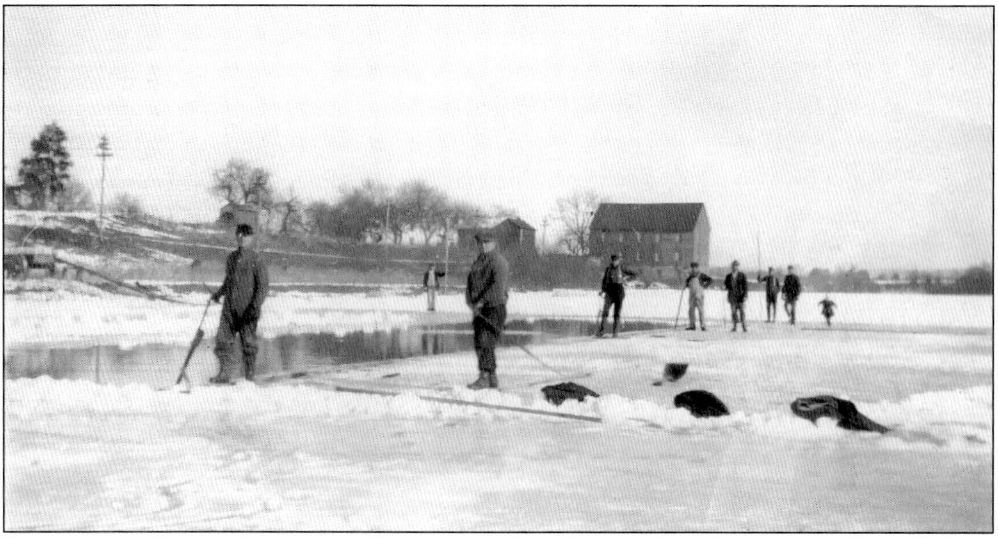

Prior to the widespread use of the electric refrigerator in the early 1950s, ice was an especially important commodity. Penns Creek ice was harvested when it was at least eight inches thick, as shown in the above photograph. It was then stored in Benner's icehouse on the east side of Tan Run. On the north bank of the creek was the town's sole gristmill (below). Between 1816 and 1823, George Orwig and George Eisenhuth built a dam across Penns Creek and a three-storey masonry gristmill. Solomon Kleckner then bought it for $5,000 and his son Joseph followed, operating the mill between 1837 and 1867. A series of owners followed, and in 1918, the mill changed from processing grain to generating electricity, becoming the Hartman Power Plant. By 1935, the structure was dismantled. The Benfer-Miller Legion Post 957 is located near the old mill site. (NBHA.)

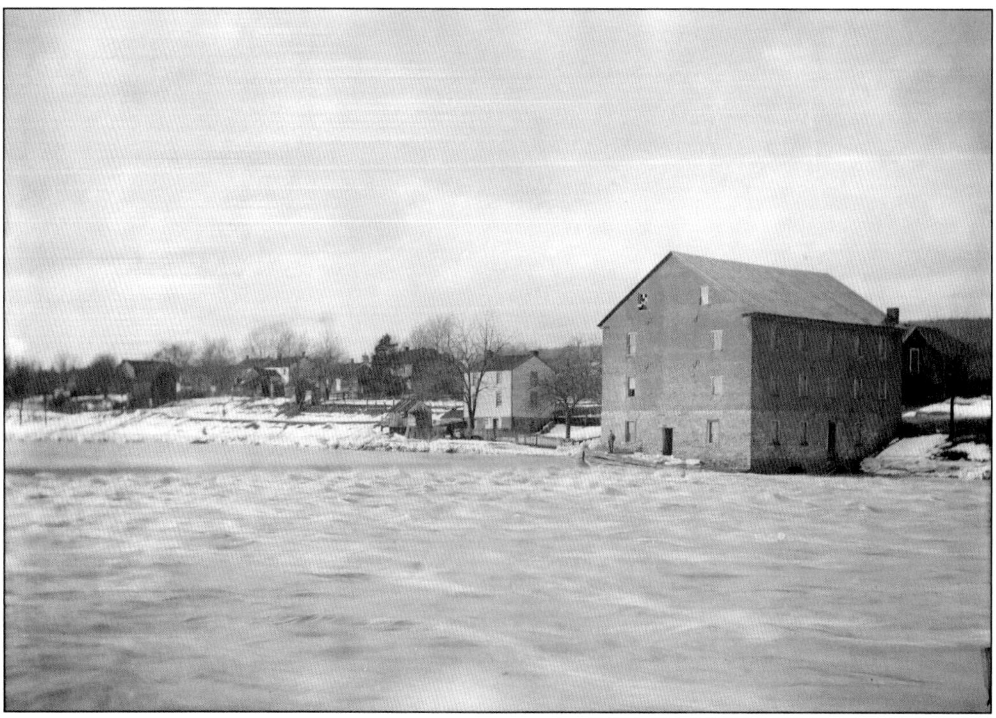

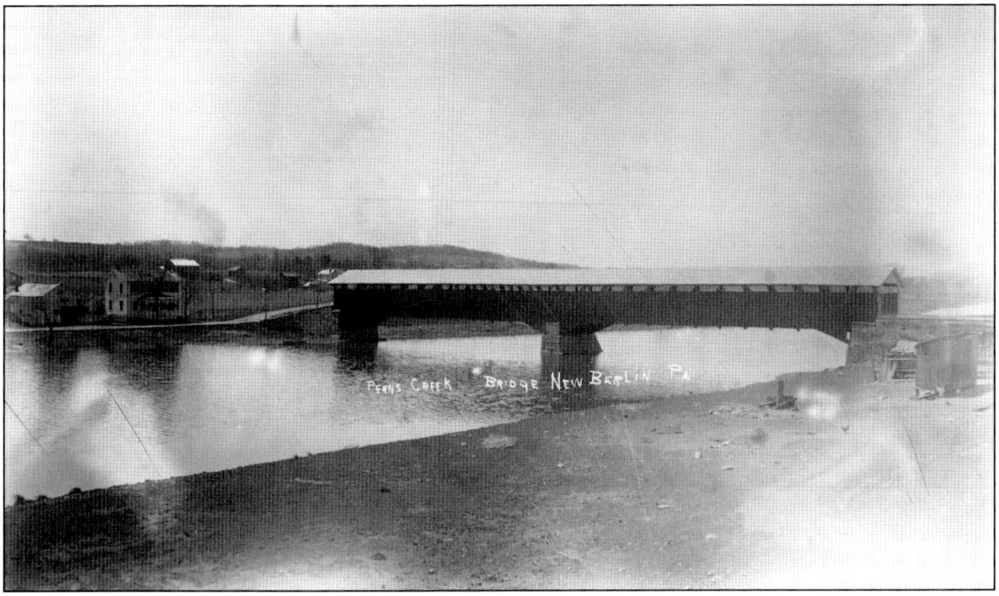

The overview of Penns Creek at New Berlin (above) was issued as a real-photo postcard by Grover Bierly, a young Mifflinburg photographer in 1915. It includes, on the far left, Jesse Cornelius's house and blacksmith shop. The Cornelius complex (below) includes wheels to be repaired at left and new wheels at right, someone with a dog, Jesse (second from left), and members of the Gutelius family. Note the sign advertising the blacksmith business above the shop's doors. It can just be seen in the landscape view above. (UCHS 79.458.3 and 80.8.9.)

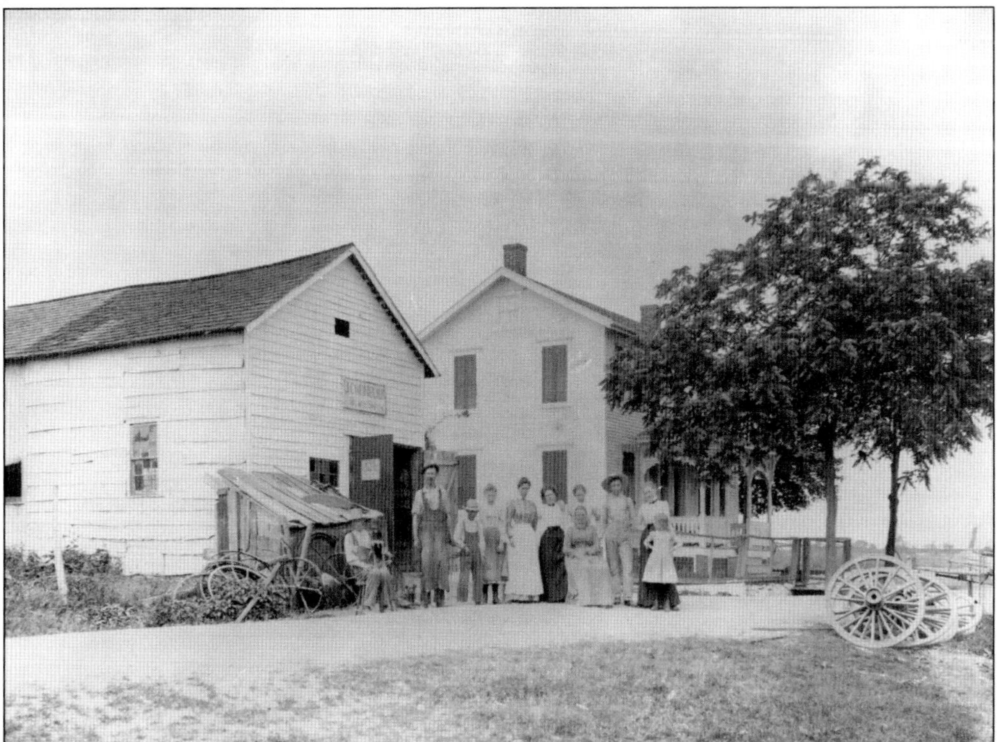

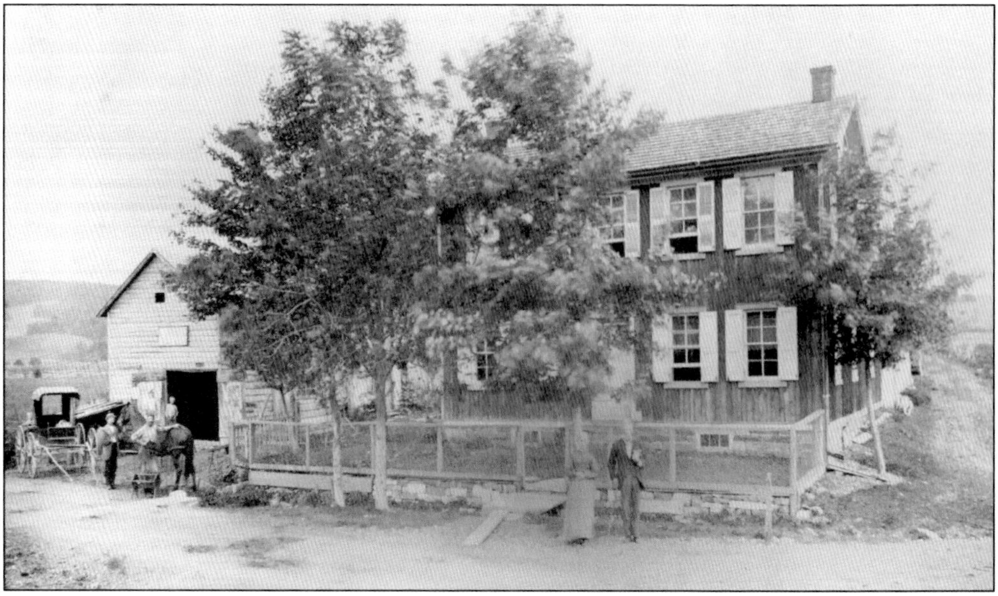

In the above photograph of the Cornelius property, Jesse Cornelius (1855–1927) poses on the left beside a horse he is shoeing. His parents, Robert (1815–1891) and Elizabeth (1812–1896) Cornelius, stand in front of the family home. In a rare interior photograph from around 1895 (below), Jesse Cornelius (left) poses with an assistant. Among the items in the shop are tire shrinkers, an anvil, hand tools, and many horseshoes. Though horseshoing and wheelwrighting would compose the bulk of a rural blacksmith's work, it is Cornelius's distinctively marked household utensils—forged wrought-iron flesh forks, ladles, skimmers, tasting spoons, and spatulas, as well as brass and iron skimmers, ladles, and small spatulas—that are sought by collectors today. (UCHS 80.8.9 and 89.5.1.63.)

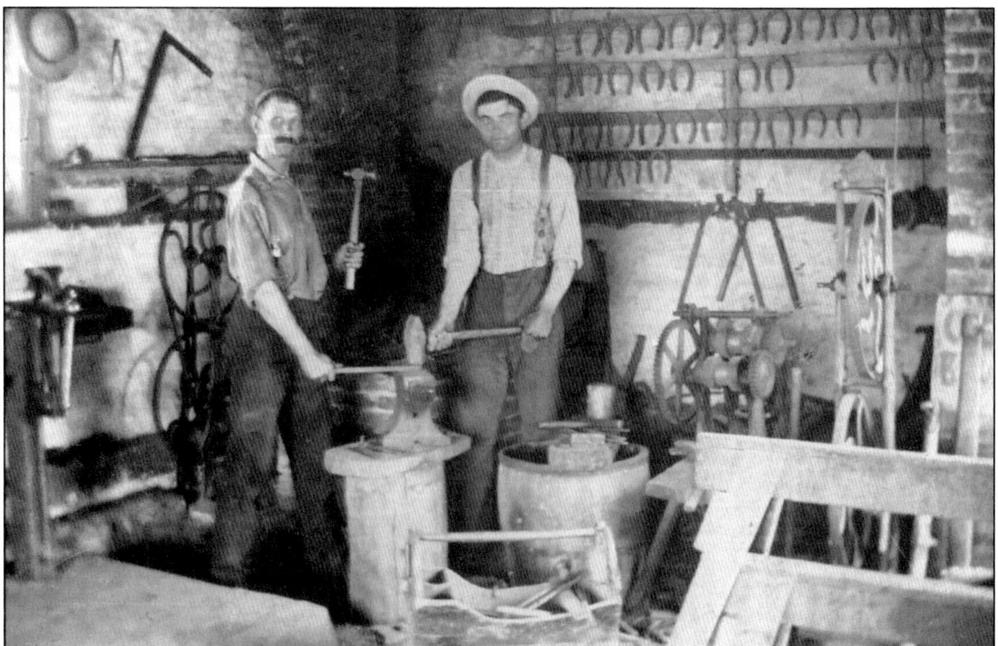

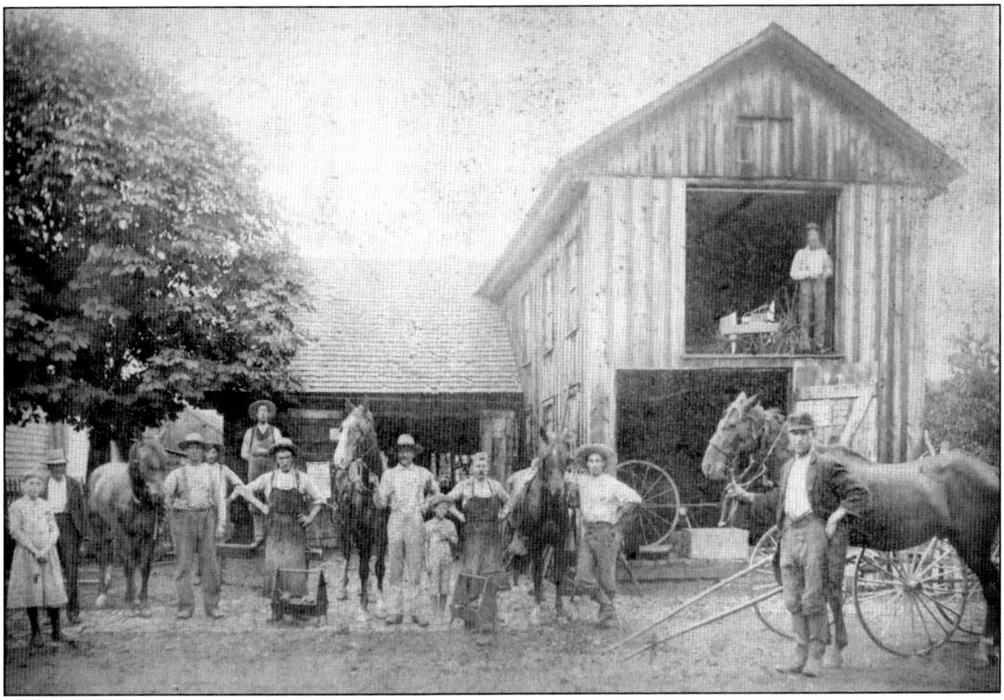

New Berlin buggies were made by Josiah Schweinhart (1815–1887) and John S. Heimbach (1824–1870) at the corner of Market and Union Streets, one door east of Baum's Hotel. Schweinhart announced his business's opening in June 1843 in the *New Berlin Union Times*. He made buggies, sulkies, and barouches and had an attached blacksmith shop (above). Schweinhart obtained the patent for a new single-tree and locking apparatus designed, he said, for vehicle safety. John Heimbach later occupied this shop. James Nagle (d. 1924) was New Berlin's tinsmith from the 1870s until 1923. The New Berlin Heritage Association had limited-edition replicas made of Nagle's tin cookie cutters, from a dove in 1990 to a bird in 2006, the originals owned by Nagle descendants. Thin, rolled sugar cookies have long been a part of New Berlin's holiday traditions. (Above, NBHA; below, UCHS 98.5.2.)

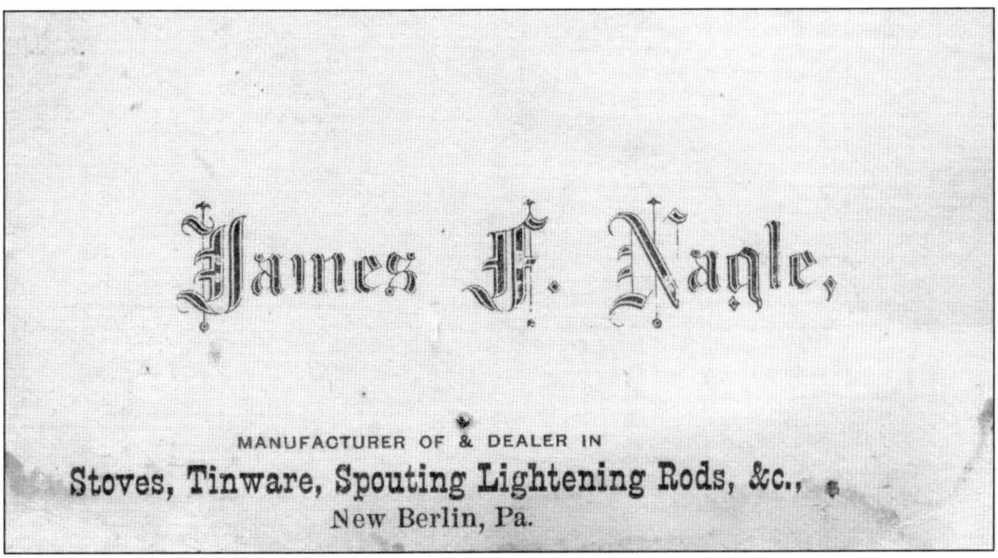

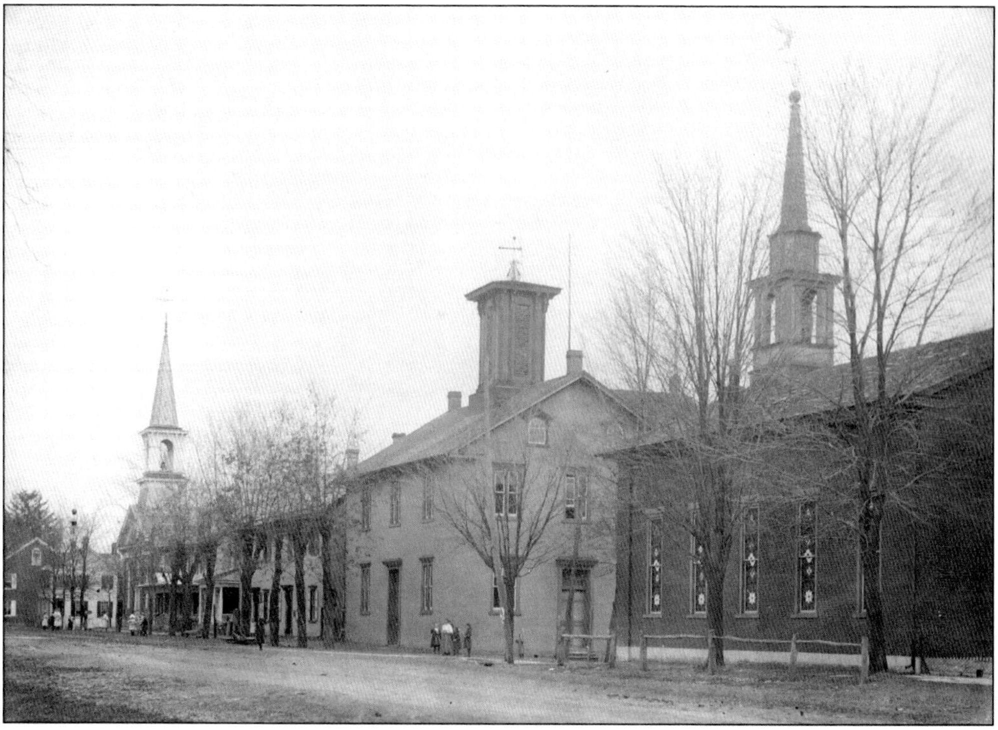

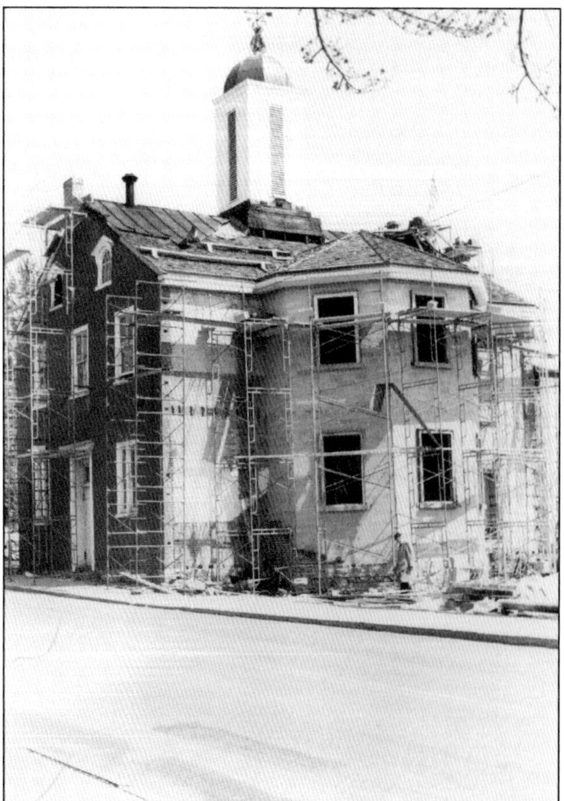

The above photograph shows the Emmanuel United Church of Christ (right) as it looked before it was rebuilt between 1912 and 1913. Down the street is the Evangelical Church when it still retained its steeple. Also shown here is the 1815 Union County courthouse (center). In 1967, the courthouse was bought for $1 by Lois Kalp of Lewisburg, who thought the Union County Historical Society would locate there. In October 1976, the society voted to gift the building to the New Berlin Heritage Association. The restoration of its cupola and the reconstruction of its apse (left), completed between 1982 and 1984, restored the original building's stateliness. Union County's first courthouse now houses the federal post office, which opened in 1988, on the ground level, and the association's museum, which opened the following year, on its second floor. (NBHA.)

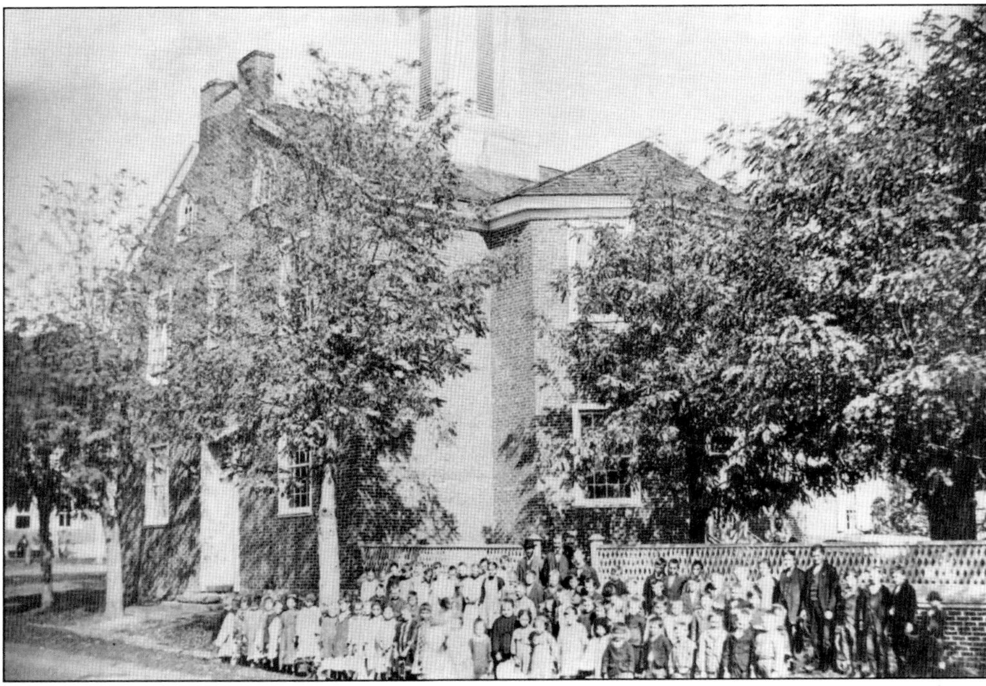

In the c. 1880 photograph above, schoolchildren pose at the rear of the original county courthouse. Their teachers, standing behind the group at center, are, from left to right, H.A. Shiffer, H.N. Cornelius, and Charles Roos. At the time of this photograph, the building's original apse was still intact. It would later be replaced with a rectangular brick addition. The courthouse had closed temporarily in 1855, when the county seat was moved to Lewisburg. The courthouse was then converted into the town's school and its cupola removed. In the below photograph, taken in 1936, teacher G. Robert Cornelius and his third-grade class pose near the corner of Market and Vine Streets. (NBHA.)

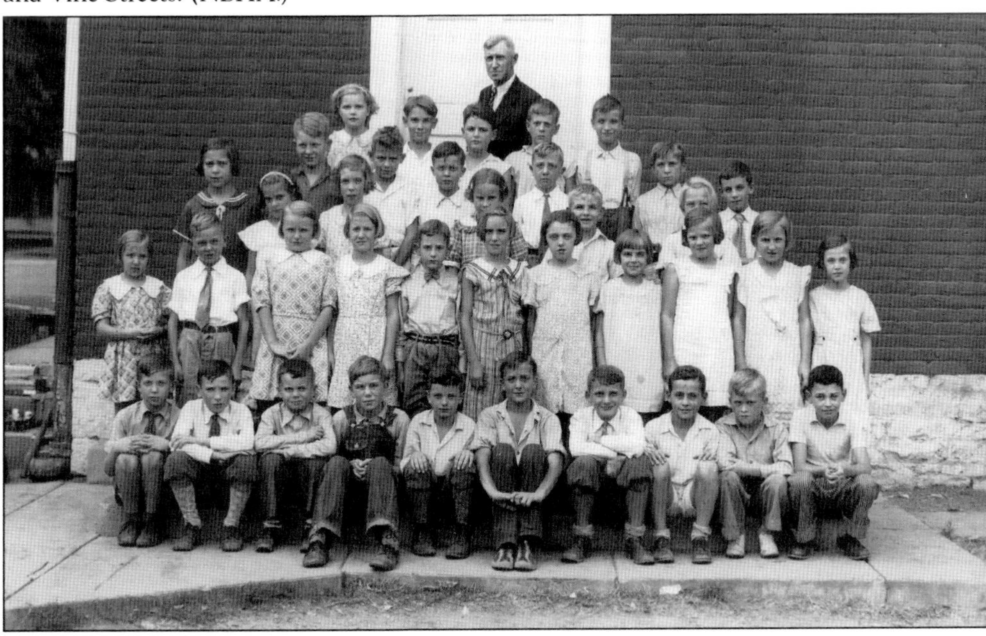

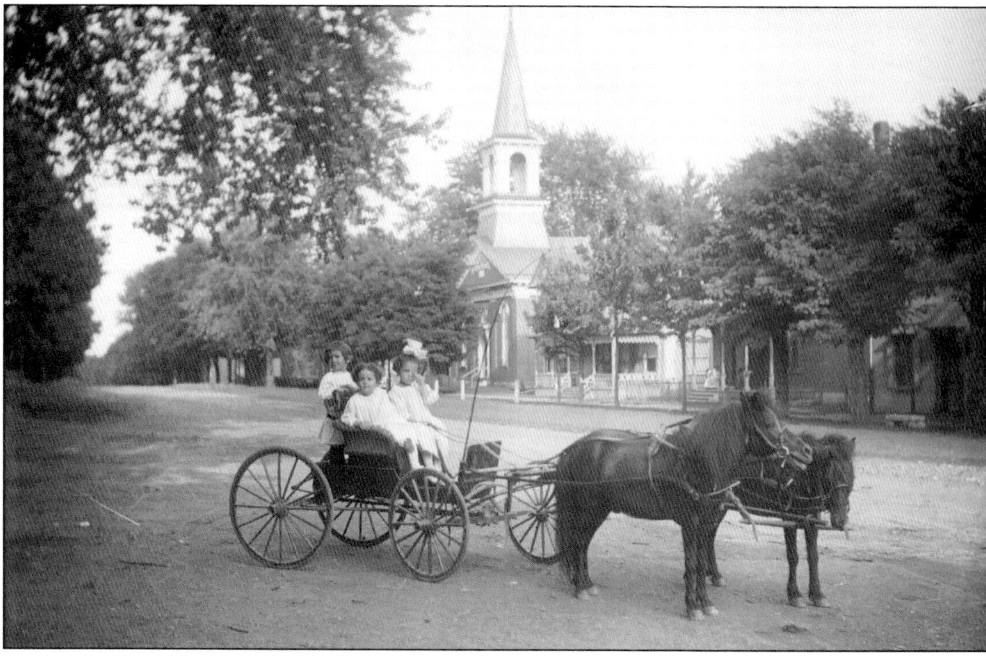

Above, Winifred Smith (with large bow) and her friends sit in S.E. Benner's pony cart in the 400 block of Market Street. The Evangelical Church is in the background. Below, the church's interior shows it decorated in September 1901 for a memorial service for Pres. William McKinley. He had been shot twice by anarchist Leon Czolgosz at the Pan-American Exposition in Buffalo, New York, on September 6, while standing in a receiving line greeting exposition visitors. McKinley initially appeared to be recovering from his wounds, but took a turn for the worse and died on September 14, 1901. (NBHA.)

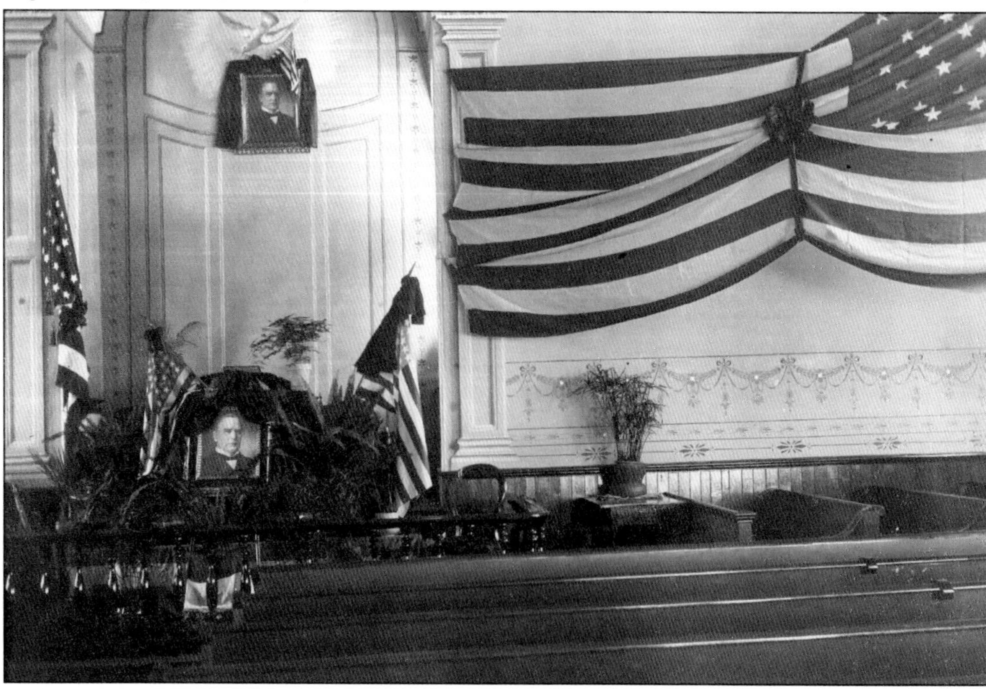

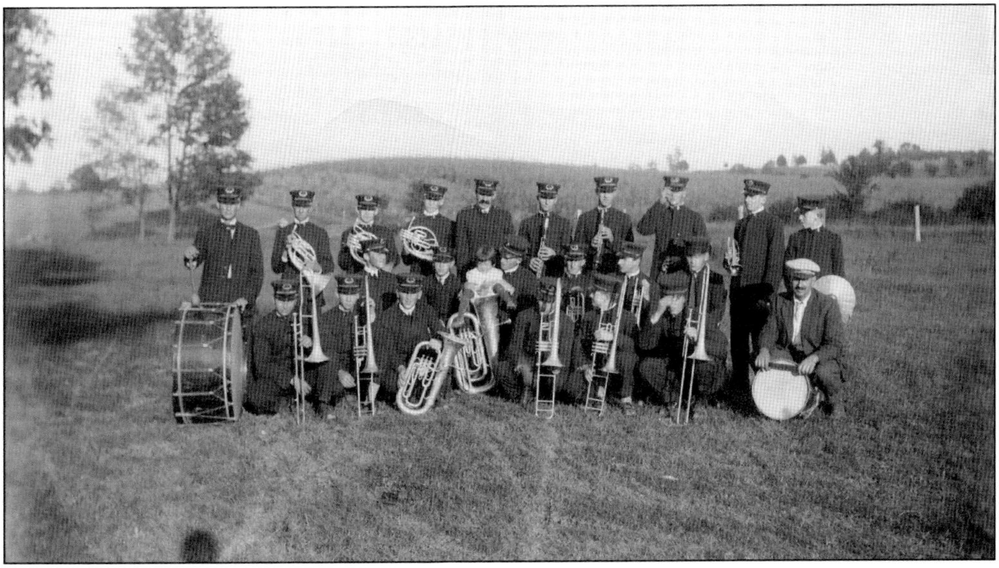

New Berlin's band, like its baseball teams, has been featured in numerous photographs. The band was formed in 1910. Pictured above, from left to right, are (first row) Ralph Arbogast, Raymond Benfer, David Arbogast, Charles Dunkle, and Frank Dunkelberger; (second row) Elmer Seebold, John Wagner, John Miller (with son Marvin sitting on horn), Ammon Maurer, David Leiby, and Murray Kline; (third row) C.O. Solomon, Mentor Sauers, Bruce Smith, Percey Maurer, band director Homer Smith, Fred Dock, Frank Beaver, Gary Engle, Luther Albert, and Henry Moyer. The band drum, prominent in the real-photo postcard below, is on display in the Heritage Association's museum. Earlier bands in New Berlin included the New Berlin Silver Cornet Band in the 1870s and C.D. Bogar's Brass Band in the 1880s. (NBHA.)

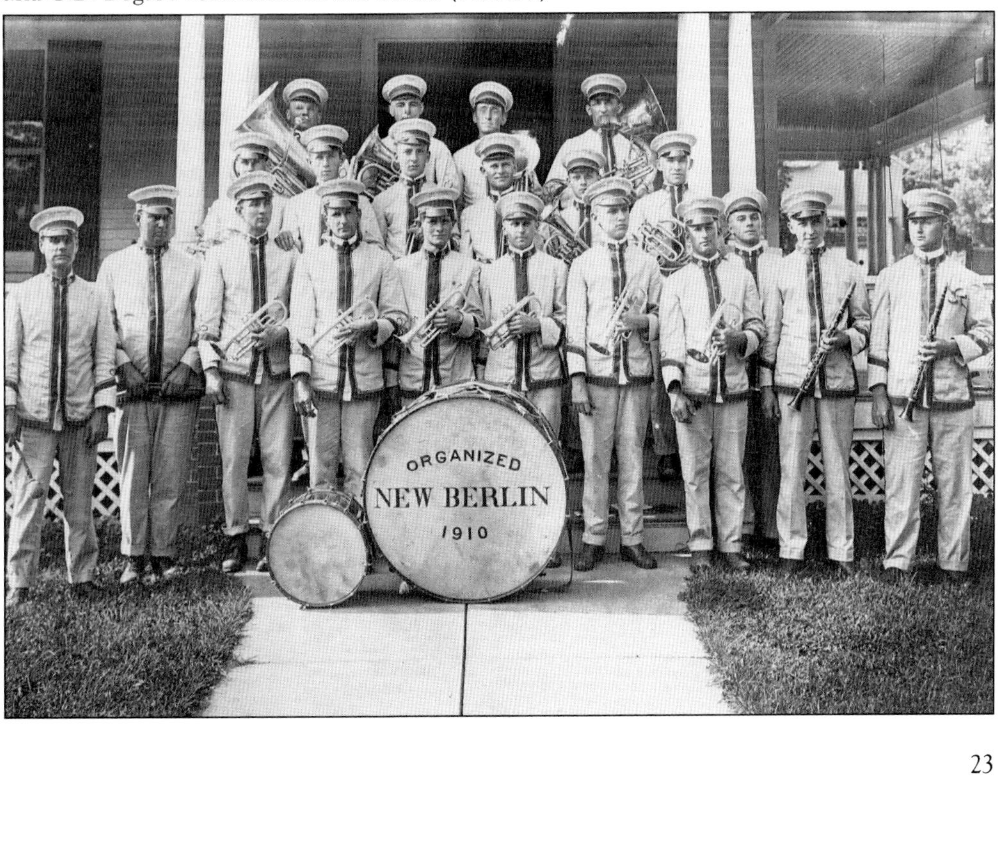

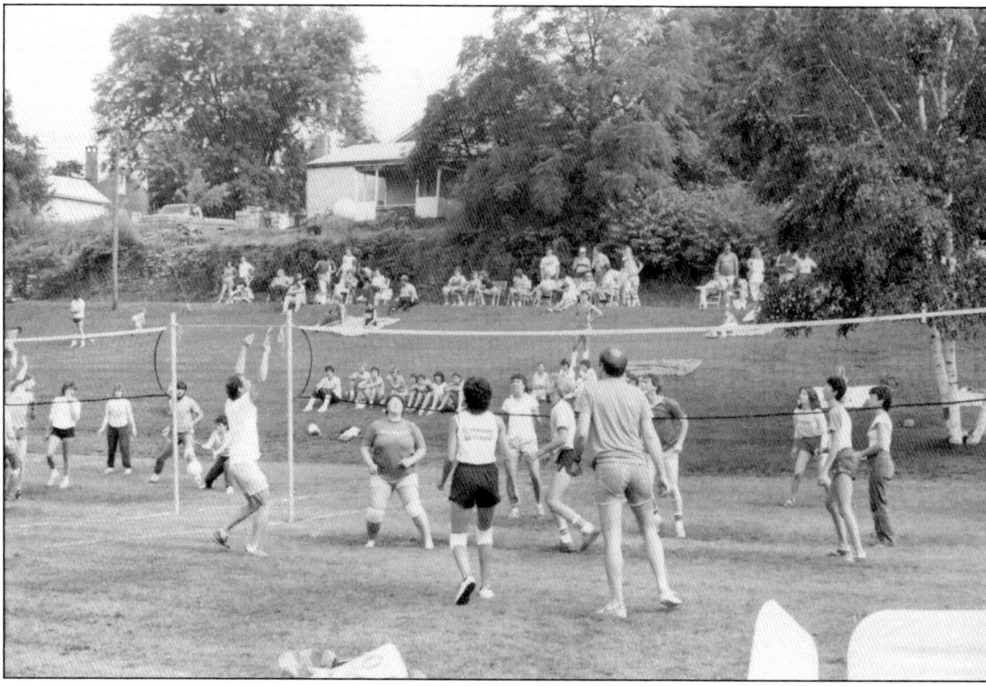

Volleyball games, fireworks displays, and various outdoor activities drew and continue to attract New Berlin families to events on the Fourth of July (above). Another favorite were pet parades, such as the one seen below in the 1970s. (NBHA.)

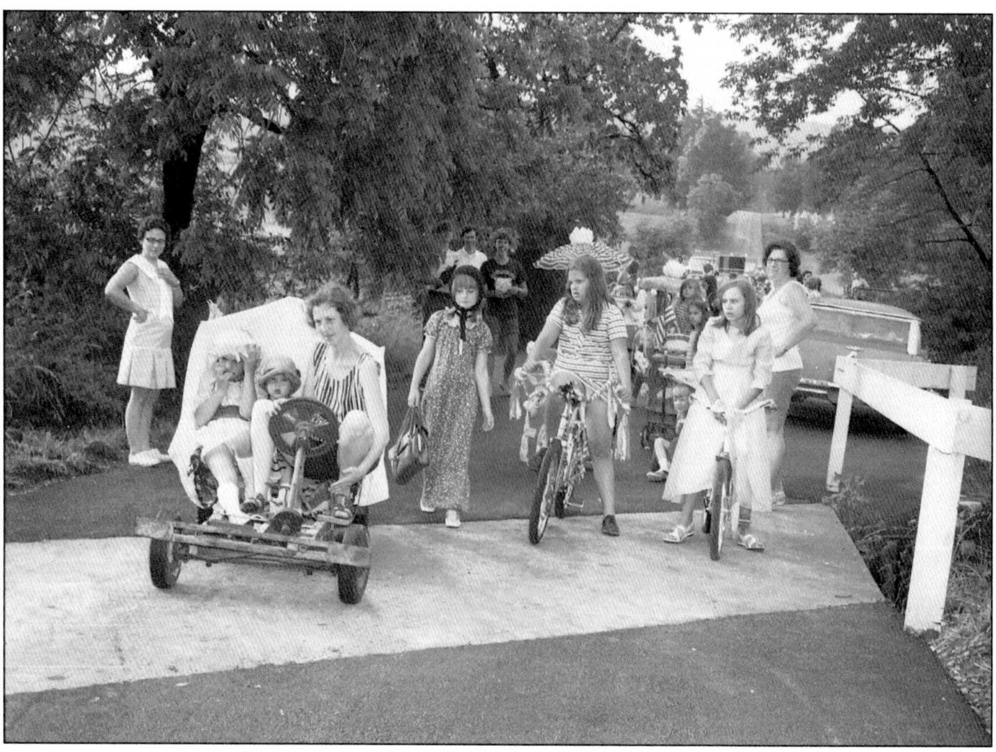

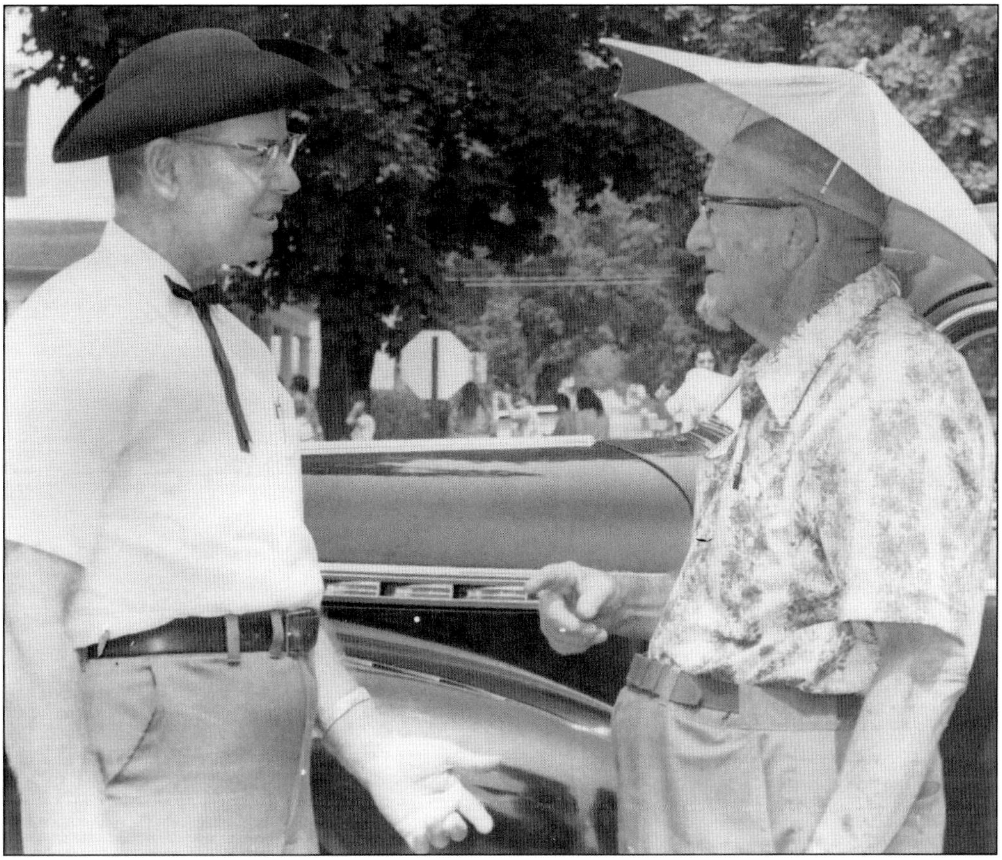

Heritage Day has been celebrated on the fourth Saturday of August for more than 42 years. It was sponsored by the New Berlin Heritage Association from 1971 to 2002 and is currently organized by the New Berlin Activities Committee. The event's founders were Donald and Ruth Spangler, Jim Wittes, Louis Eaton, Marie Wolfe, Richard Jones, Joan Maurer, and Gloria Maize. In the above photograph, former mayor John Knouse (right) makes a point to local auctioneer Earl Eash, who called the auction for many years. The daylong event began to raise awareness about New Berlin and contributed funds to town projects, including the restoration of the original 1814 courthouse below. (NBHA.)

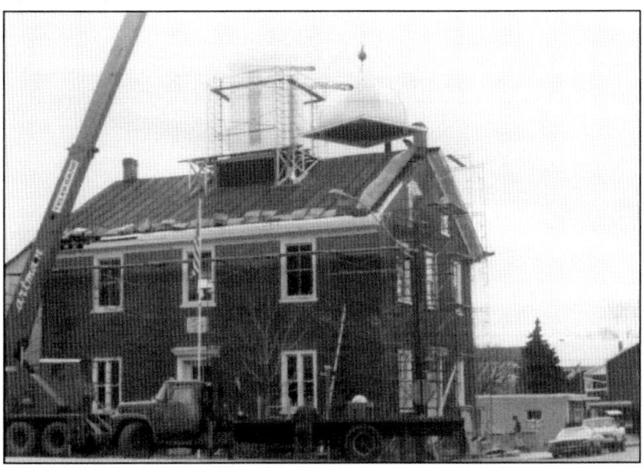

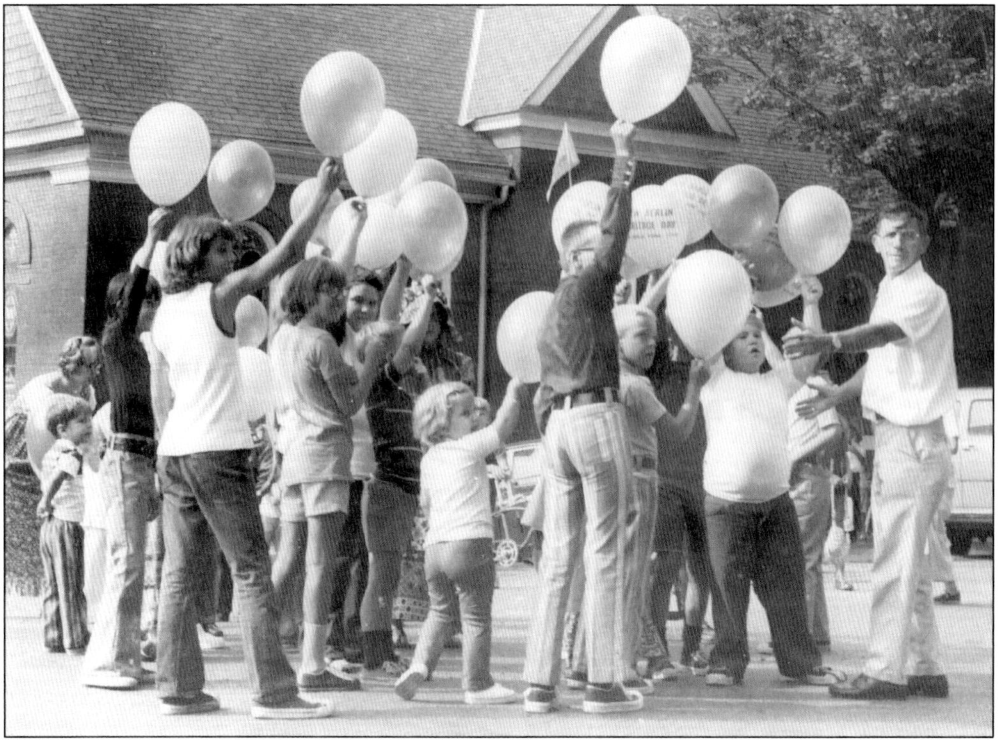

In the above photograph from 1973, New Berlin Heritage Day organizer Louis "Bud" Eaton (1921–2006) stands at right, preparing to give the signal to participants to release their balloons with paper messages inside. Balloons were found as far away as Catawissa, Columbia County. In a recreation of past New Year's celebratory acts, an anvil shoot was executed on the square, in which two large blacksmith anvils were placed one on top of each other with black powder in between. The powder was then lit, creating a large bang. Below, Mary Poppins, as portrayed by Dolores "Lori" Snook, was another crowd-pleaser in the early New Berlin Heritage Days. (NBHA.)

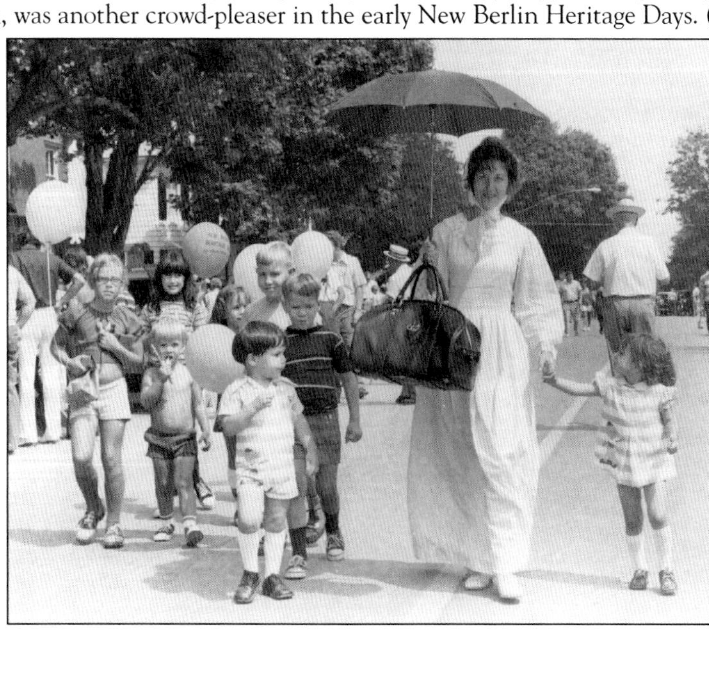

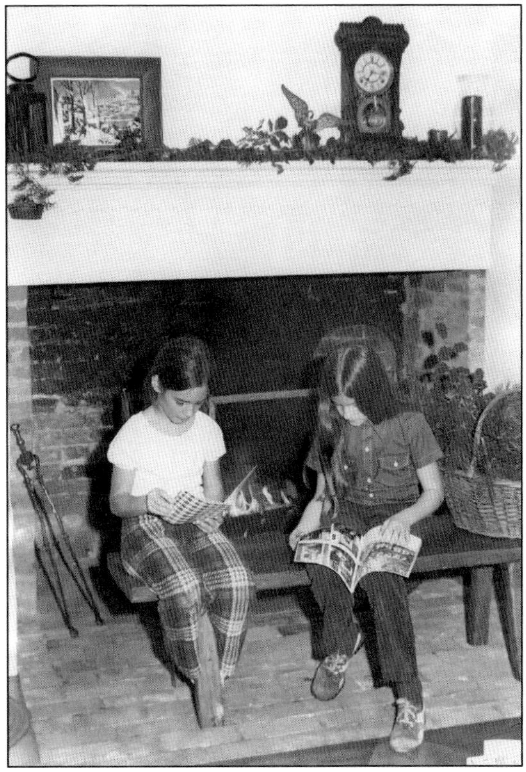

The Heritage Christmas House Tour in 1973 included the home of Elmer and Joan Maurer. In the right photograph are the Maurers' daughter Amy (left) and a friend, Christine Spangler. Rev. Mark Michaels (below) slept overnight that year with the Heritage Association's exhibit, housed in the Sunday school addition of the Lutheran church. This was another fundraiser for the restoration of the 1815 courthouse. (NBHA.)

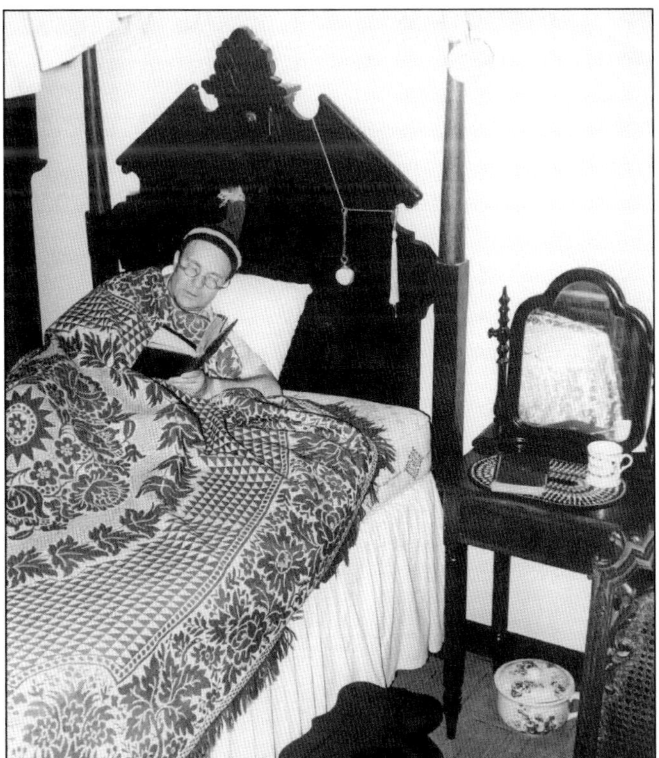

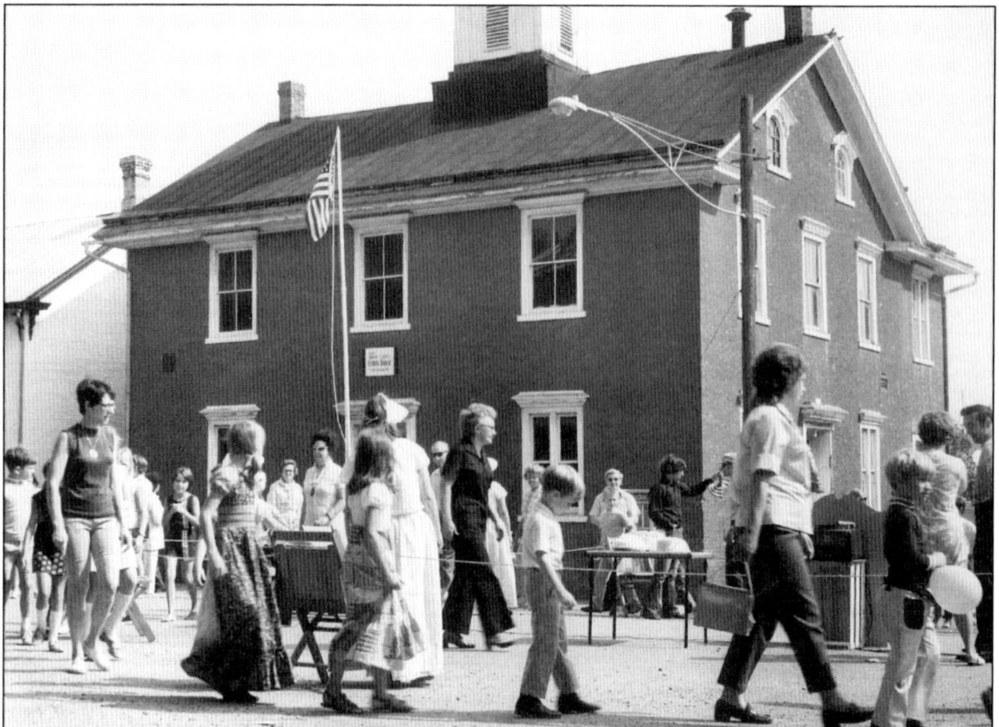

Other favorites at the first New Berlin Heritage Days were the cakewalk and the chicken barbeque, headed by Donald and Ruth Spangler from 1971 to 2002. In 1971, the dinner, for $2.50, included half a chicken with baked beans, a buttered roll, coleslaw, and a slice of pie. The barbeque was sometimes sold out by noon. Since 1974, the auction of donated items has been held on or near the town square. In later years, a large gazebo occupied the central town intersection, where questions could be asked by visitors, quilt raffle tickets were sold, signed and numbered tin cookie cutters were dispensed, and the Union County Historical Society's annual historical calendar would debut. (NBHA.)

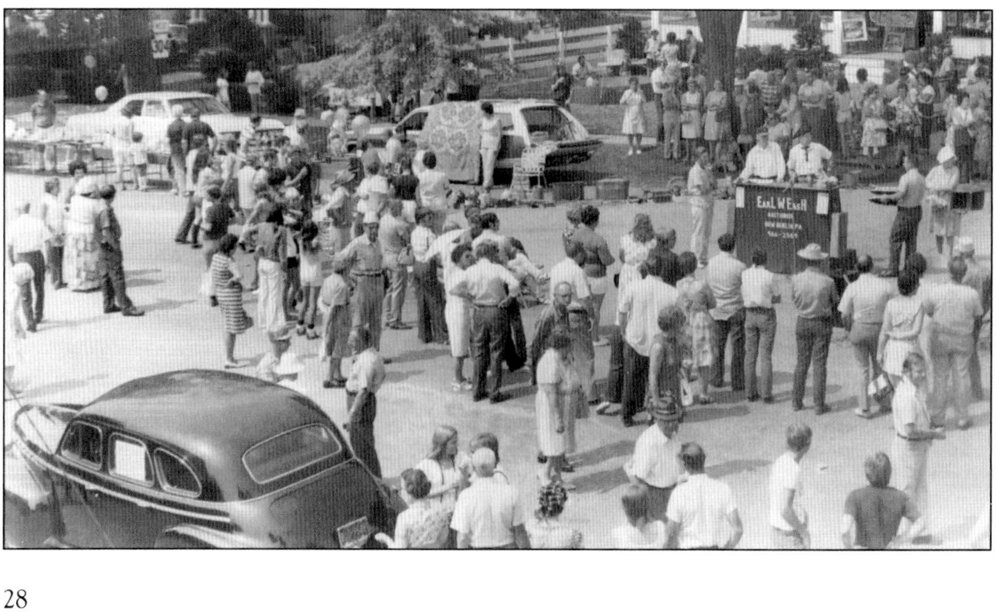

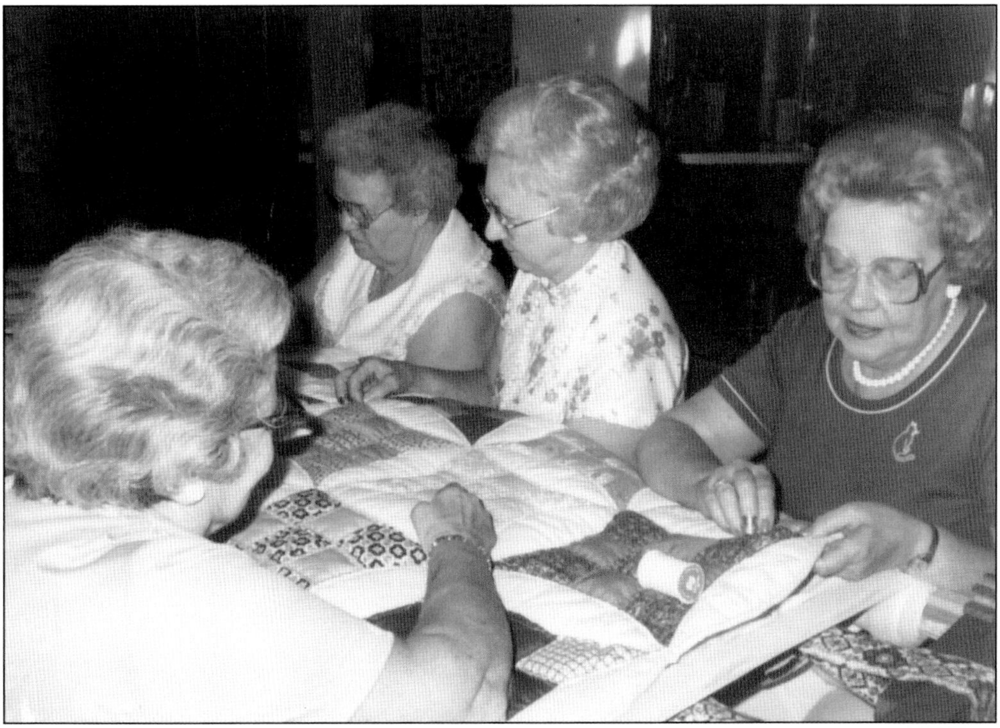

New Berlin's long tradition of group quilting was revived in 1972 as the United States bicentennial approached. Josephine Spangler led the group. In the above photograph, the ladies at the quilt frame are, from left to right, Margaret Solomon, Mary Wetzel Moll, Edith Solomon, and Dorothy Eaton. Others in the group were sisters-in-law Margaret and Miriam Seebold. Quilts still raise funds for community projects. Mellie Leiby used an older "Fruit in the Basket" quilt as a backdrop for an infant's portrait. This was sometimes done in rural "studio" portraits. (NBHA.)

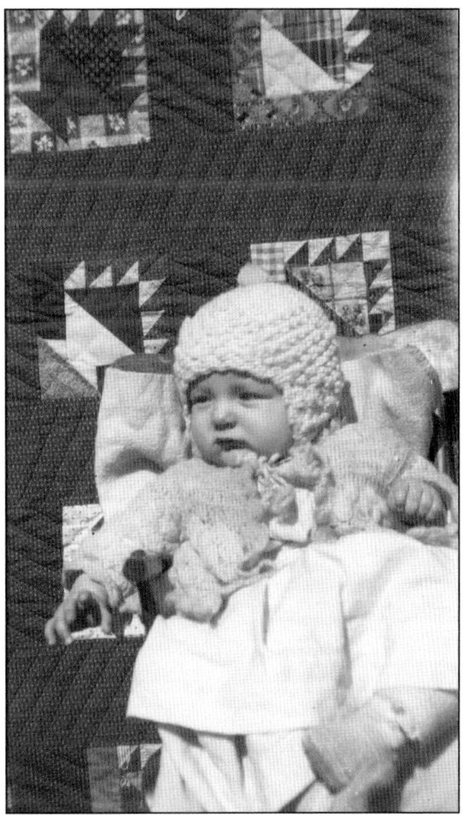

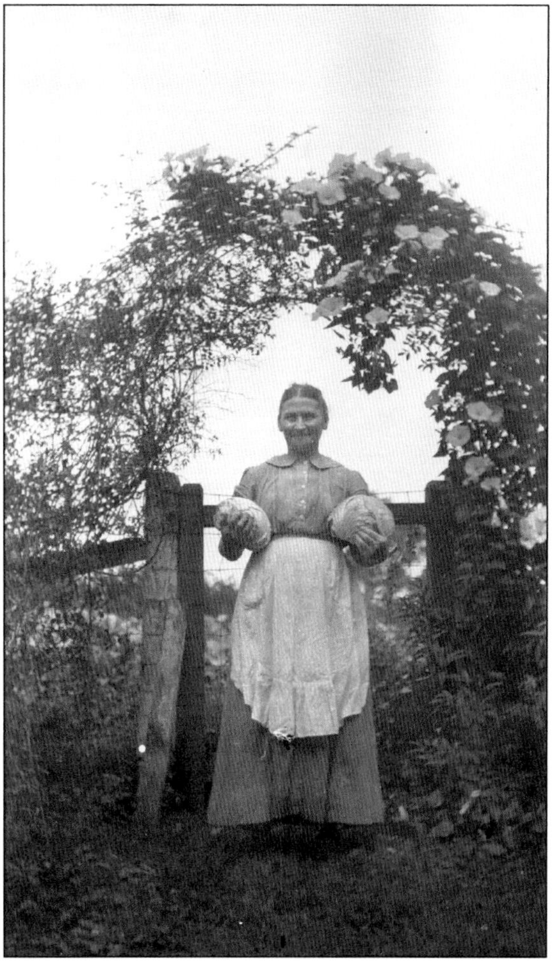

Amateur photographer Mary Fayetta Kline (1889–1980) was born near Kratzerville, Snyder County, into the farming family of George and Mary Alice Kline. She married David Leiby in 1921. Known as "Mellie," she enjoyed taking photographs with her box Brownie, documenting everyday rural life in the New Berlin area. These scenes are typical of her photographic work in the 1930s and 1940s. (NBHA.)

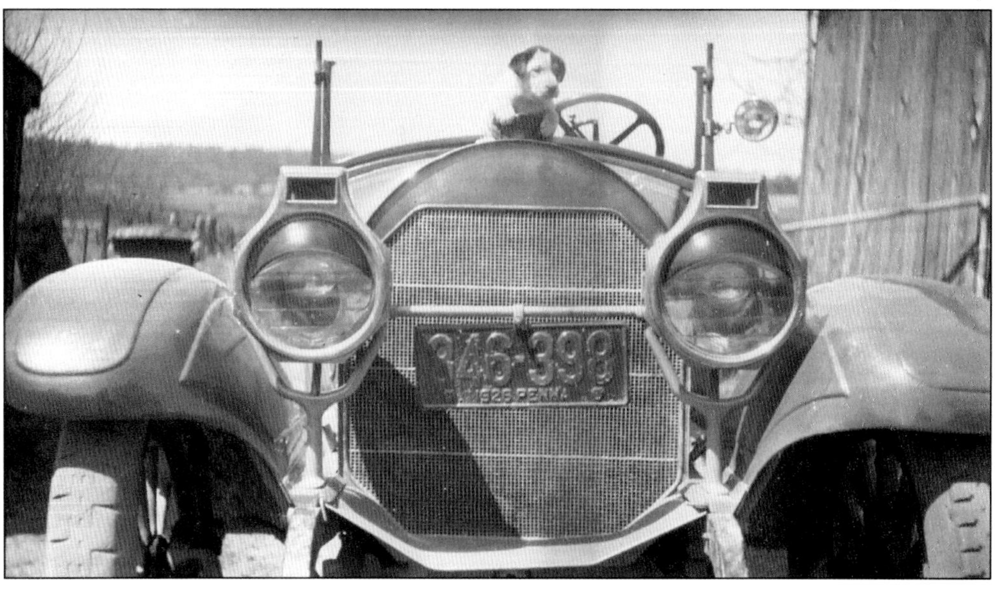

“Mellie” Leiby became a charter member of the New Berlin Heritage Association in 1971. She and her husband, David, collected many local Native American artifacts: arrowheads, drills, net weights, and even a pipe stone that she found near Penns Creek in the spring after fields were plowed. Before the days of no-till farming, such artifacts could be found on plowed fields along creek and river overflow areas or at locations like Delta Place outside of Lewisburg. Mellie and her brother Murray Kline were both history enthusiasts. Mellie’s interests included birds, and she was a member of the National Audubon Society. Portraits of animals, people, and produce were among hundreds of images of life in the Buffalo Valley that Mellie Leiby captured on film. (NBHA.)

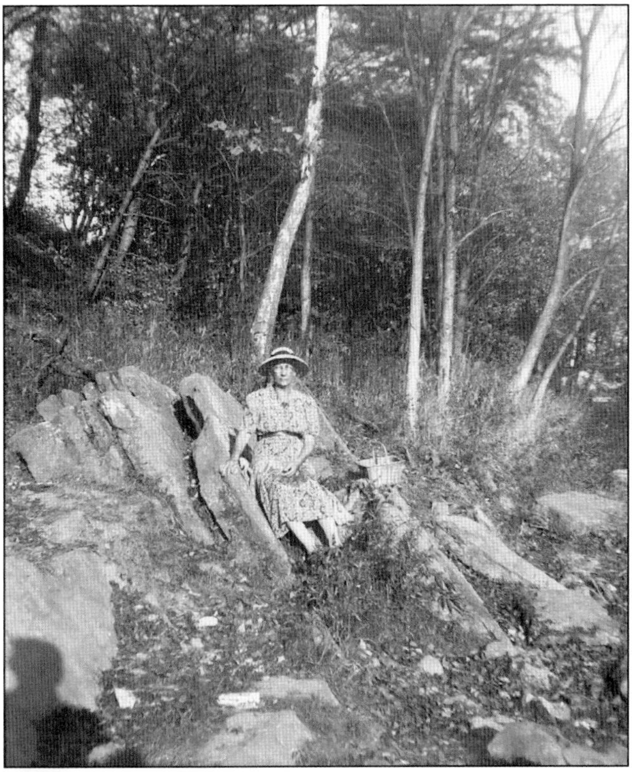

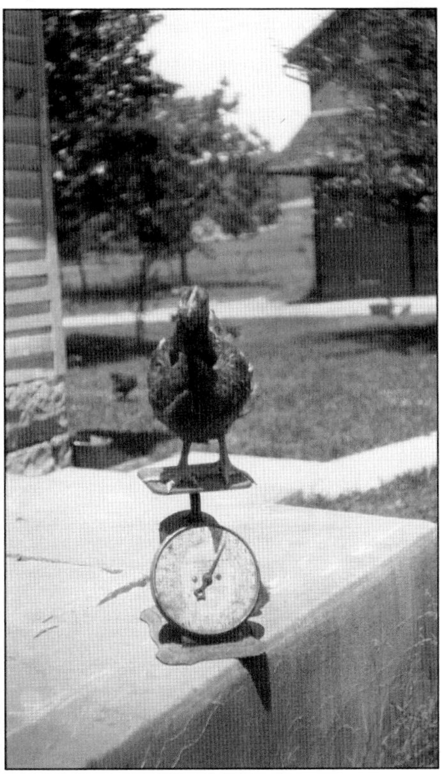

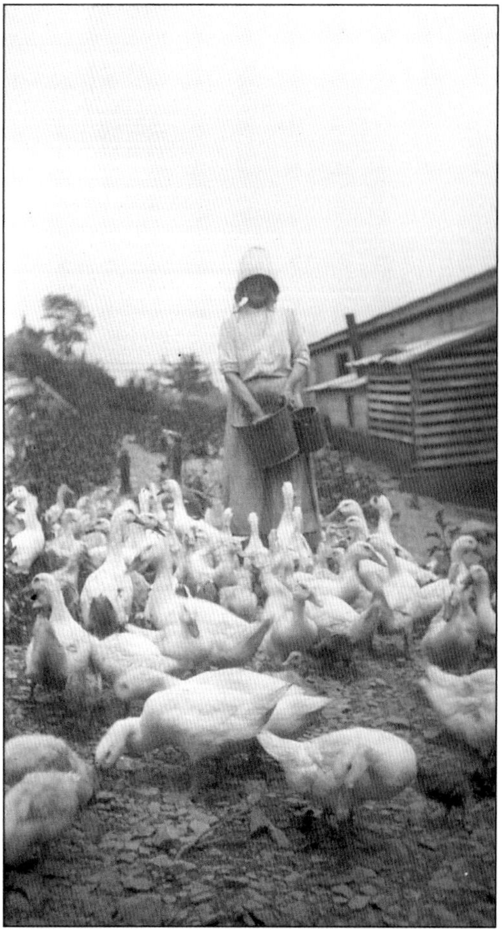

Farm scenes by Mellie Leiby included, animals, people, and buildings. One portrait subject was the distinctive wooden octagonal barn with its central silo, formerly owned by Mellie Kline's parents, George Kline (1856–1938) and Mary Alice Smith Kline (1860–1940). The barn (below), now owned and operated by Dennis and Mary Jo Spangler, still stands one mile east of New Berlin's main square, on the north side of Route 304. The octagonal barn is one of a few that were built in central Pennsylvania. The photographer's brother Murray operated the farm after the death of his father and, in 1947, bought it at public auction. Murray's grandnephew currently runs this farm. (NBHA.)

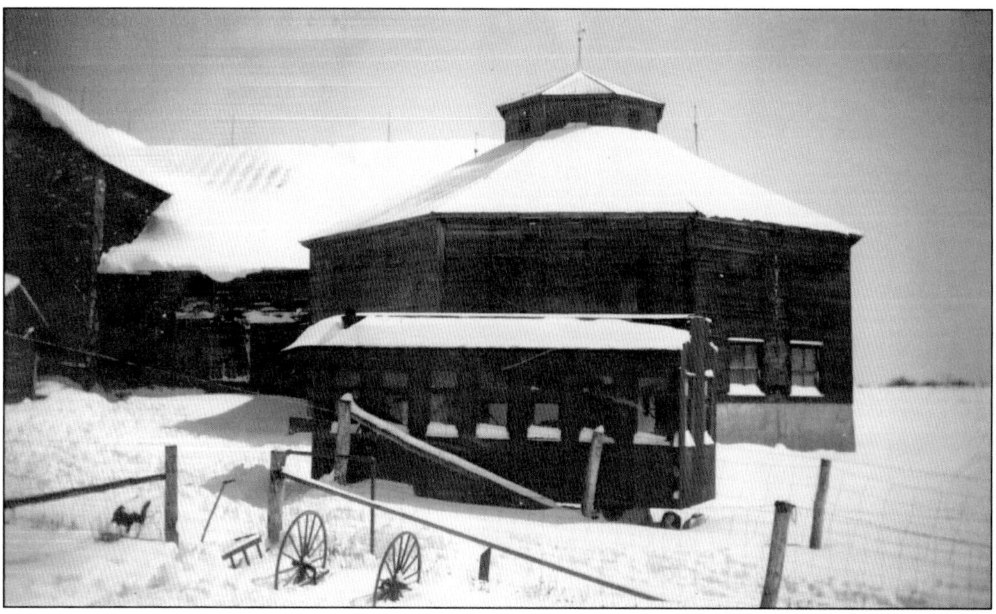

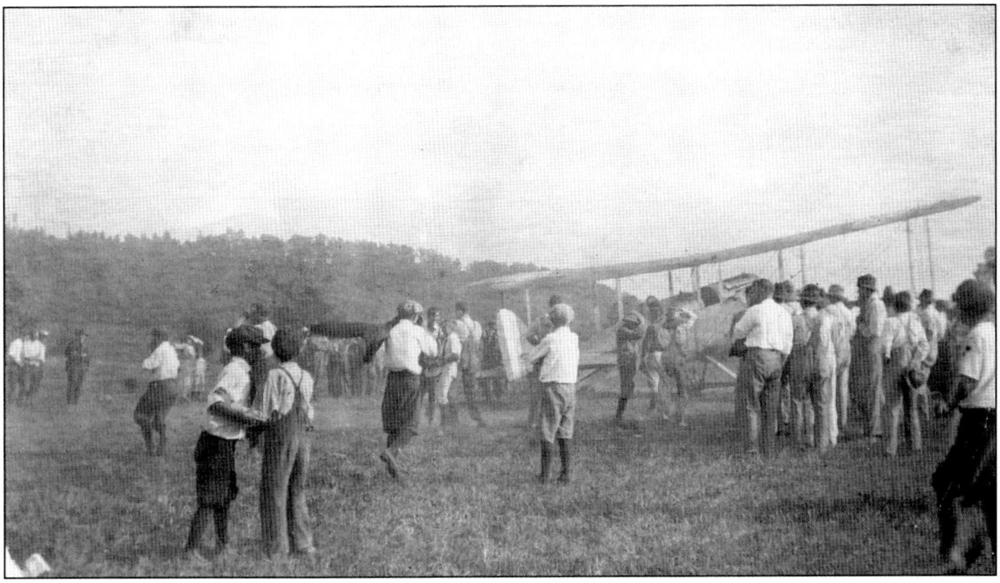

In the above photograph, onlookers gather at the site of an airplane crash in Murray Kline's farm field. Below, residents pose at another airplane crash. Both photographs were taken by "Mellie" Kline Leiby around 1920. The appearance of an airplane would have been a new and exciting phenomenon at that time. (NBHA.)

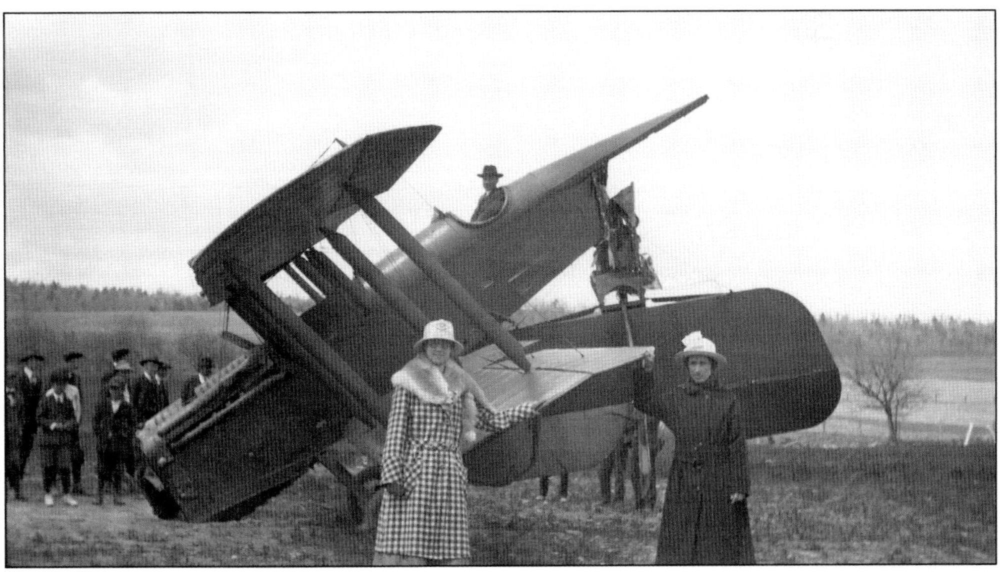

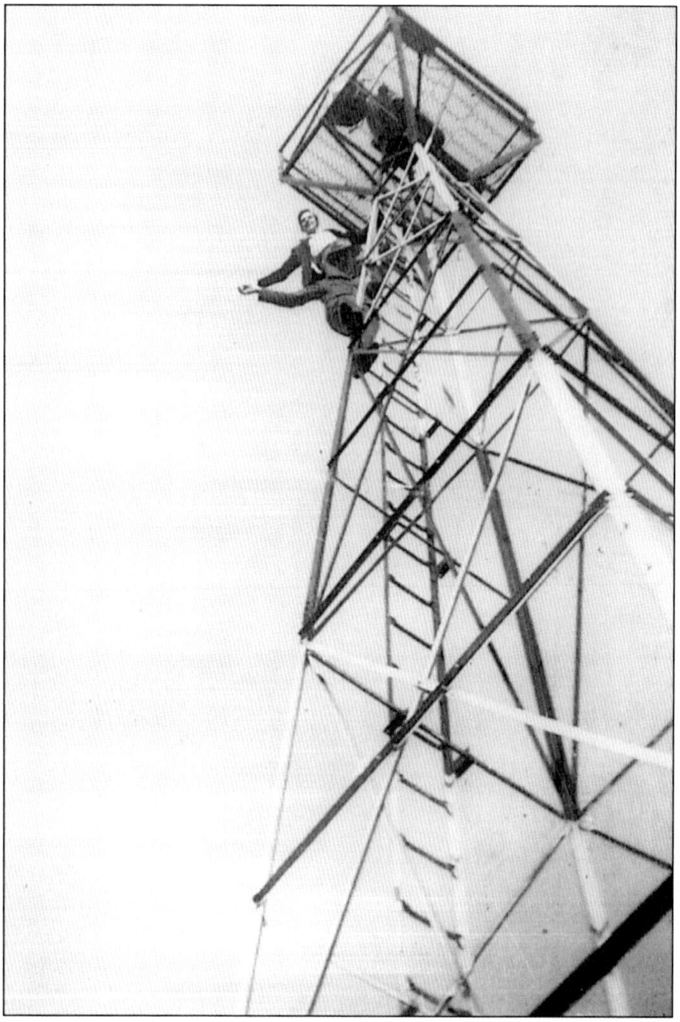

The mail plane beacon on New Berlin (also known as Shamokin Mountain), left, was photographed prior to its being dismantled on January 18, 1957. It and three other beacons—at Elysburg, Mahoney City, and Woodward—had stood since the 1920s. But all were decommissioned in 1957. The Laurelton beacon remained operational. Ruth Spangler remembered walking up the mountain and paying a nickel or a dime to watch television in the beacon house. As it was one of the few televisions in New Berlin, there would often be a dozen or more teenagers gathered around it. No matter what was playing, this was the place to be. The below photograph, from the slope of Shamokin Mountain and looking south, was taken a decade before the beacon was built. (Left, Marvin Wagner; below, NBHA.)

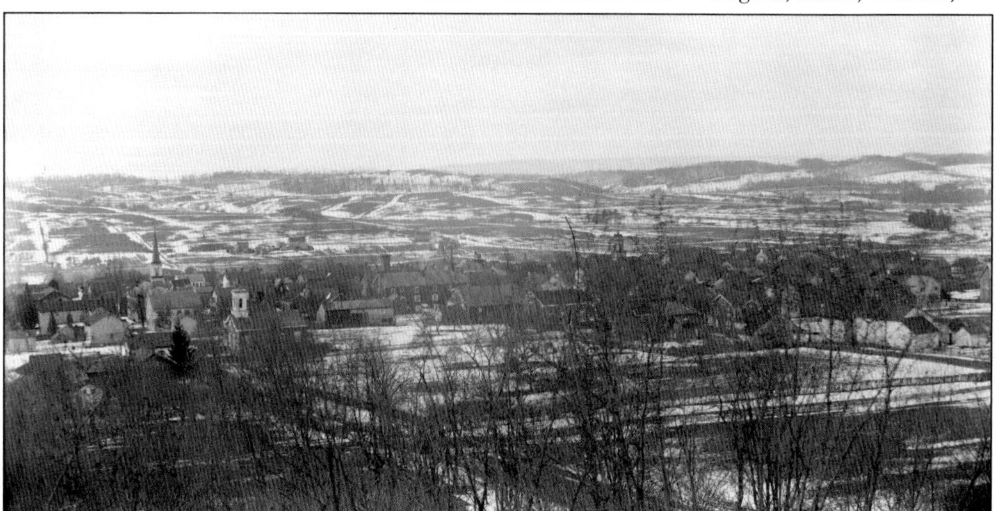

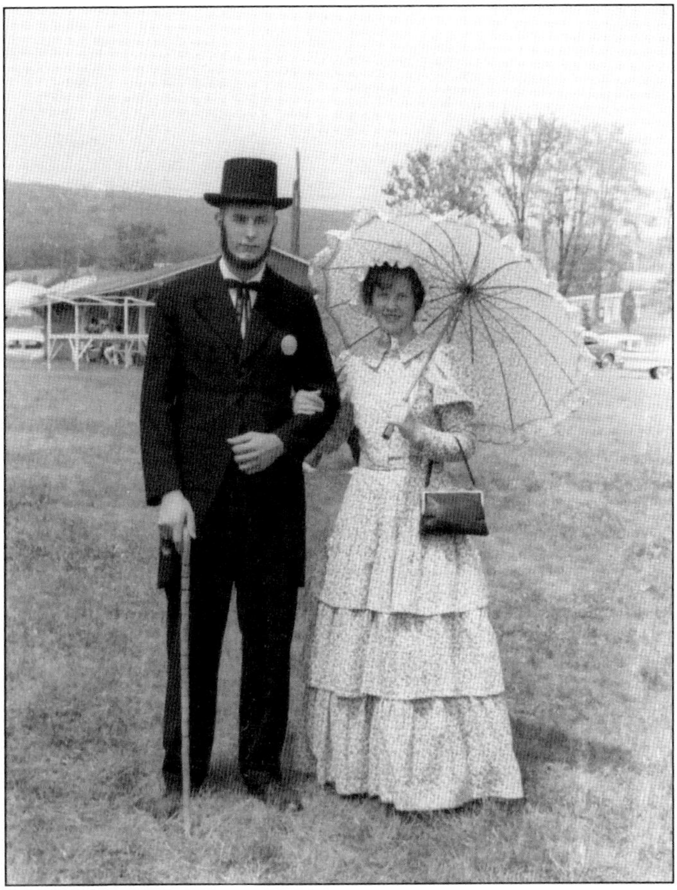

Right, Ruth-Alice Seebold and Gary Spangler pose during Union County's sesquicentennial celebration in 1963. Ruth-Alice is wearing a dress and carrying a parasol made for the occasion by her mother, Margaret (Dotterer) Seebold. Gary is sporting a Brothers of the Brush sesquicentennial tie. Judging of the beards of New Berlin's Brothers of the Brush took place on the carnival grounds' stage. The contestants pictured below are, from left to right, George Wetzel Jr., Orville Spangler, Elmer Lohr, Alvin Spangler, David Black, three unidentified men, Marvin Maurer, unidentified, Richard Jarrett, and Gary Spangler. Rev. Andrew Horn is kneeling and talking to Carl Reich. (Gary and Ruth-Alice Spangler.)

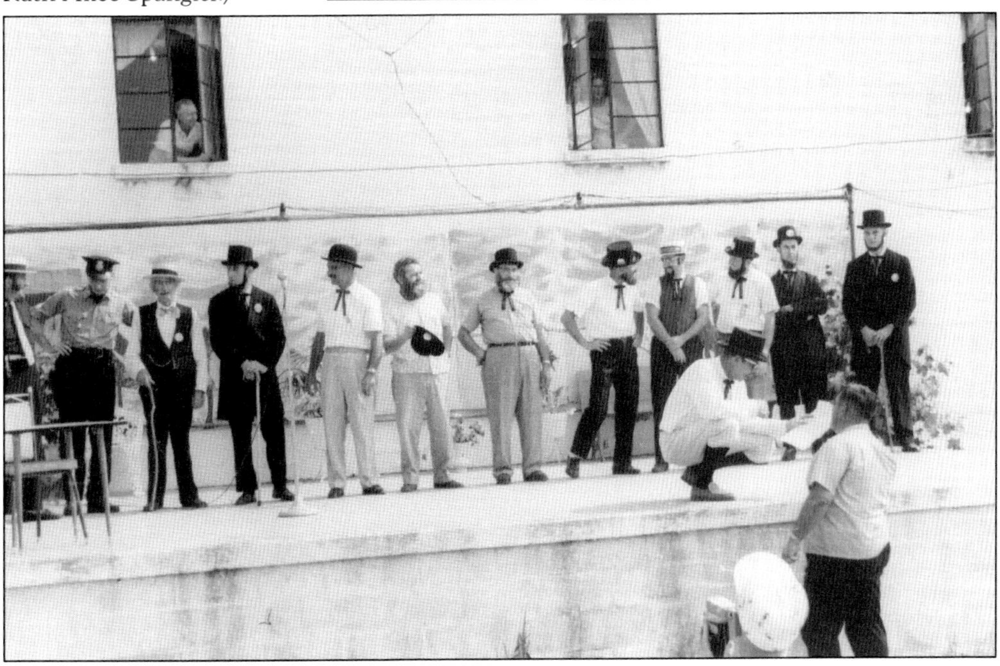

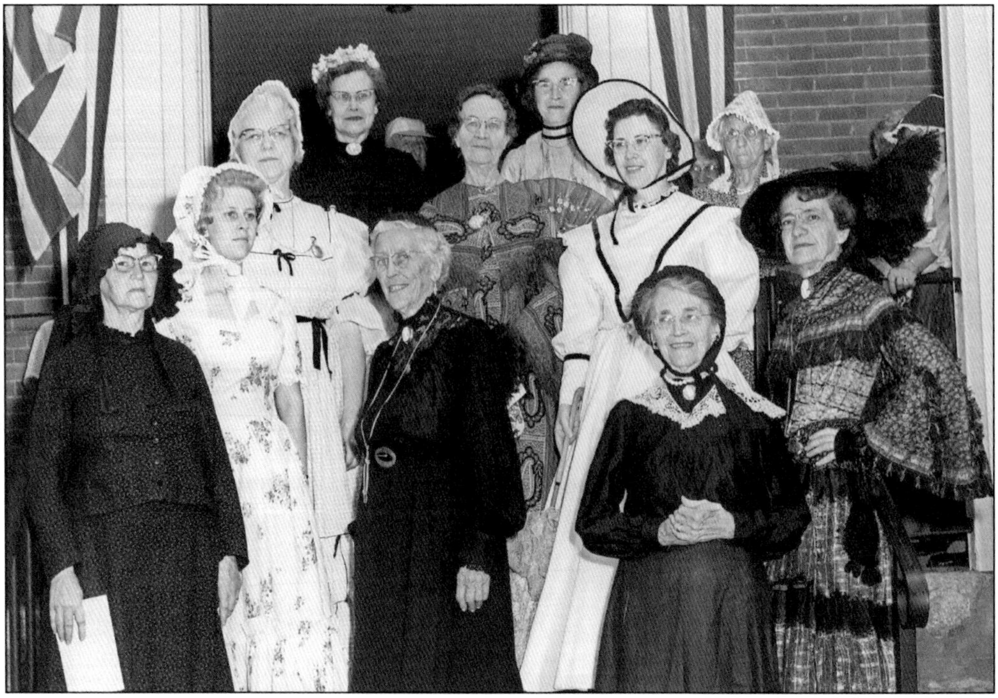

Sesquicentennial celebrants in 1963 are, from left to right, (first row) Hilda Musser, Cora Seebold, and Esther Miller; (second row) Mary Jane Smith, Arlene English, and Winifred Smith; (third row) Ethel Moyer, Edith Wunderly, and Mary Miller; (fourth row) Josephine Spangler and Kathryn Hackenburg. (NBHA.)

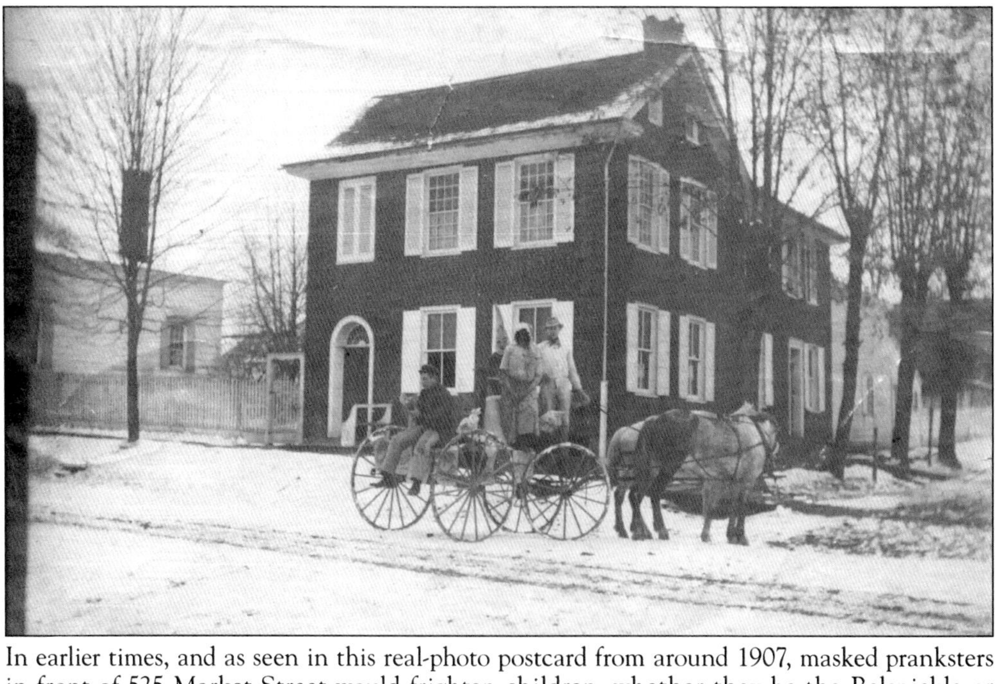

In earlier times, and as seen in this real-photo postcard from around 1907, masked pranksters in front of 525 Market Street would frighten children, whether they be the Belsnickle or ragamuffins. (NBHA.)

Archie Miller, on the violin, and Lawrence Lawson, on the mandolin, were musicians who learned their art from traditions passed down by word of mouth. They played into the 1980s, when appreciation for their skill was especially keen. In the right photograph, they pose in front of the original Union County stone jail (note the bars across the windows), on the northwest corner of Market and Plum Streets. Harry D'Addario (below), another New Berlin resident, was a master fiddler. He and his brother Marty D'Addario, from Middleburg, were featured on the album *Oh Mother It Hurts Me So*, recorded by the Oral Traditions Project of the Union County Historical Society in 1980. (NBHA.)

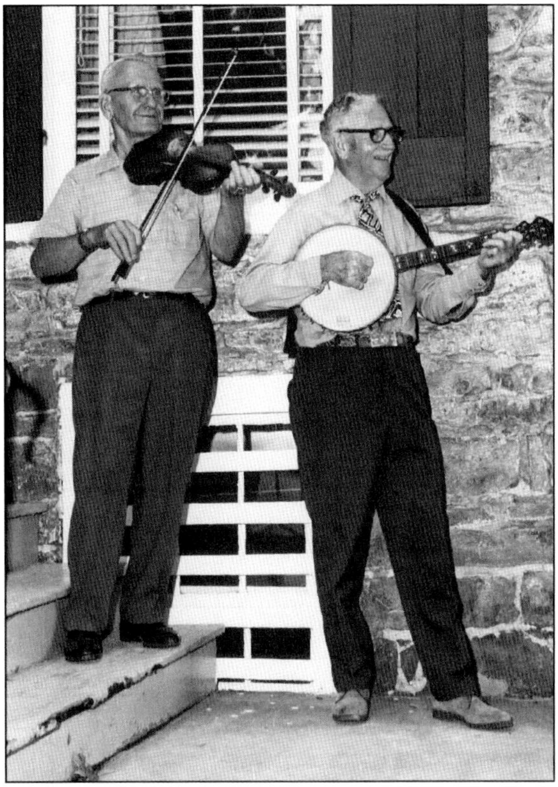

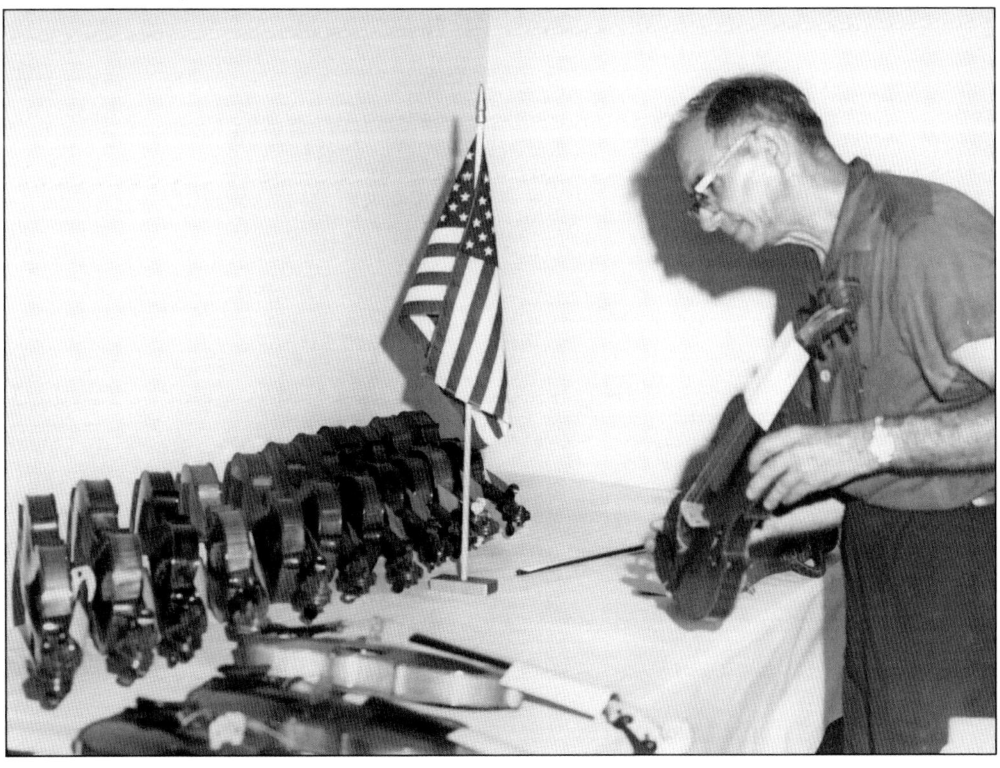

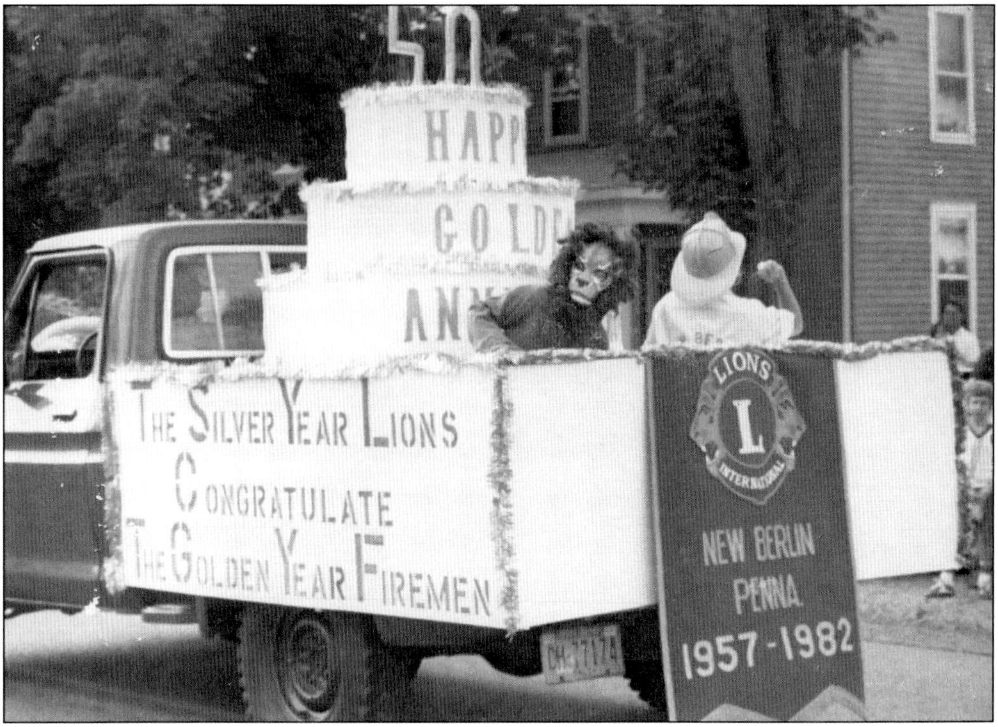

A parade was held in New Berlin commemorating both the golden anniversary of the New Berlin Fire Company and the silver anniversary of the local chapter of the Lions Club. These parade photographs from 1982 were taken by staff of the *Union County Journal*. The weekly county newspaper transitioned to become the *Lewisburg Daily Journal* in 1987 and then merged with the *Milton Standard* in 2003 to become *The Standard Journal*. The New Berlin Fire Company's founders still living in 1982 were, from left to right, as follows: Harry D'Addario, Roy Kline, Archie Miller, Carl Moyer, Ellsworth Snook, and David Solomon. (Above, UCHS 2009.1.6; below, NBHA.)

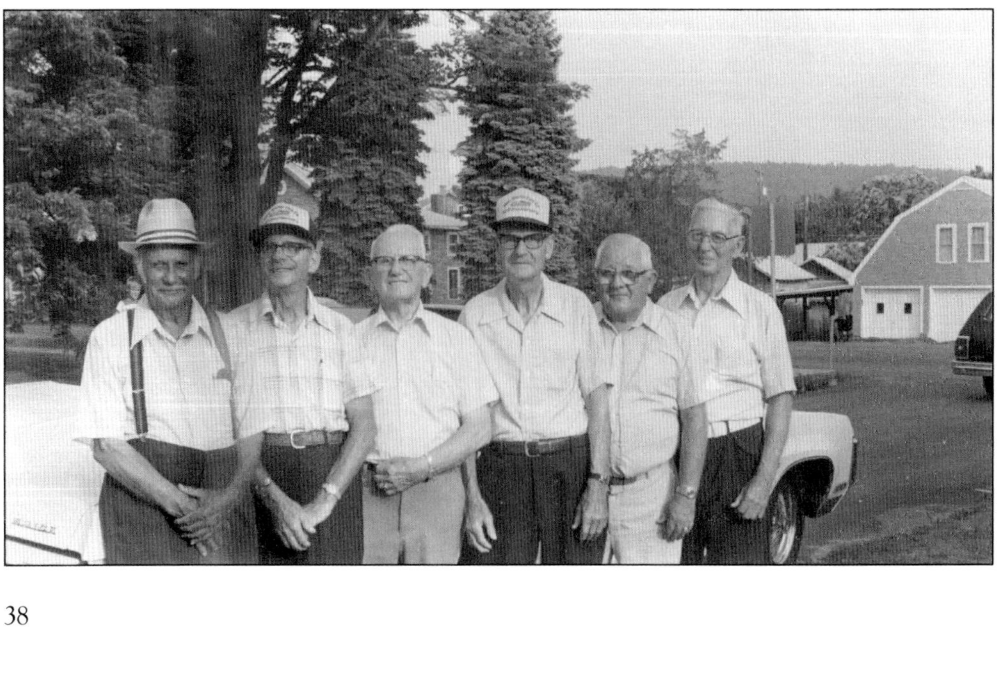

The Evangelical Church, one of five church buildings in town, stood at the southwest corner of Market and Plum Streets. It was photographed by Mifflinburg amateur photographer Grover Bierly in 1915 (right). This was the second building on the site, the first being a 34-by-38-foot log building constructed in 1816 and razed in 1873 to make room for the larger, brick building. Today, the former church, without its original steeple, is home to The Integral Yoga Center at 428 Market Street. The Lutheran church, built in 1867, was also photographed in 1915 by Bierly. It is the subject of the real-photo postcard below. An adjacent home on the east side of the Messiah Lutheran Church was razed in 1963 to allow for an addition housing a parish hall and seven classrooms. (UCHS 79.458.7 and .4.)

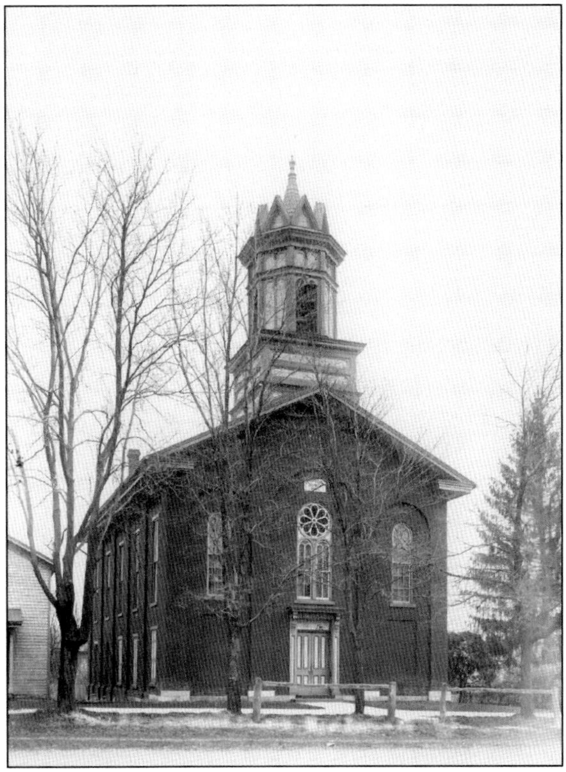

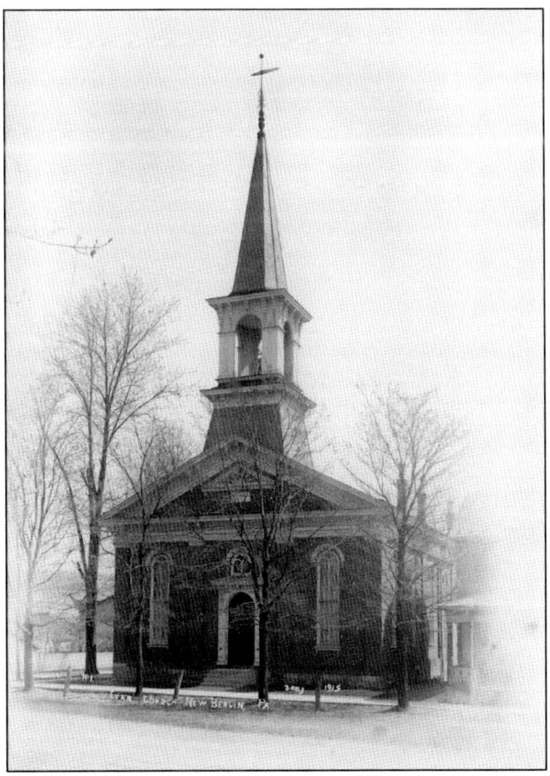

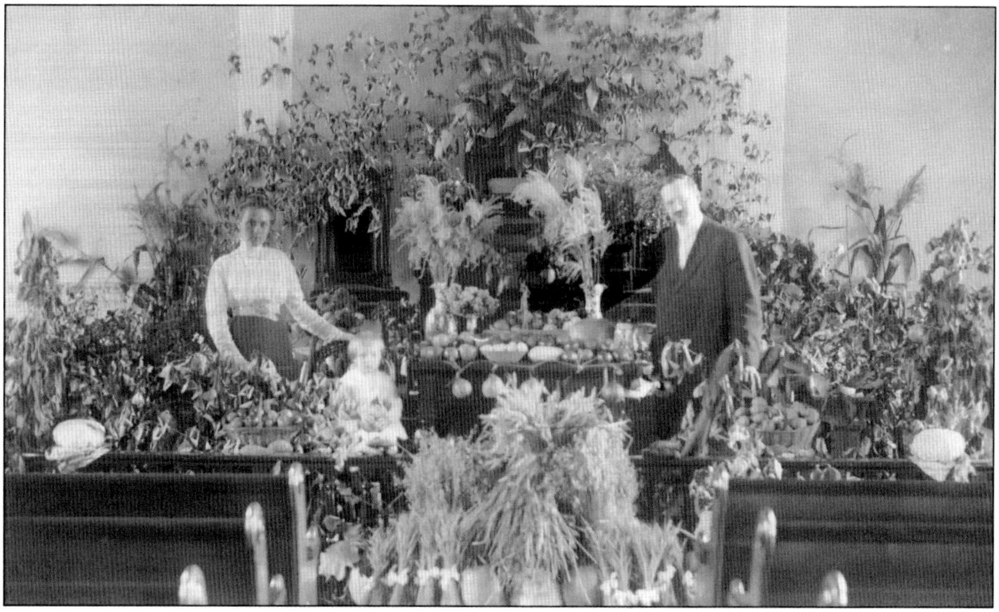

Above, a photograph of Harvest Home decorations at the Messiah Evangelical Lutheran Church includes the Reverend H.L. Gerstmyer and his family. The ups and downs of the Gabriel weathervane began when it was mounted on the steeple of the town's original Lutheran and Reformed church in 1822. After the split between the congregations, Gabriel was removed in 1910 while a new church, renamed the Evangelical Church, was built. In 1976, Gabriel found a temporary repose in the front yard of the parsonage of Nevin Maurer (below). It resided in the basement of the Evangelical Church before being remounted. In 1985, however, the 1822 angel was taken down again because of reports that old weather vanes were subject to theft. A replica of Gabriel was made, and the original was placed in the sanctuary. (NBHA.)

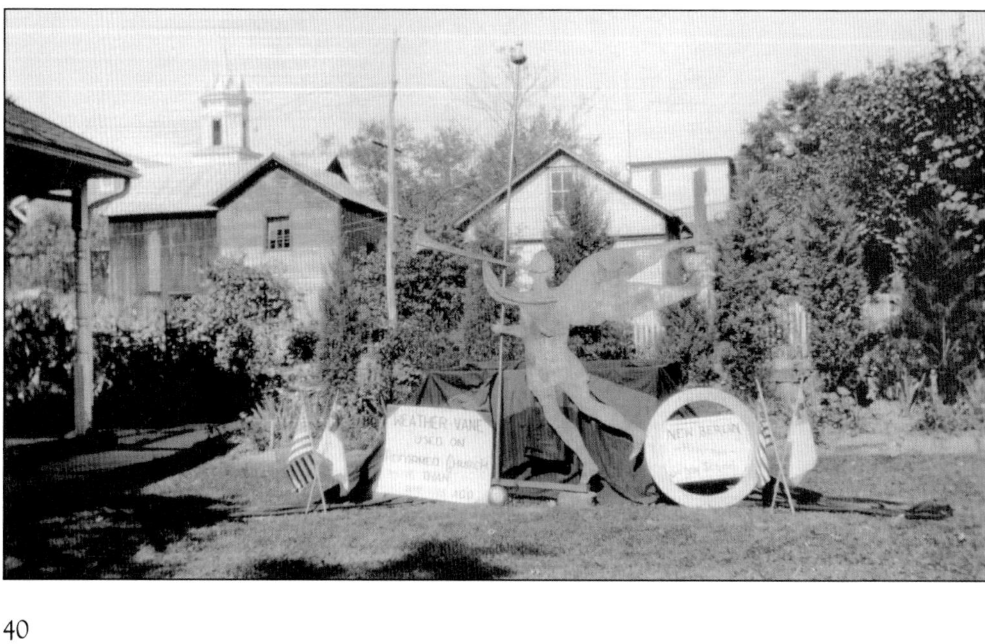

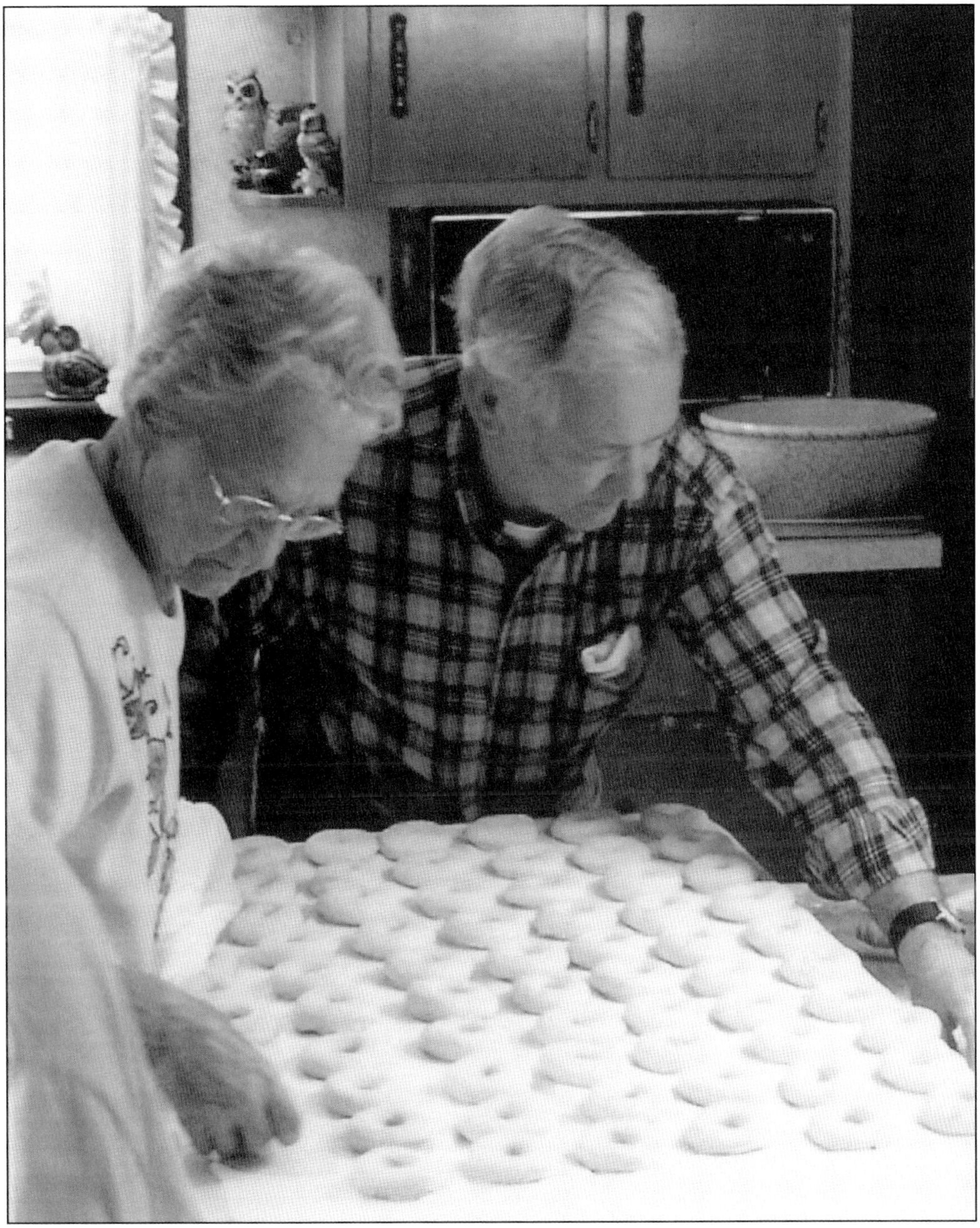

The 50-year-old Donut Day tradition began in 1958, when Catherine "Cass" Maurer's son Elmer, the New Berlin Explorer Scout advisor, needed a fundraiser for his troop. Cass had watched her mother make donuts and had helped Ethel Herman make them at the Kratzerville Reformed Church. So, every cool month of the year, in the basement of The Emmanuel Church, Cass headed the fundraising donut effort, along with Mary Moll, Ellen Ulrich, Gertie Beaver, Annie Ulrich, Kass Hackenburg, Ethel Moyer, Dot Eaton, Elmer Maurer, and his brothers. Pictured here in 2008 are Cass and her son Robert Maurer, of Mifflinburg. Cass and a crew of 10 still fried about 100 dozen rounds starting at 5:00 a.m. Two helpers mixed the batter, two rolled and cut the dough, one or two did the frying in lard, two sugared, and two bagged, sold, and delivered donuts fried for Fastnacht Day, also known as Shrove Tuesday, Mardi Gras, or Fat Tuesday. (John Showers.)

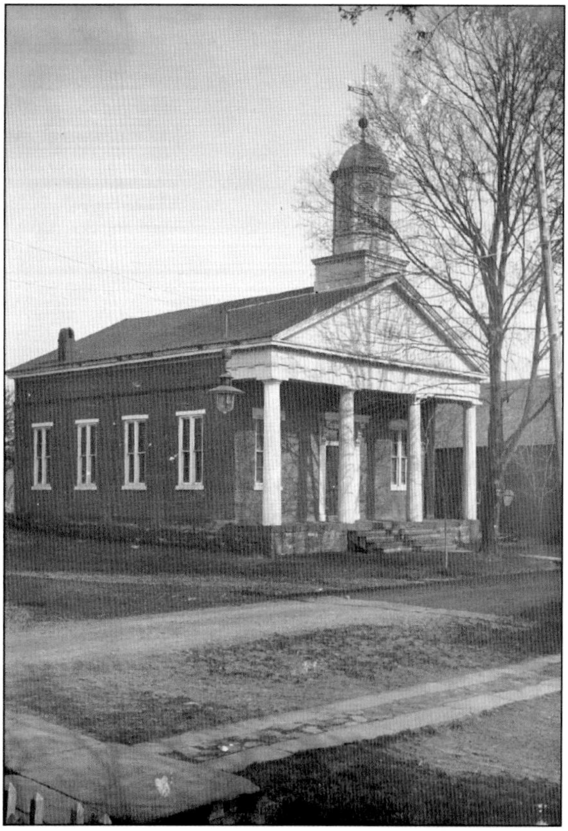

The exterior of the Presbyterian Church on Vine and High Streets remains mostly unchanged from the 1915 photograph, left, by Grover Bierly. Its interior (below) was also photographed. James Merril, John Lashells, and Joseph Stillwell were the first elders of the church, which was built in 1844 by a small congregation. No longer a place of worship as of 1944, it now serves New Berlin as its community center. The New Berlin Borough Council meets there monthly, along with other groups. It was refurbished, then rededicated on August 19, 2007. Major funding came from the Pennsylvania Historical and Museum Commission, the Degenstein Foundation, a Community Development Block grant, and two Community Revitalization grants. This was augmented by community fundraising events and a large bank loan to complete the project. (NBHA.)

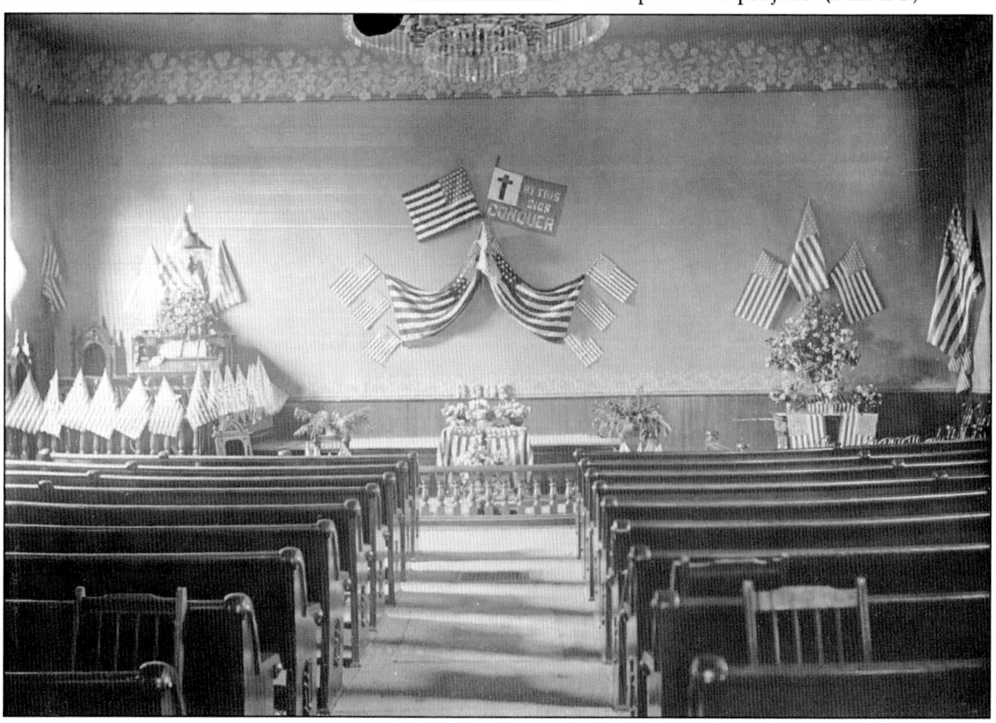

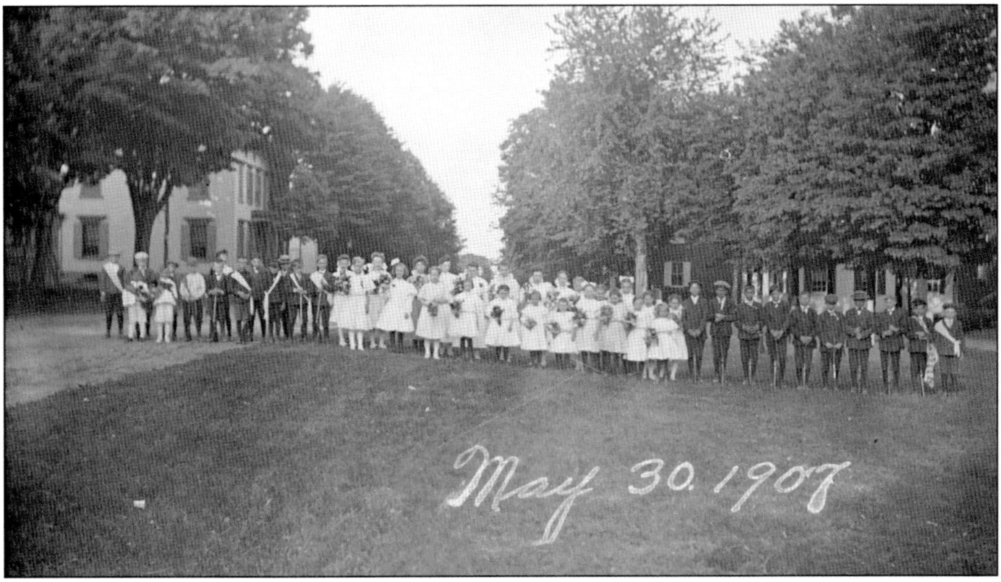

In towns large and small, residents love parades, whether the occasion is Memorial Day, Flag Day, or a homecoming. These photographs were taken during a Memorial Day parade in 1907. A *carte de visite* (below) by New Berlin photographer Charles H. Venus (1872–1959) presents Odd Fellows on Flag Day, June 8, 1898. A flag ceremony was also held annually on Memorial Day. In the below photograph, Johnny Roshorn, the maker of the flag, stands at center left. Capt. David Mitchell (d. 1904), a Civil War veteran of Company D, 208th Regiment, is on the right. The Odd Fellows building is seen in the background, on the south side of Market Street between the Reformed and Lutheran churches. David Heckendorn (d. 1864) had a photography studio in New Berlin prior to Venus. (NBHA.)

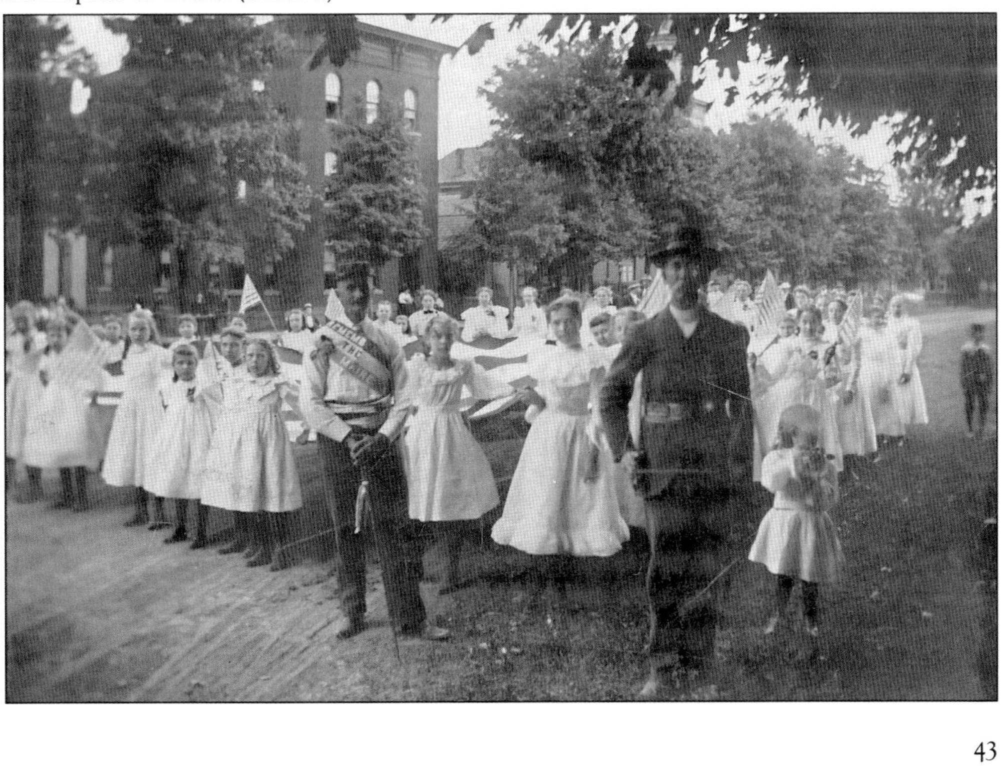

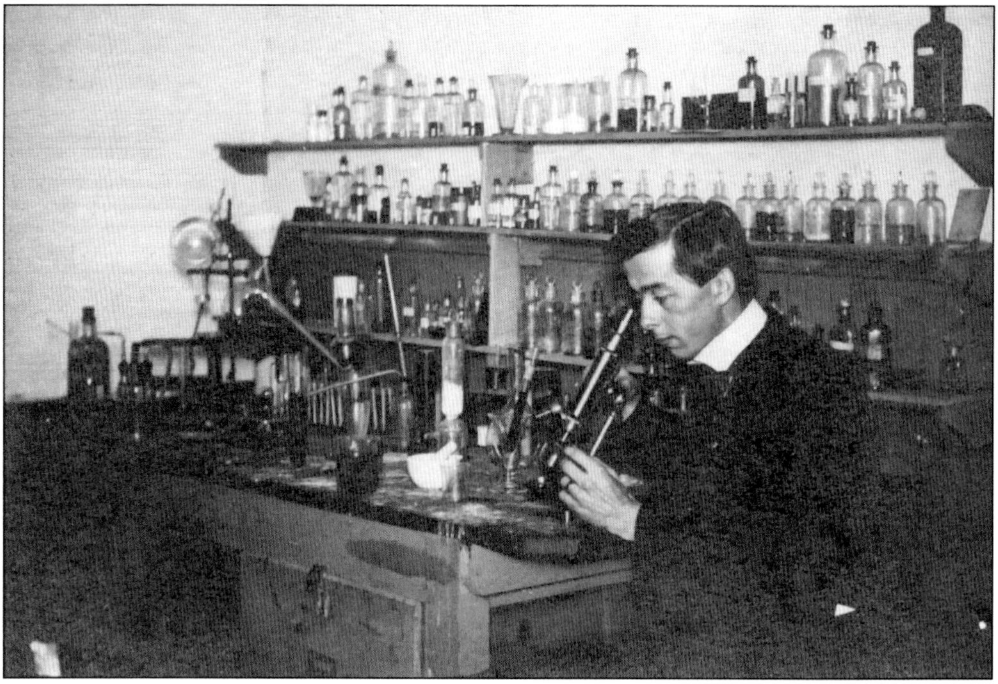

The Union Seminary, established in 1856, was the Evangelical Church's first institution of higher learning. It was reorganized as Central Pennsylvania College in 1887. Between 1902 and 1911, it served as a private high school, again called the Union Seminary. The New Berlin Heritage Association has a large collection of photographs from the Central Pennsylvania College days that include the physics lab, chemistry lab, classes, and graduating seniors as well as its band, orchestra, and football and baseball teams. Albright College in Berks County, Pennsylvania, was named for Jacob Albright (Albrecht), who inspired the Evangelical Church movement in New Berlin and Dry Valley starting with a series of visits in 1806–1807. Converts who were particularly influential were Martin and John Dreisbach, John Aurand, and Michael Maize, all of Limestone Township or New Berlin, Abraham Eyer of Winfield, and John Ranck of White Deer. (NBHA.)

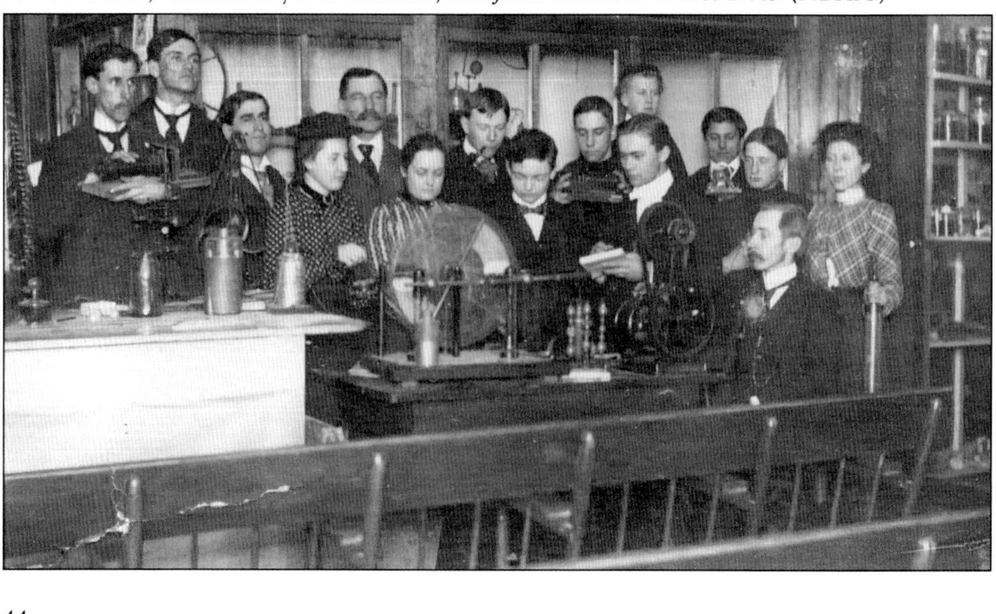

After 1886, the four-story building included a new dormitory floor, while classrooms, a study, and the chapel were housed below. Central College, as it was then named, eventually consolidated with Albright College. The photographs on this page were taken during the building's last years as a private high school. In this photograph, Jay Arthur Napp is pictured on the right in a dormitory room around 1908 or 1909. The Union Seminary football and baseball teams often played local high schools, including Mifflinburg High School. The *Mifflinburg Telegraph* noted on May 18, 1906, "Mifflinburg crossed bats with Union Seminary at New Berlin last Saturday and were defeated by a score of 8-5."

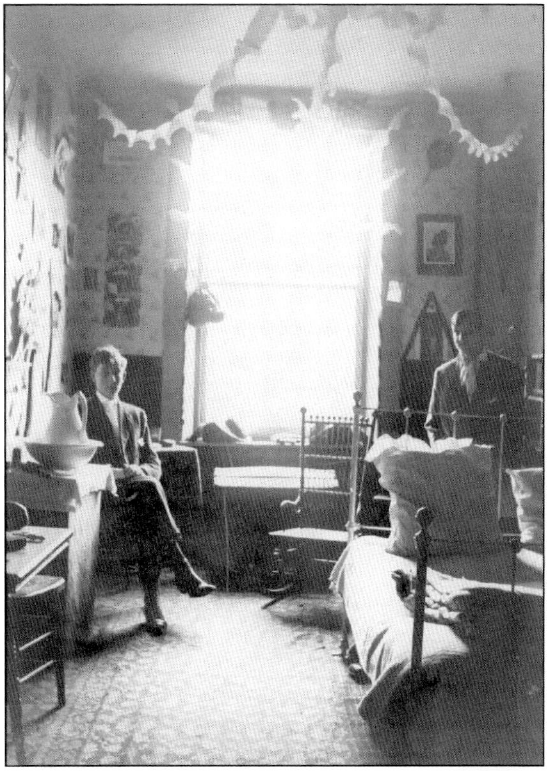

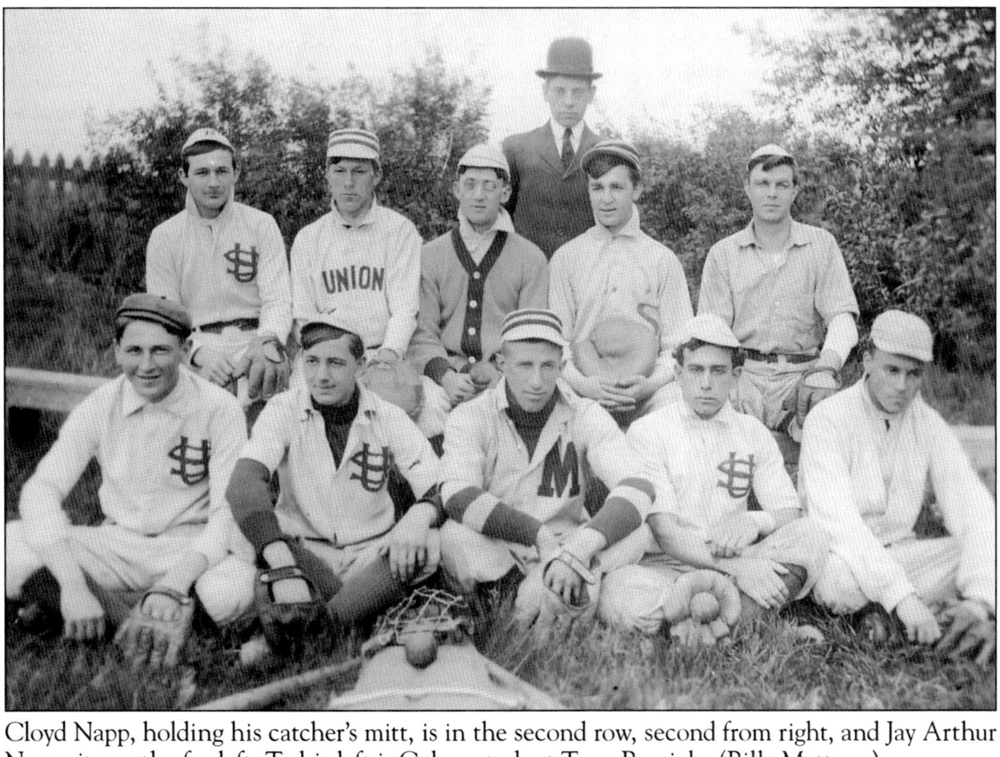

Cloyd Napp, holding his catcher's mitt, is in the second row, second from right, and Jay Arthur Napp sits on the far left. To his left is Cuban student Tony Bossiale. (Billy Mattern.)

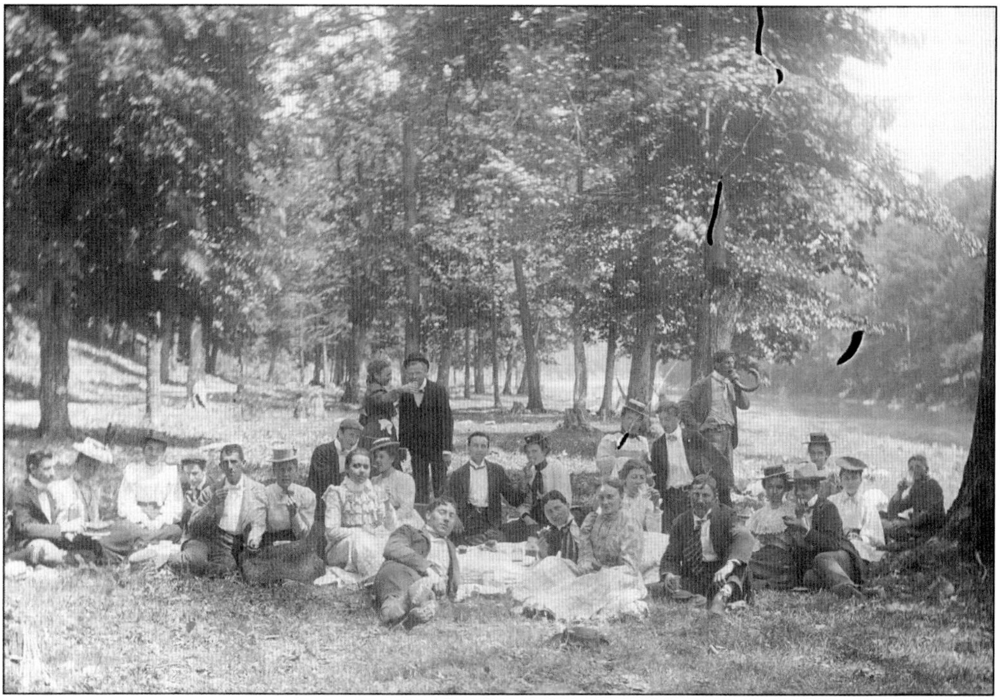

New Berlin photographer Charles H. Venus photographed a Central College group picnic above Sampsell's Dam on May 30, 1899. Students were often photographed in classes, as well as during leisure moments, such as fishing, boating, cycling, or, as in the below photograph, cutting capers for the photographer in the 1890s. (NBHA.)

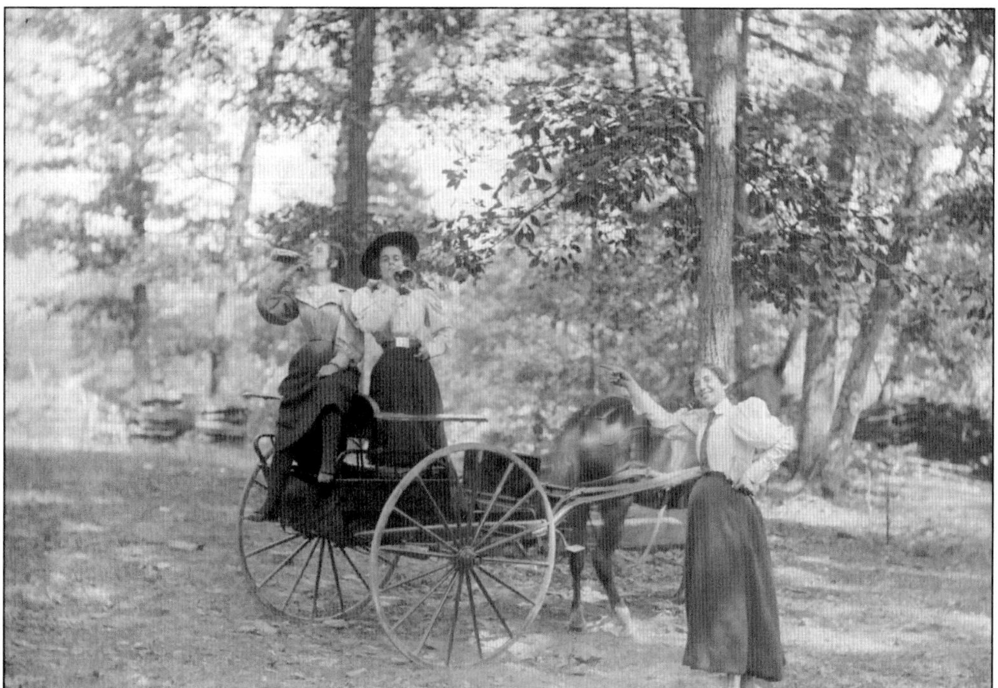

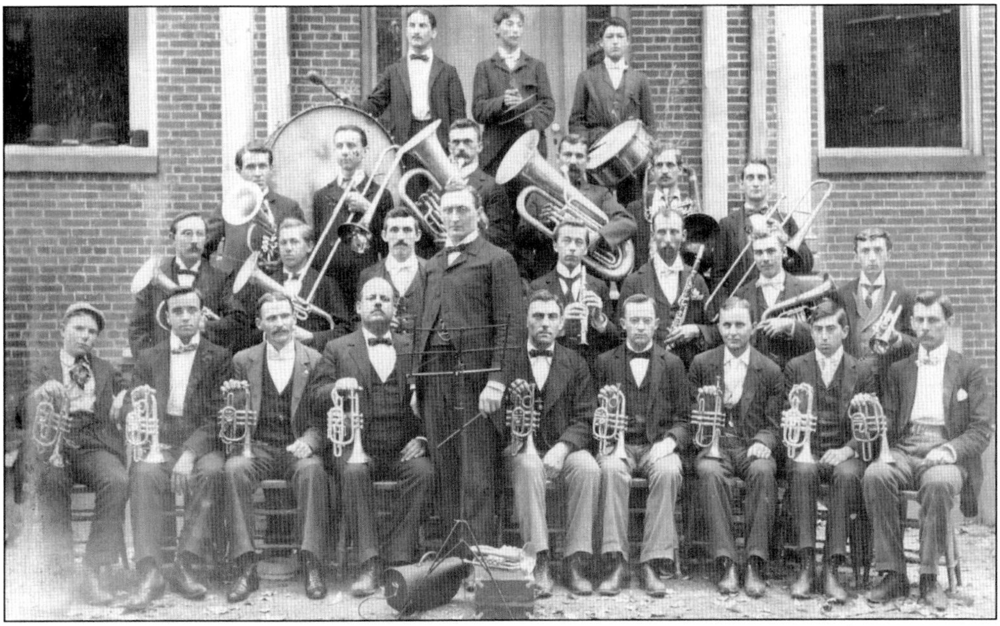

The Central College band included area scholars and those from other towns and states. Posing here are, from left to right, (first row) ? Reamer, H.C. Stover, ? Kingler, unidentified, ? Keiss (conductor), ? Winter, unidentified, ? Mock, ? Kreitzer, ? Kniss, and ? Keaffer; (second row) Guy Stover, ? Carmany, ? Smith, ? Venus, ? Ledkichler, ? Lovel, and ? Hoch; (third row) ? Wetzel, ? Hurd, ? Stine, two unidentified men, and ? Guthrie; (fourth row) ? Sakeld, ? Orwig, and ? Oldt. (NBHA.)

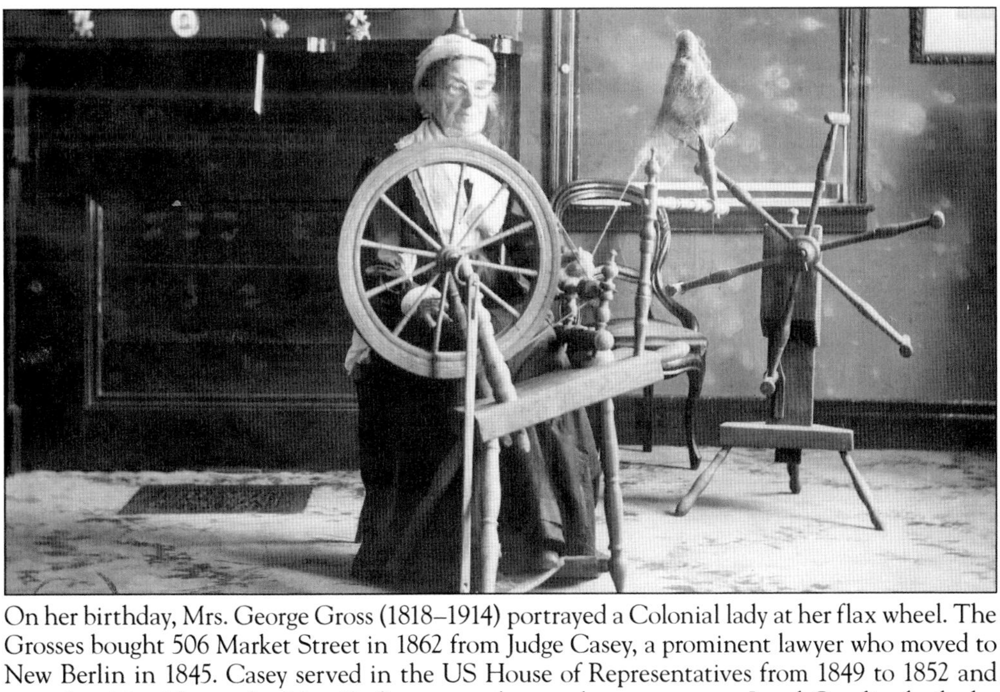

On her birthday, Mrs. George Gross (1818–1914) portrayed a Colonial lady at her flax wheel. The Grosses bought 506 Market Street in 1862 from Judge Casey, a prominent lawyer who moved to New Berlin in 1845. Casey served in the US House of Representatives from 1849 to 1852 and moved to Harrisburg after New Berlin was no longer the county seat. Israel Gutelius built the house around 1845. (NBHA.)

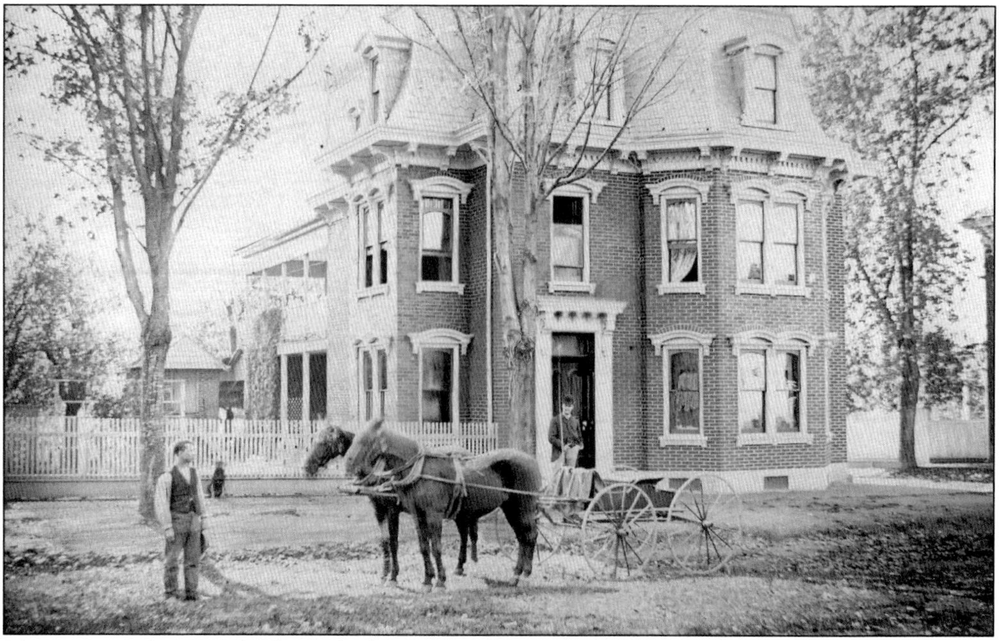

The c. 1906 photograph above, looking west on Market Street, shows the home of New Berlin native son and physician Dr. Harry Mauck Wilson (1877–1916). It is one of a few New Berlin structures built in the 1880s, as evidenced by its mansard roof. The newly reorganized Central Pennsylvania College (below) also had a mansard roof on its new fourth floor, built when the former Union Seminary building was remodeled between 1883 and 1886. This building was razed and the New Berlin Elementary School of the Mifflinburg School District was built on the site in 1953. The last classes were held there in June 2012. The building's new use has not been determined, but the site has historically been designated for educational purposes since the seminary's first transfer of title. (NBHA.)

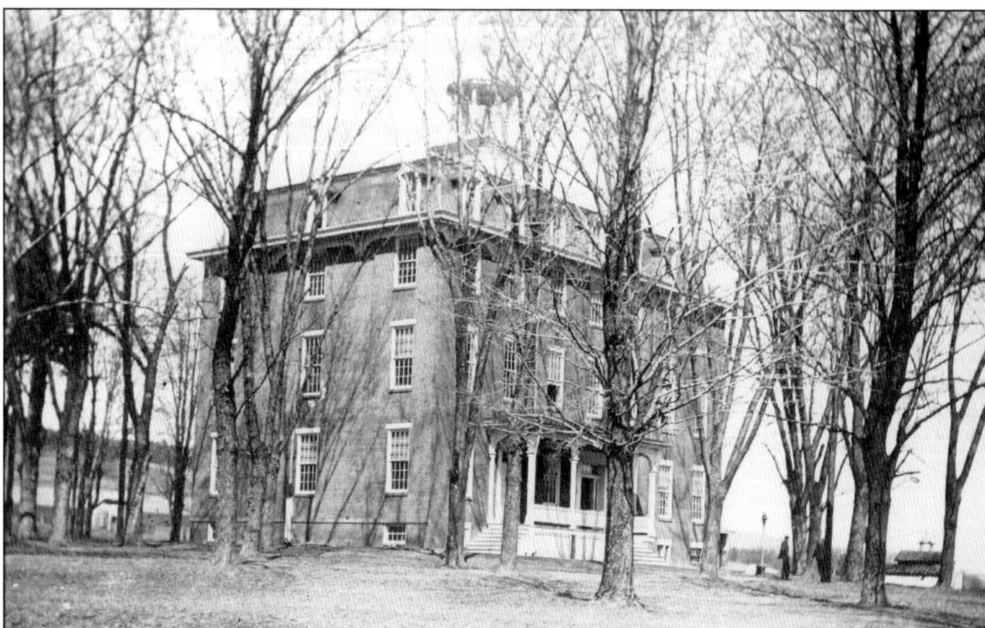

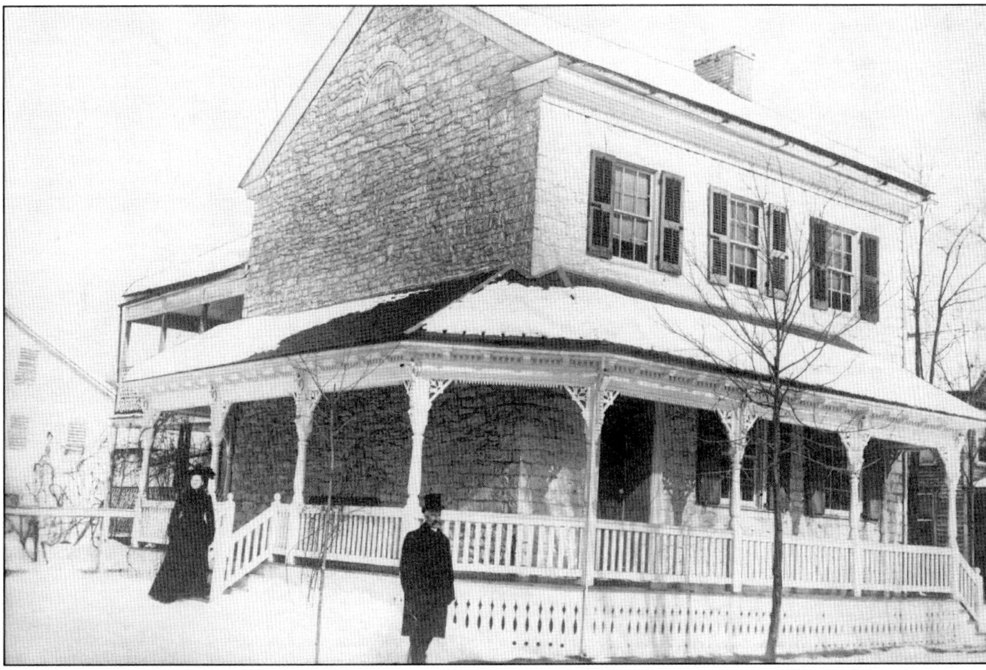

Edward and "Lizzie" (Manbeck) Seebold are seen in the above photograph at their home on the northwest corner of Front and Walnut Streets around 1905. One of two limestone homes in New Berlin, the residence was built by William Kessler (the date stone reads "1814 WK"). Kessler owned a tannery behind the house and was also Union County commissioner (1819), treasurer (1823–1825), and justice of the peace (1833). In 1835, Abraham Schoch, one of three generations of tanners, lived there and ran the tannery. The stone for the house may have come from Henry Gross's land west of town. Sam Schoch had a tannery on Tan Run and lived on Front Street near his brother. The below photograph, taken on Market Street, includes Mrs. Charles Border on the far left, Mary Ellen Harbacher in the cart, and Anna Horlacher beside the child. (Above, UCHS 2012.4.3; below, NBHA.)

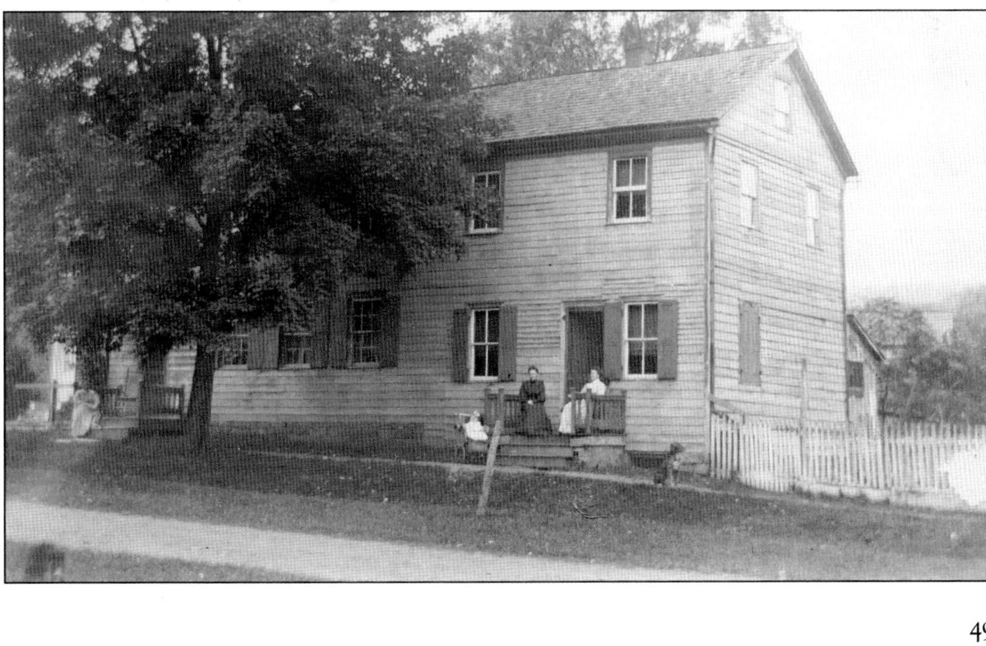

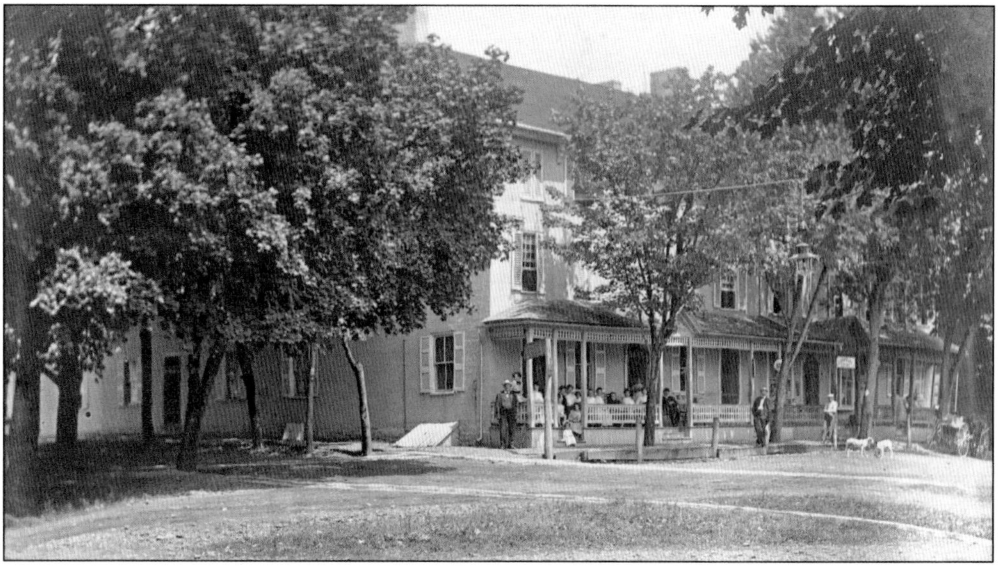

Union Hotel was photographed before and after a devastating fire on December 8, 1912. It had been constructed by Christopher Seebold in 1818, and was later enlarged by owner Michael Kleckner (1807–1887). Five arched doorways were focal points in its handsome facade. The blaze began at 11:45 p.m. on December 8 and was out of control before outside help could arrive. Having rained earlier that night and with no wind, the fire did not spread. The home, partially seen on the far right in the below photograph, and an auxiliary building later belonged to Robert W. and Grace Miller. In the 1970s, Grace Miller used the side building, formerly the office of the *New Berlin Reporter,* as a restaurant called The Towne House. Today, both buildings belong to David and Sally Farmer. (Above, NBHA; below, UCHS 86.3.8)

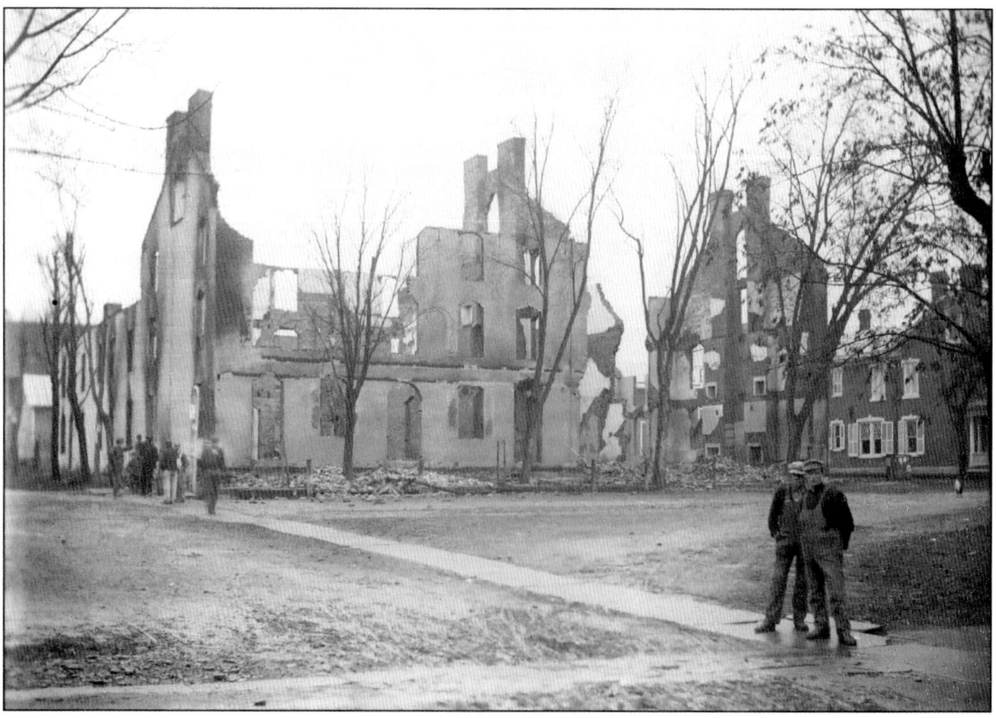

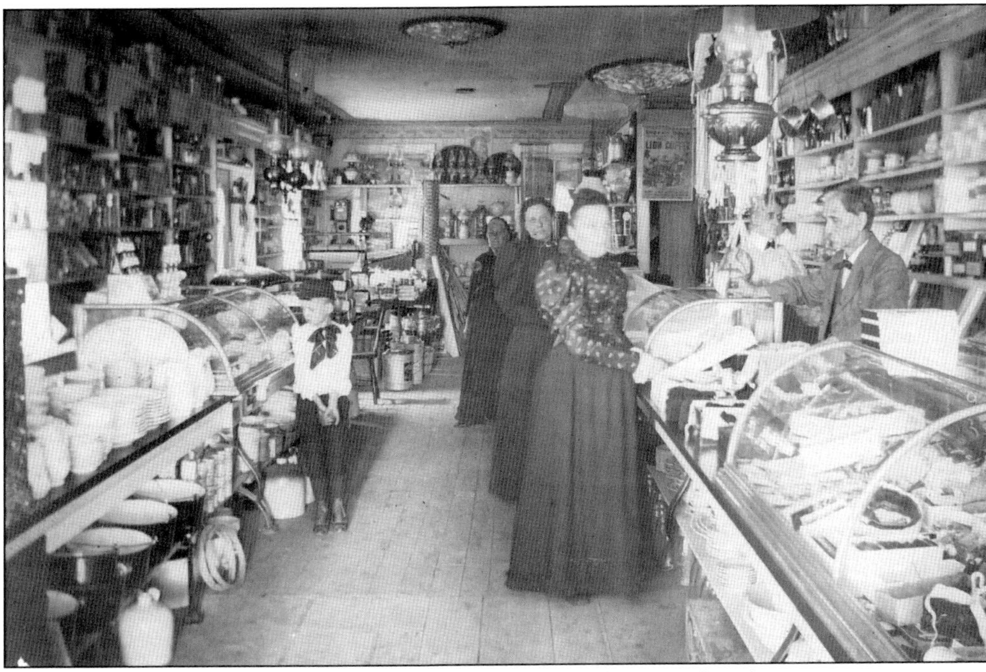

Above, a cabinet photograph, taken by Charles H. Venus of New Berlin, shows a rare interior view of a commercial establishment. This is George Rothfon's store, which sold groceries, hardware, Queensware, drugs, medicines, and chemicals, at 307 Front Street. Another interior view (below) is of a printing shop, probably Homer Smith's on Market Street. He printed the *New Berlin Reporter* until 1930. (Above, UCHS 2009.6; below, NBHA.)

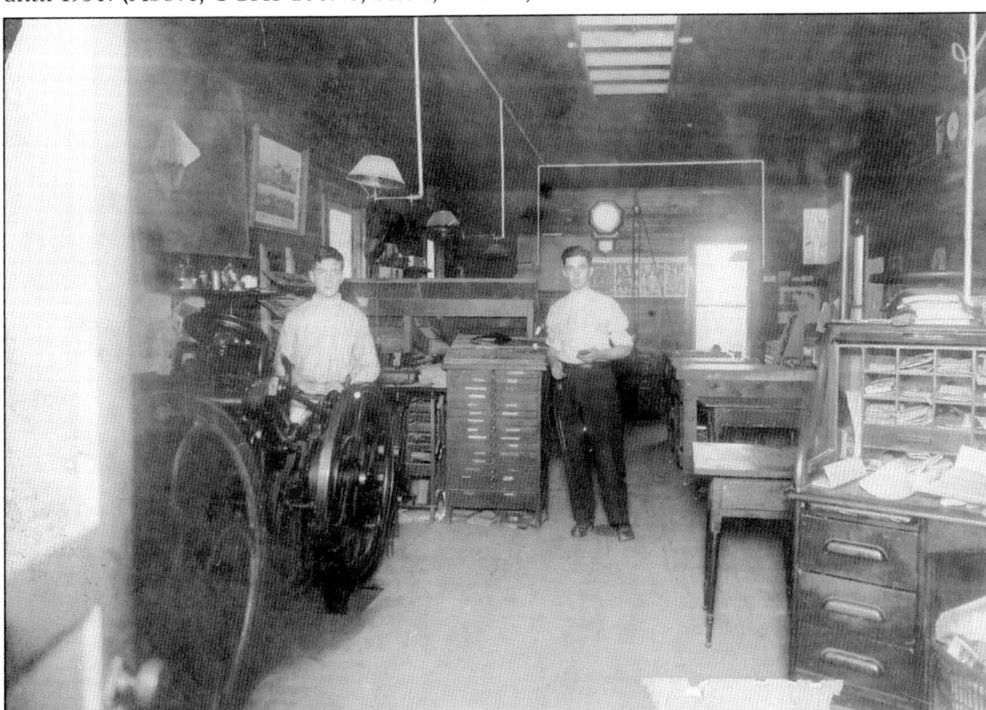

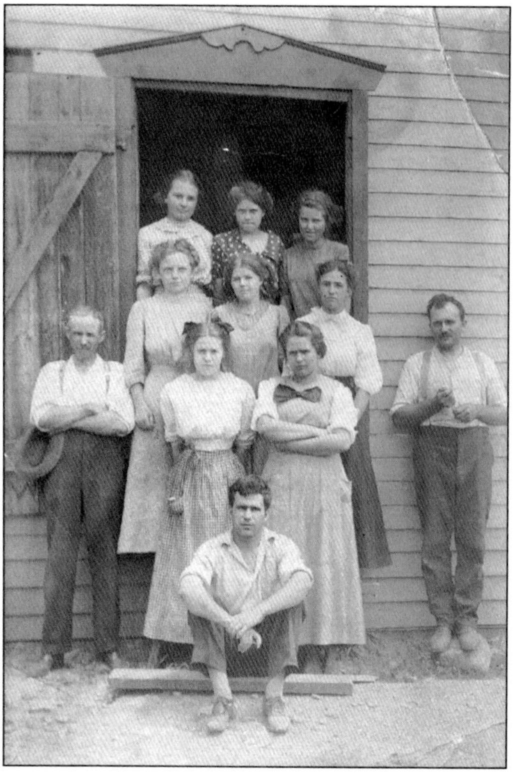

The first stocking factory in Union County was located in New Berlin, in the 300 block of Front Street. Employees of the factory are seen in the left photograph. Later clothing firms established in town included two hosiery mills, a silk mill, a shirt factory, the New Berlin Garment Factory, Middleburg Sportswear, Sew-Comp, and, most recently, Tara Lee Sportswear in 1978. Textile production in earlier times had been in homes and by itinerant weavers who made coverlets and woven yard goods. Below, on April 14, 1898, umbrella-holding spectators view the smoldering remains of the stocking factory's fire. (Left, UCHS 85.23.2; below, NBHA.)

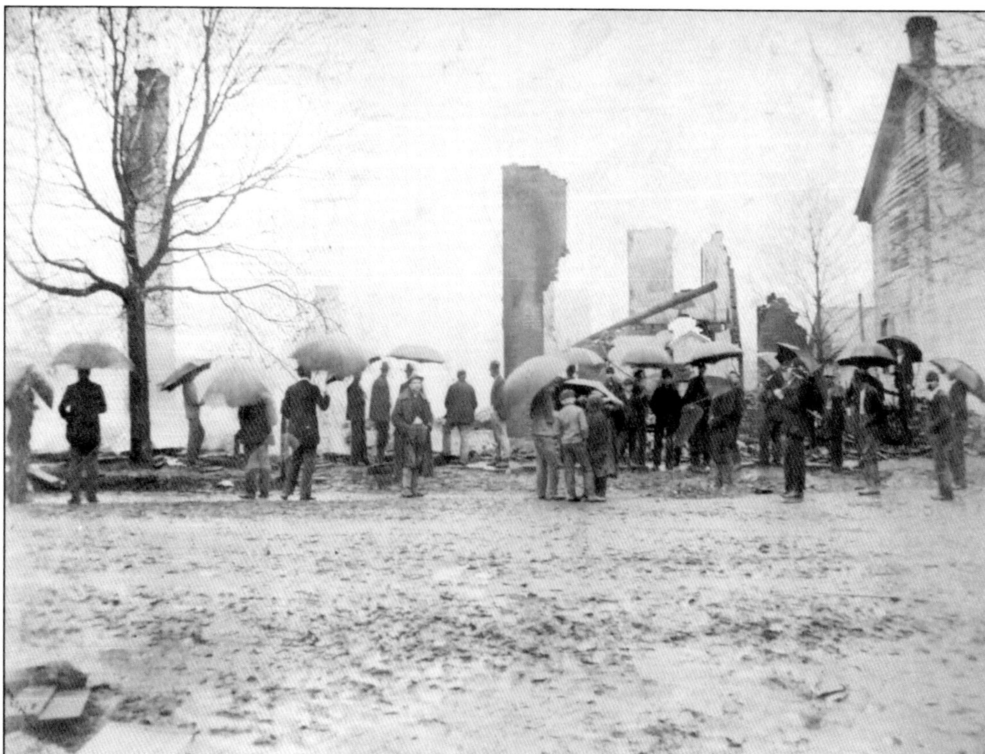

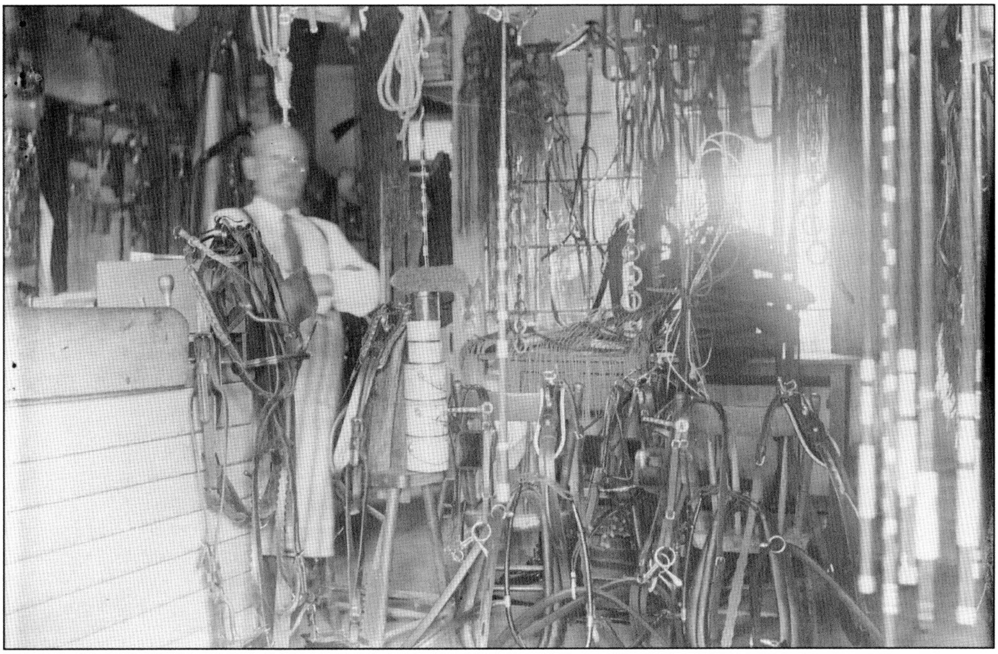

Calvin Bogar's harness shop, at 407–409 Front Street, is seen in the above photograph from 1908. Calvin D. Bogar (1851–1923), a saddler and harness maker through the 1910s, was a grandson of George Bogar, who purchased the property in 1825. The canvas work glove shop of Francis Bause (c. 1849–1947), below, is seen around 1910. It was located on the southeast corner of Market and Walnut Streets, across from the Rosedale Dairy. In 1916, it became the home of David and Sadie Maurer. For many years, Bause was also a trustee for New Berlin's Christ Evangelical Lutheran Church. (NBHA.)

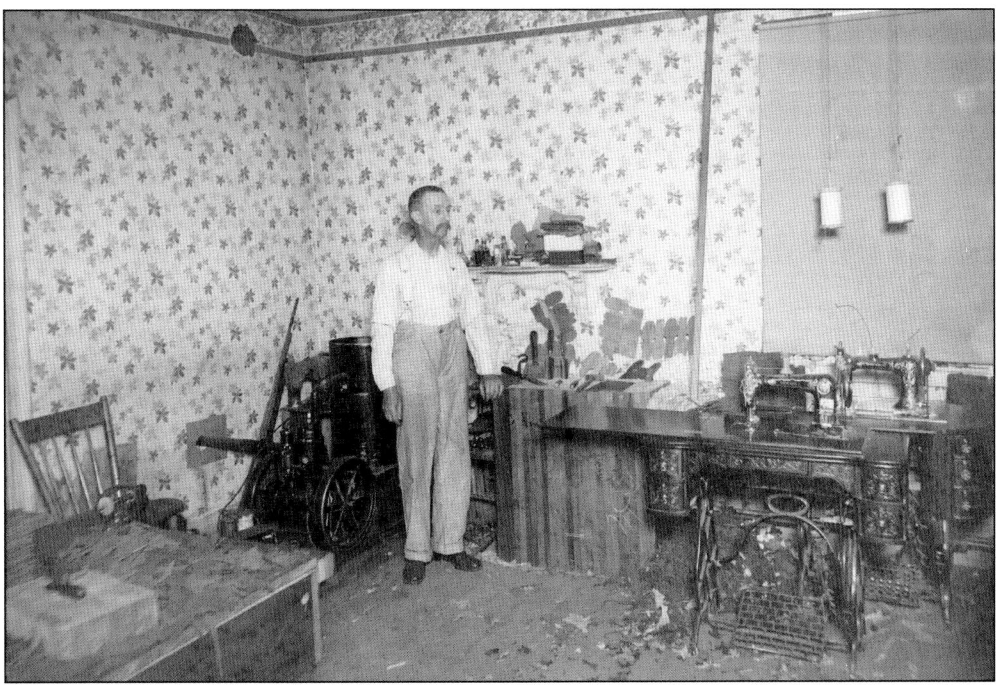

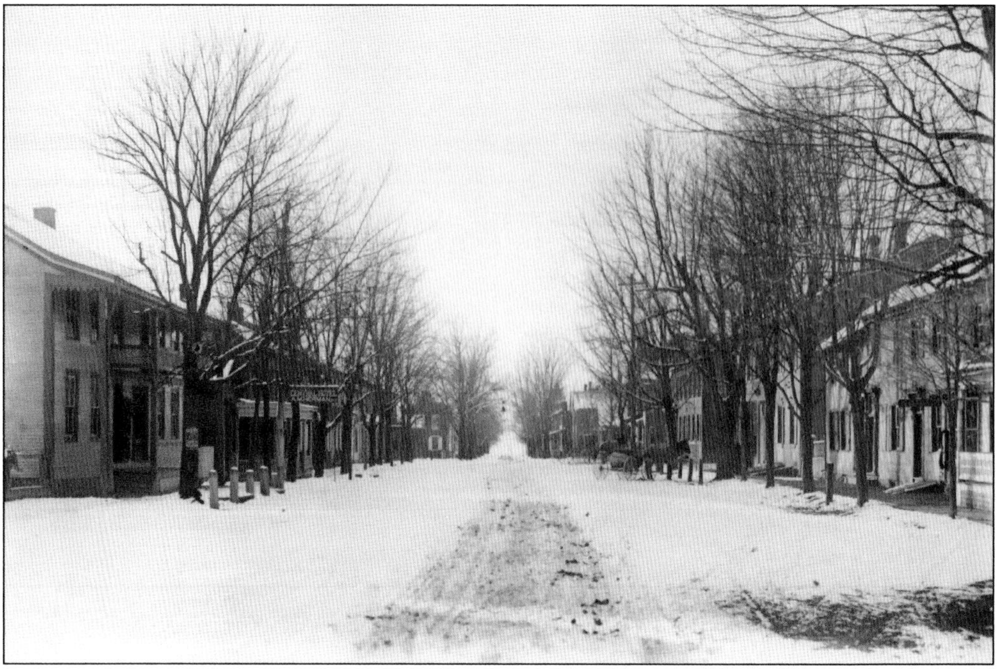

Country streets were often lined with trees. Barely visible on the left, even through winter leafless trees, is the sign for the Central Hotel. It was located on Front Street. A year and a half after the Union Hotel burned to the ground, the Central Hotel suffered the same fate. The latter was labeled a "suspicious fire," and the hotel's owner, A.M. Herman, was charged with arson. (NBHA.)

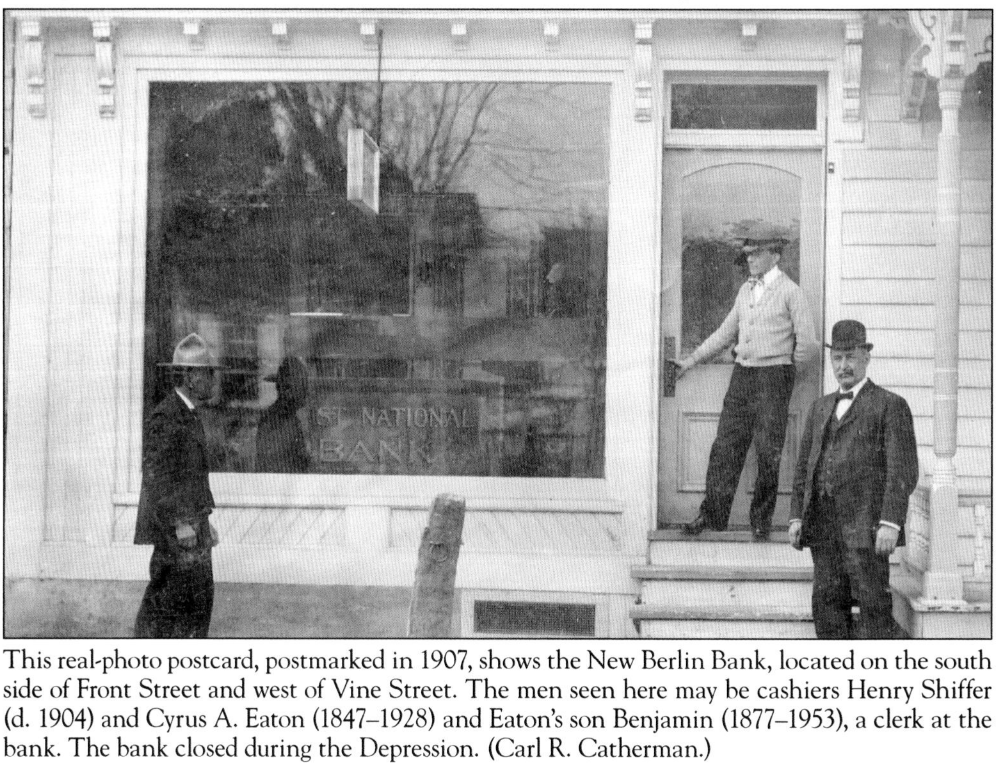

This real-photo postcard, postmarked in 1907, shows the New Berlin Bank, located on the south side of Front Street and west of Vine Street. The men seen here may be cashiers Henry Shiffer (d. 1904) and Cyrus A. Eaton (1847–1928) and Eaton's son Benjamin (1877–1953), a clerk at the bank. The bank closed during the Depression. (Carl R. Catherman.)

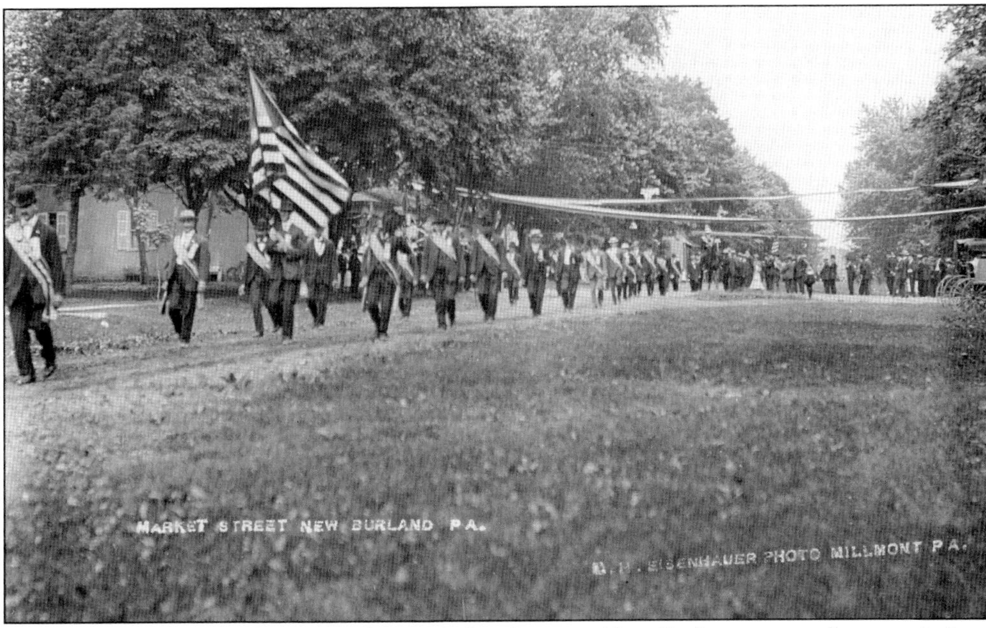

This view of a Memorial Day parade on Market Street in New Berlin was issued as a real-photo postcard by Millmont photographer Urs H. Eisenhauer around 1909. This is the only known example of Eisenhauer's work in New Berlin. Behind the buggies on the right is the original county courthouse, and across the street, barely seen, is the Union Hotel. The parade marchers are headed west toward Union Street. (NBHA.)

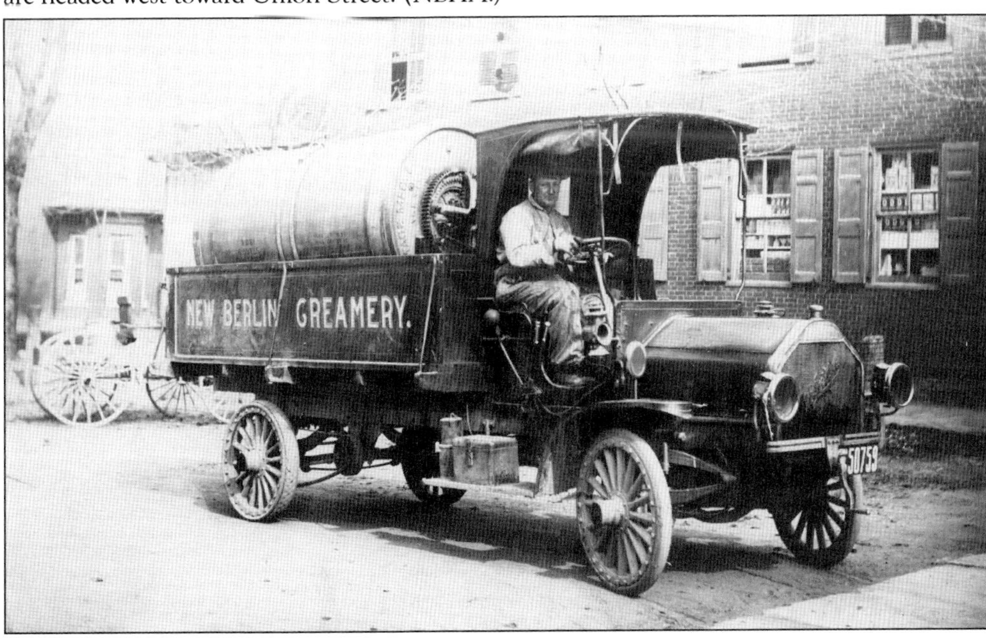

In New Berlin, organized dairy collection started with the Creamery. Owner Frank L. Maurer sold fancy separator butter, eggs, and poultry for about 15 years from his location on Walnut and Market Streets. Charles Oldt collected the milk from nearby Snyder County dairy farmers. Maurer also operated a general store at Front and Vine Streets. The New Berlin Creamery was bought by Harry McClow, who ran the business from around 1917 to 1924. (NBHA.)

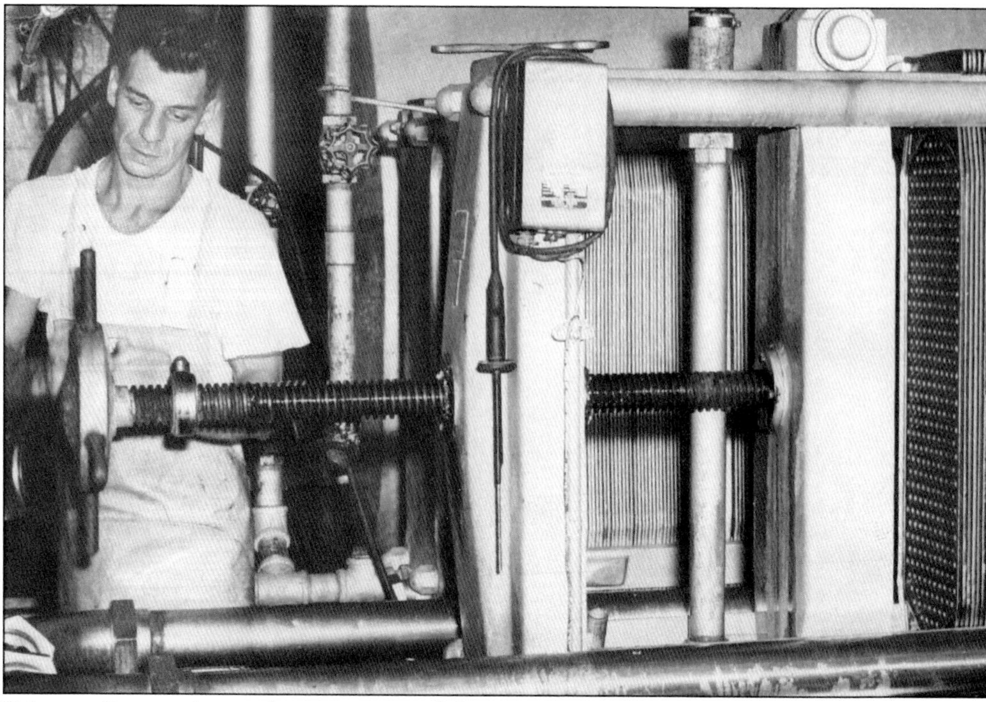

Ephraim Quat took over the creamery with his sons Arnold and Jack while a third son, Leon, a New York attorney, was a silent partner. Pratt Townsend was the business manager. The business prospered under these men, who hired as many as 55 employees at Rosedale. The dairy helped sustain New Berlin during the Depression. Workers from around 1930 included Raymond Aurand, Eddie Brouse, Simon Conrad, Harry D'Addario, Bill Faber, Ben Hollenbach, Russell Keister, Ralph Kline, Art Leitzel, Jacob and John Miller, Lamont Musser, Ambrose Oldt, Russell Ramsey, John Ripple, Lester Snook, Reno Spangler, and Pratt and Ralph Townsend. In the above photograph, a worker wraps cheese. In 1946, the Rosedale Dairy baseball team (below) was the West Branch League champion team. Baseball was an important community sport, and New Berlin fielded good teams. (Above, NBHA; below, UCHS 82C.46.22A.)

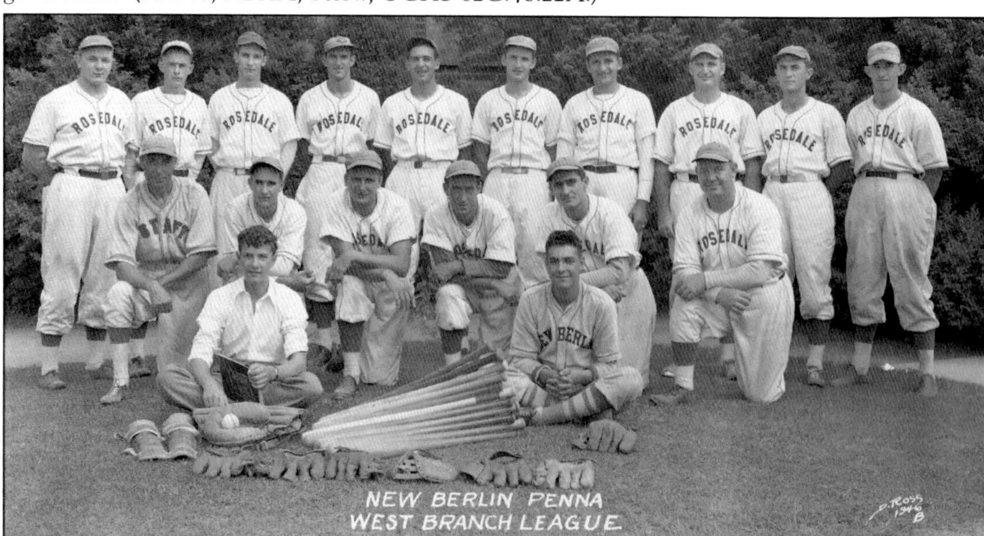

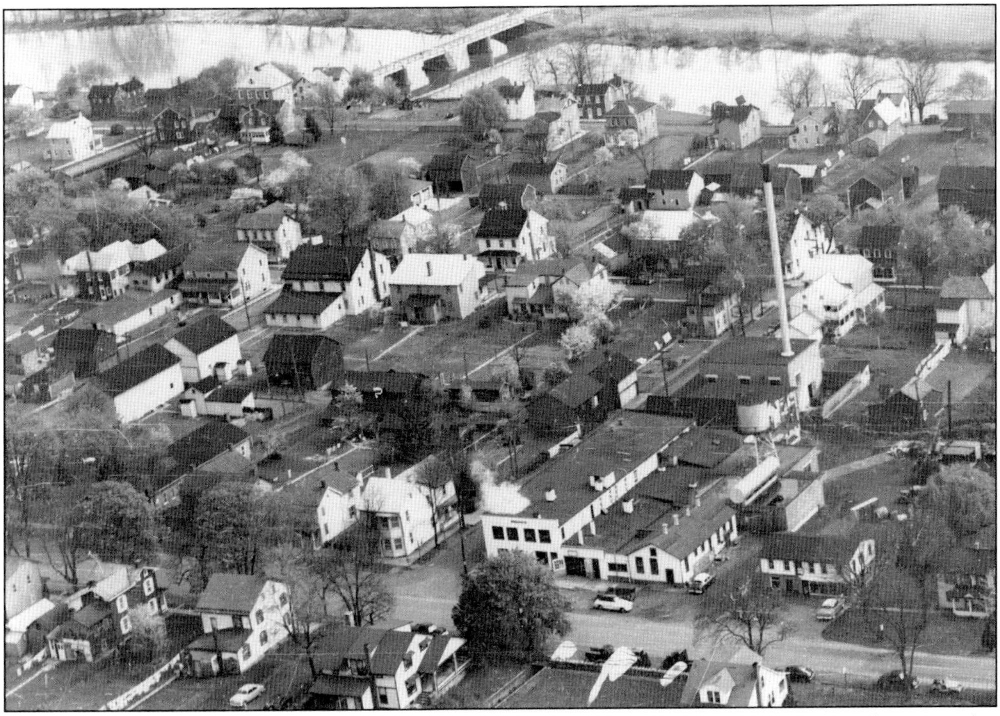

The above aerial view of town includes Rosedale Dairy, the large two-story complex near the lower right-hand corner. Its cream cheese was sold in rectangular wooden boxes printed in blue for Philadelphia Cream Cheese, red for a pimento cheese, and green for scallion cheese. Other types packed in tins were large curd farmers' cheese, lion's cheese called *schmere kase*, dried curd bakers' cheese, and popcorn cheese (one-half square curds in cream). Rosedale cheese was sold in Pennsylvania's coal region, Philadelphia, New York, and Baltimore. Condensed milk and yogurt products were added in the 1940s and 1950s. The dairy, active through 1962, was demolished by Keister Construction, which built a HUD housing project called the Rosedale Apartments on the cleared site. In the below photograph, milk cans to be delivered are lined up on the conveyor belt at the dairy. (NBHA.)

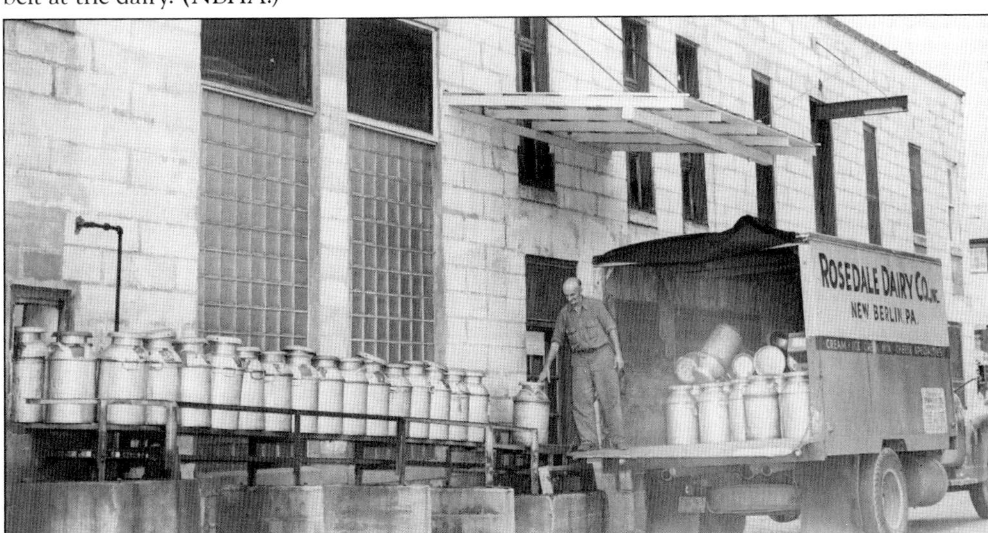

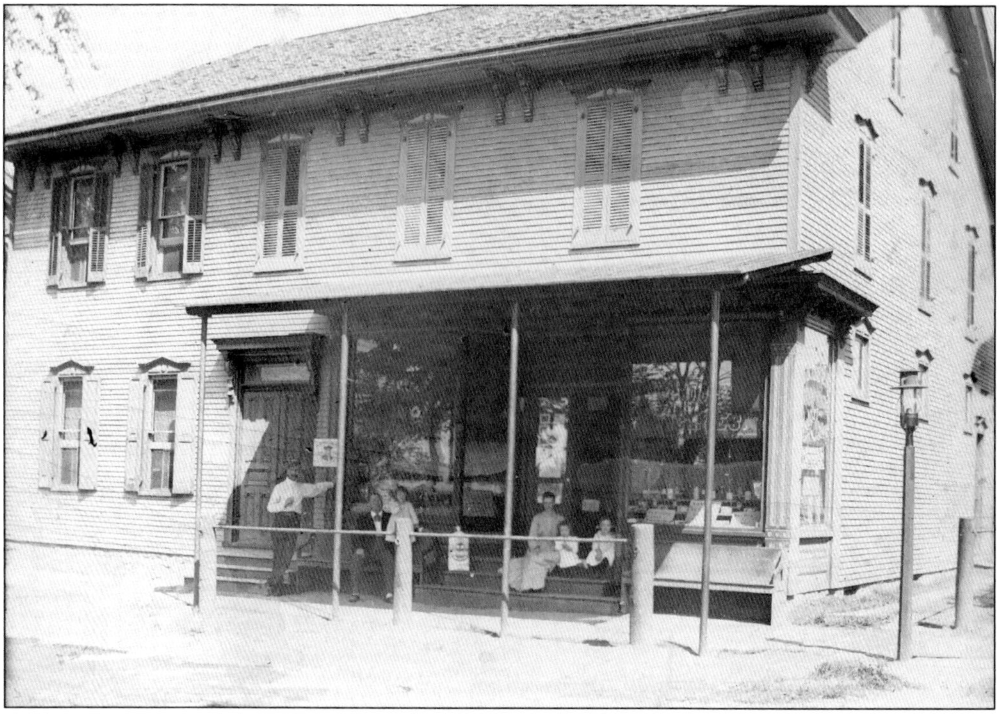

Although many workshops have existed in New Berlin over its two centuries, in 1910, only a few stores served the city. Among these establishments were Ritter's Store and Meat Market at 225 Front Street (originally Winter's, and currently Willow's New and Used furniture). Druggist James Theodore Smith and his son Homer were photographed at the apothecary at 207 Market Street (below). The Smith house and shop were built in 1872 by James's father, John Smith, who operated a shoe shop there. (NBHA.)

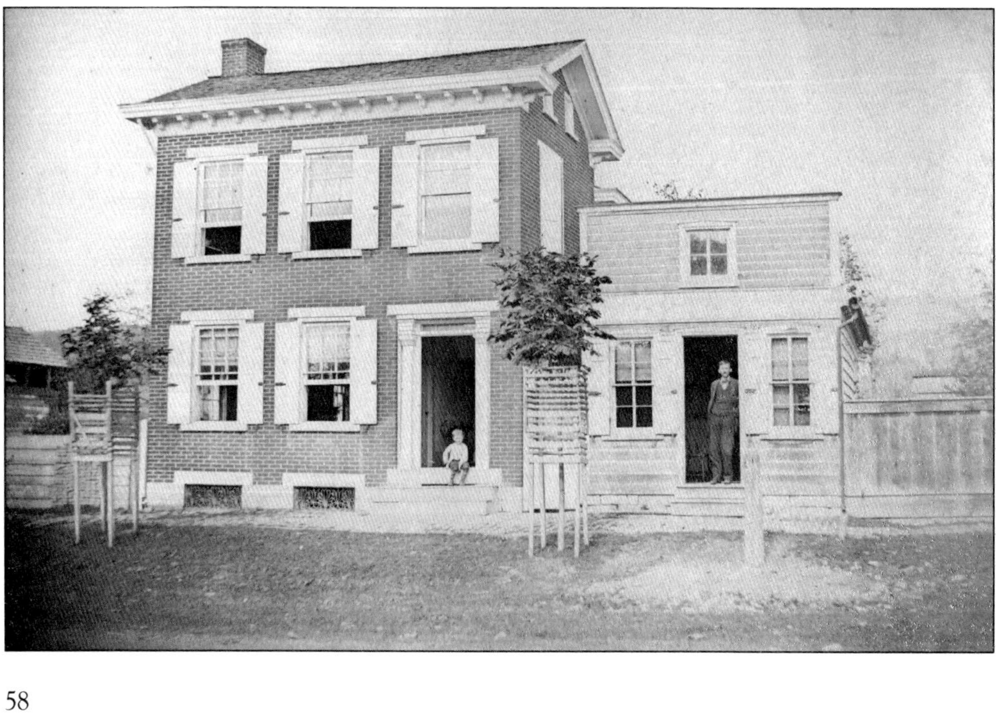

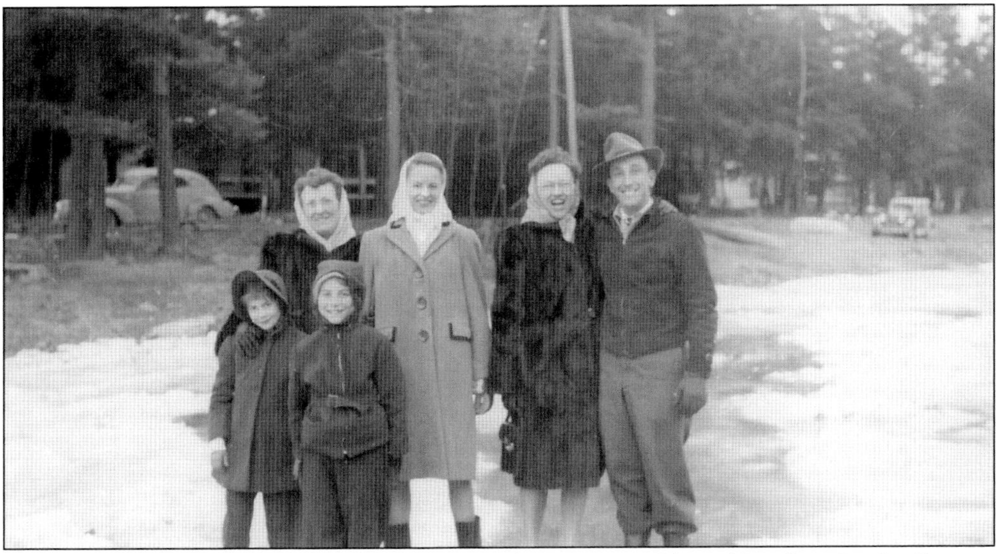

Participating in a family outing (above) at Sampsell's Dam on Wildwood Road are Sandie Showers Cannon, Vivien Showers Gross, Joanne Gross Rittweger, and Jean and Harlan Showers. This photograph was taken sometime prior to Harlan's joining the Army in 1943, bound for Southeast Asia. Below, store proprietors Harlan F. (1913–1982) and Jean (Klase) Showers (1915–2000) stand at the entrance of their general store in New Berlin with their son John R. (1952–). A general store from the early 1900s, the establishment operated as the Showers Brothers Store in 1946 by John C. and Harlan F. Showers. Harlan and Jean ran it together until Harlan's death. It then operated under three successive owners until 1998, when the entire building was converted to its original hotel use as part of The Inn at New Berlin and called by its original name, The Samuel Aurand Hotel. (John Showers.)

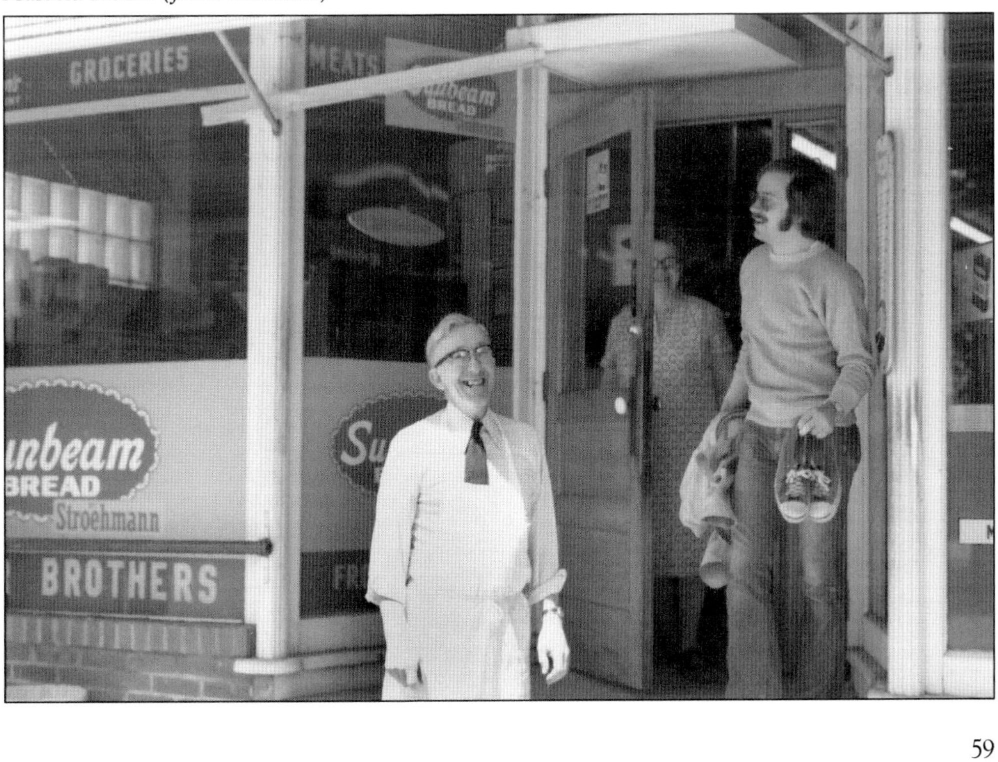

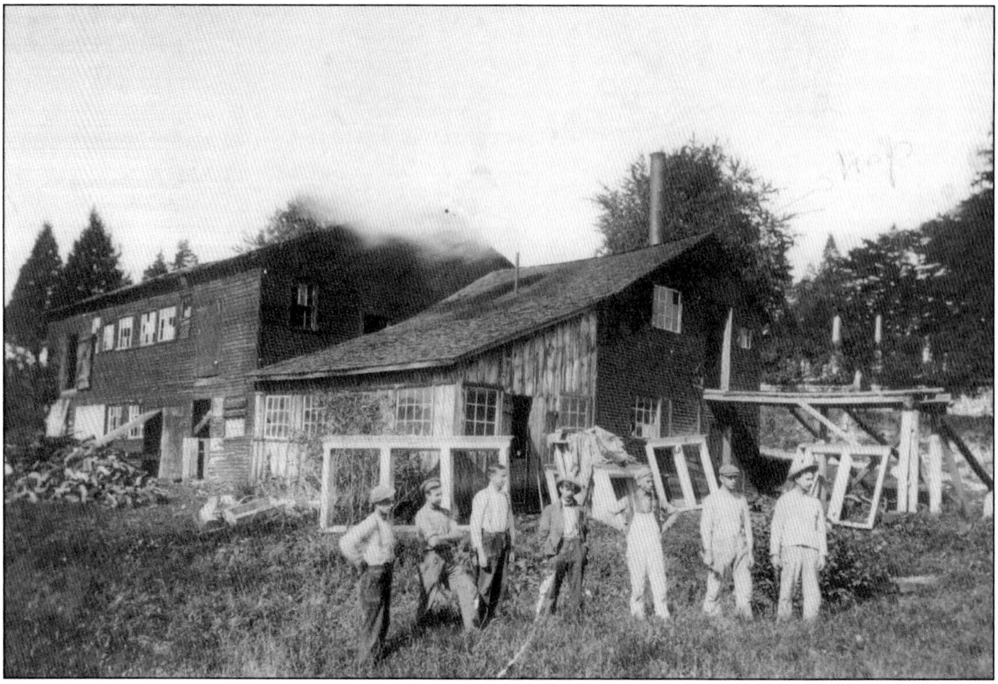

Solomon's sawmill, shown above in 1920, was at the foot of the New Berlin cemetery and north of Liberty Street. The workers shown here are, from left to right, Henry Oscar Solomon, John Ritter, Fred Solomon, Calvin Wetzel, William Walker, Guy Engle, and William Solomon. A second sawmill, owned by Enos Oldt, was closer to the base of the Shamokin Mountain, as seen in the cabinet photograph below. A third mill was across from the gristmill and above the mill dam on the Snyder County side of Penns Creek. (Above, NBHA; below, UCHS 2011.42.19.)

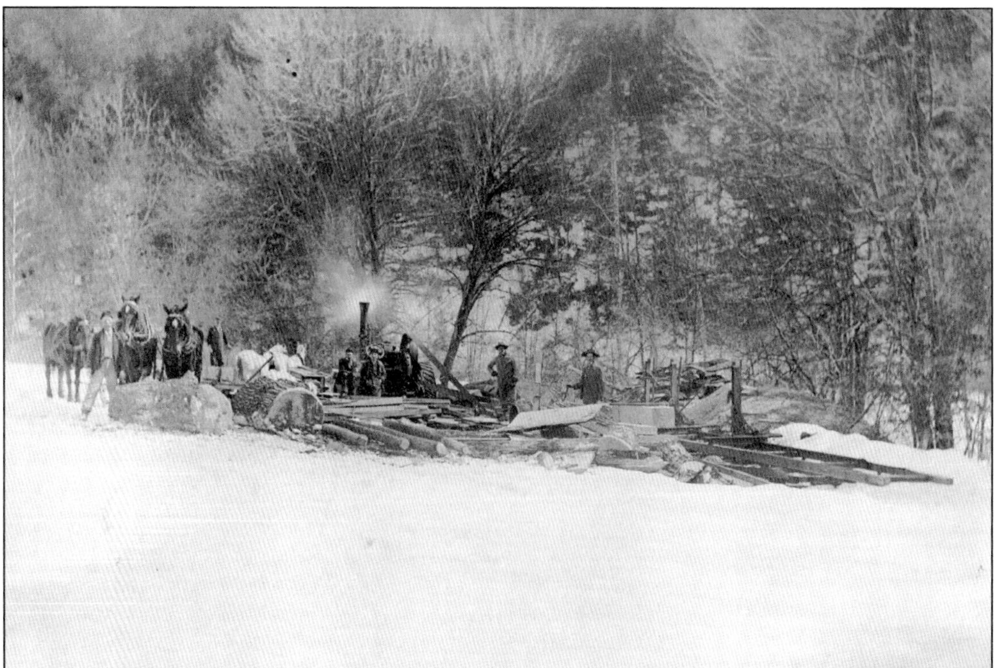

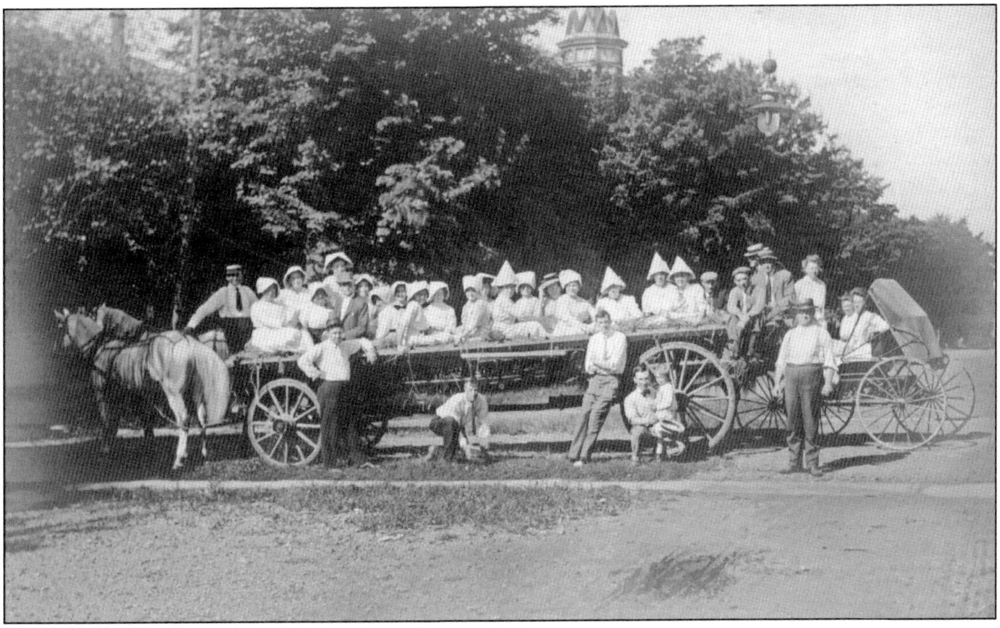

Above, farmer Ammon Maurer's large wagon and team proved handy in carrying hat-wearing revelers, including Irwin Stover and John and Eddie Schochs. The Lutheran Church steeple can be seen above the trees in this photograph, taken at Market and Vine Streets. A large group assembly from the 1910s was the subject of the real-photo postcard below. Shown here are dining, kitchen, and sleeping tents pitched on the Commons above Penns Creek. The New Berlin Railroad station is just visible along the postcard's right edge. In 1795, the Commons was given to the borough of Longstown (New Berlin) by town founder George Long and his wife for use as a common cow pasture. Now it serves as an open space and site for numerous recreational activities on the Fourth of July. (UCHS 2004.21.1 and 2005.28.8.)

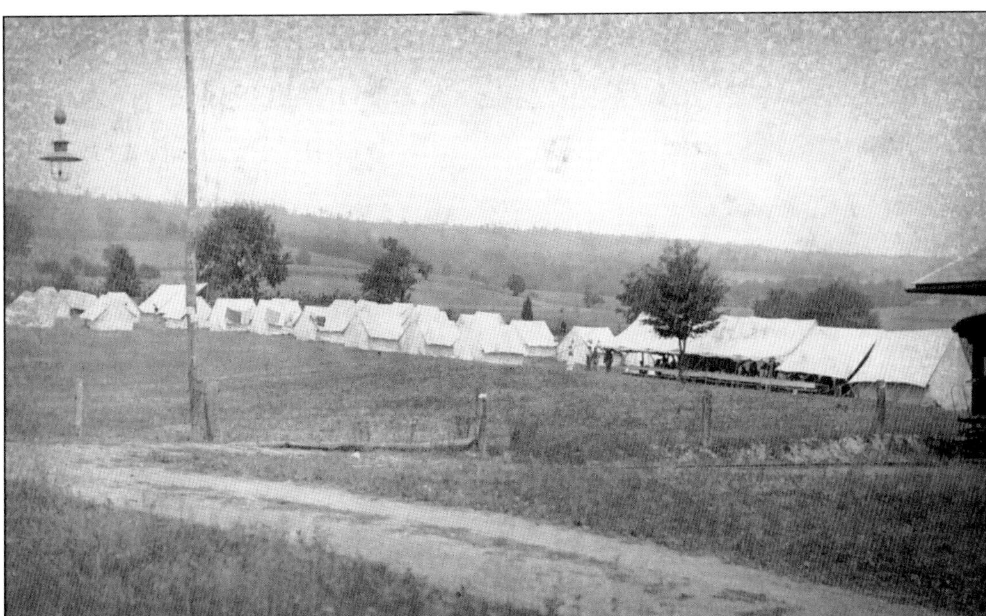

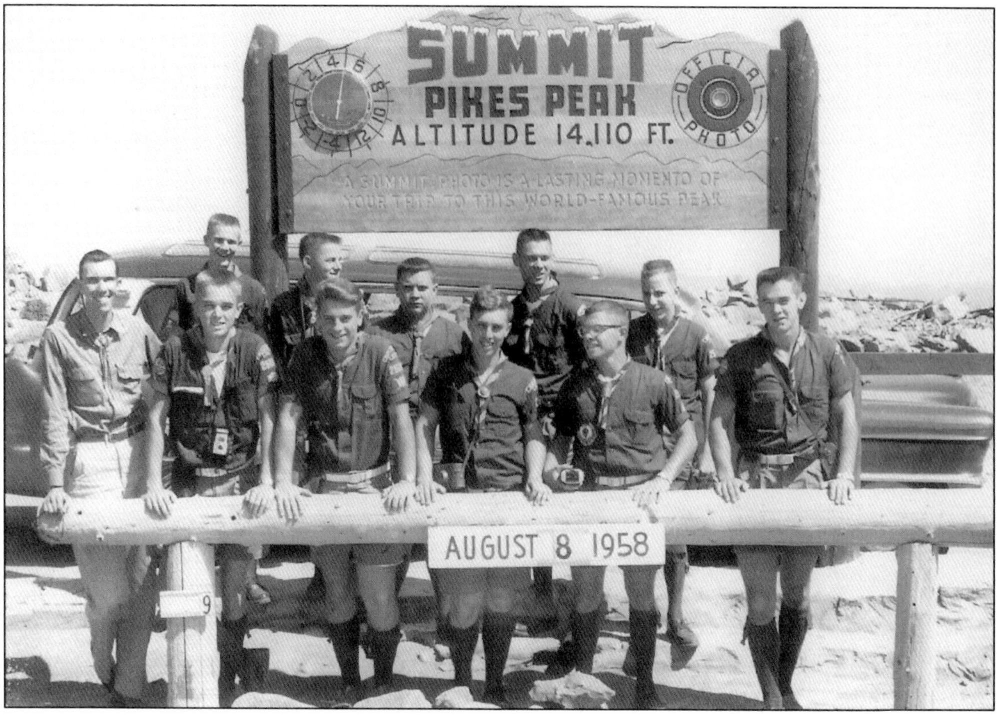

New Berlin's Explorer Scouts went to the Philmont Scout Ranch in Colorado for their first cross-country trip. In the above photograph, they are at the summit of Pike's Peak in the summer of 1958. Shown here are, from left to right, (first row) unidentified car driver, Wayne Miller, Jon Lawson, Eugene W. Keister, Richard DeVett, and Ernest Maurer; (second row) Rodney Kline, Edwin Hollenbach, Lewis Maize, advisor Elmer Maurer, and Philip Snook. Missing from the photograph are Kenneth Ulrich and John Reidell. Elmer Maurer was New Berlin's longtime postmaster. New Berlin Girl Scouts were organized by its first leader, Cora Snook, around 1935. The Girl Scouts shown below were photographed together in 1947. (NBHA.)

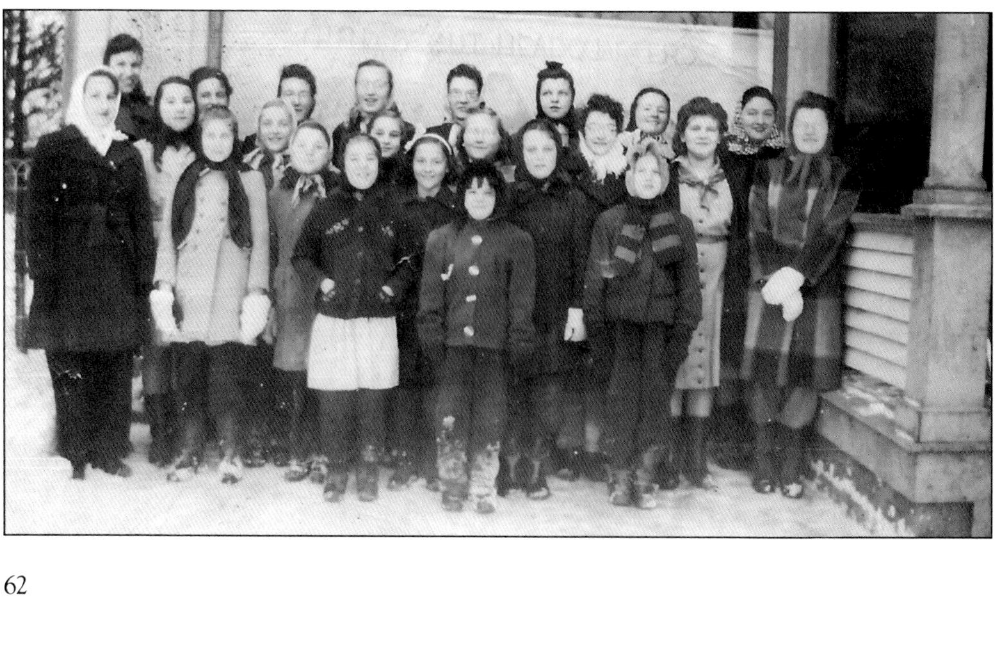

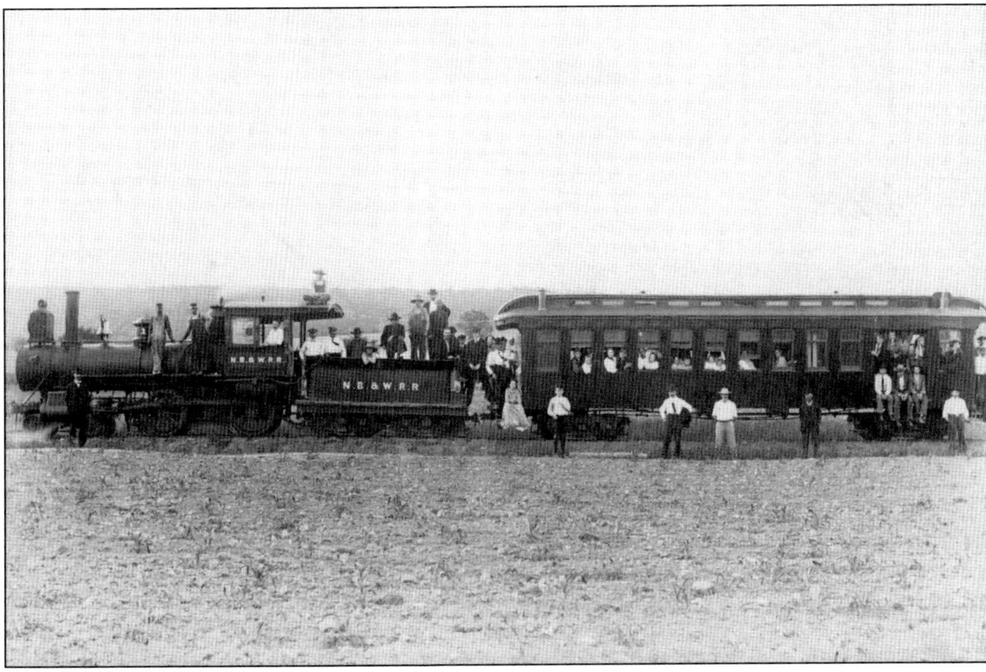

Passenger car travel between New Berlin and Winfield commenced on June 14, 1905. It was hoped that a rail line would infuse new life and commerce into New Berlin and Dry Valley, the former having been bypassed by the Philadelphia & Reading along the Susquehanna and the Lewisburg/Tyrone—later called the Pennsylvania—line through the center of the Buffalo Valley. The printed New Berlin/Winfield train schedule listed all its stops in the eight-mile run, including four round-trips on weekdays and two on Sundays. The line's primary freight was agricultural produce in the summer and timber in the winter, but there were not sufficient quantities to justify continued use. The "jerk water line," as it was called by some, ceased running in 1916, a financial failure that never realized the town's earlier dreams. (Above, NBHA; right, Jim Walter.)

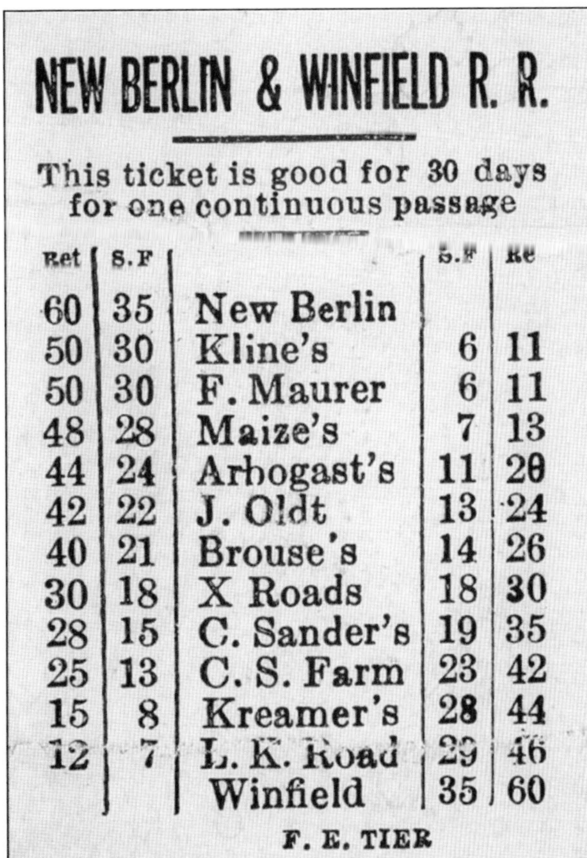

NEW BERLIN & WINFIELD R. R.

This ticket is good for 30 days for one continuous passage

Ret	S.F		S.F	Re
60	35	New Berlin		
50	30	Kline's	6	11
50	30	F. Maurer	6	11
48	28	Maize's	7	13
44	24	Arbogast's	11	20
42	22	J. Oldt	13	24
40	21	Brouse's	14	26
30	18	X Roads	18	30
28	15	C. Sander's	19	35
25	13	C. S. Farm	23	42
15	8	Kreamer's	28	44
12	7	L. K. Road	29	46
		Winfield	35	60

F. E. TIER

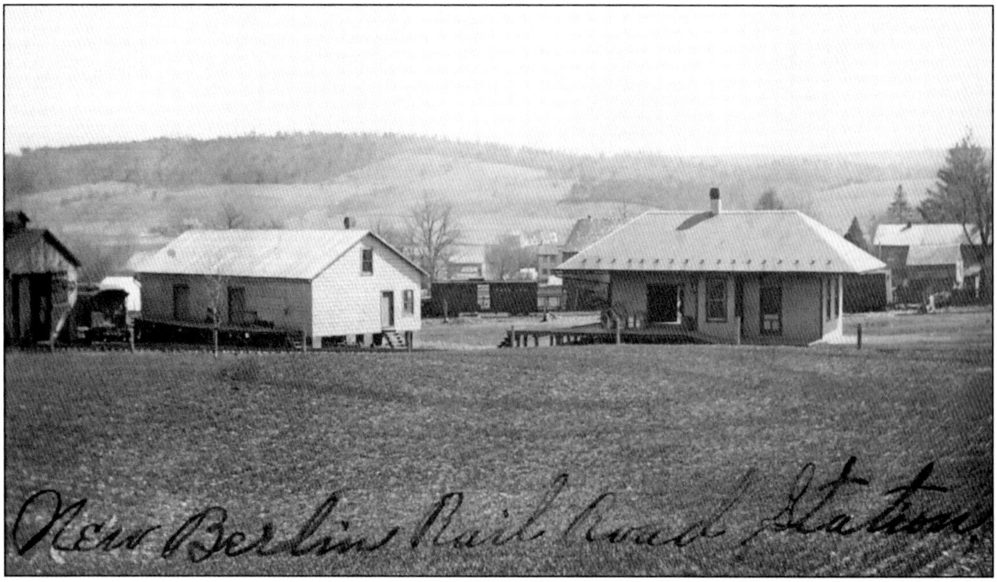

The New Berlin train station was located at what became the first QE/Playworld site north of Maize Alley. At this site were railroad shops, a coal yard, and a freight and grain house. Some of these structures are seen in these real-photo postcards, one of which is postmarked "9/18/1906." As anticipated, the introduction of a rail line to New Berlin brought new businesses, including a bank, and strengthened others, but the revenues were not high enough, and within seven years, its future looked bleak. Mid-year 1914, the freight income totaled $2,234 and passenger travel brought in $3,251—not much more than that year's operating costs of $4,931. Maintenance was deferred. The last train ran on September 19, 1916, and, four days later, the line was foreclosed for $11,500. Engine No. 2 is shown in the below photograph. (UCHS 2005.48.6 and 2010.21.180.)

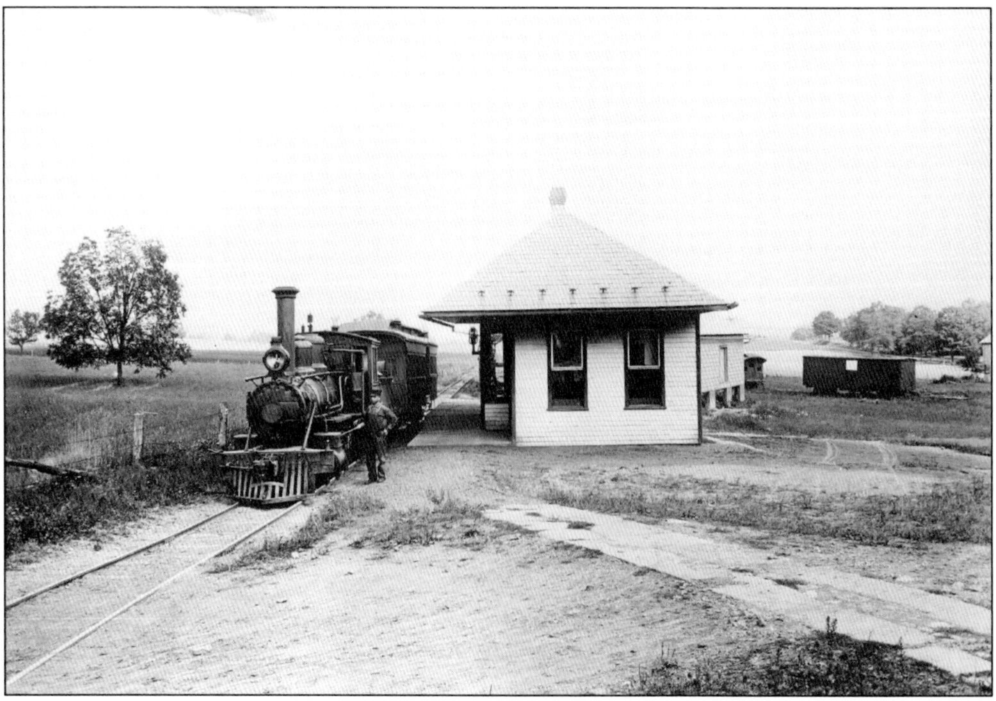

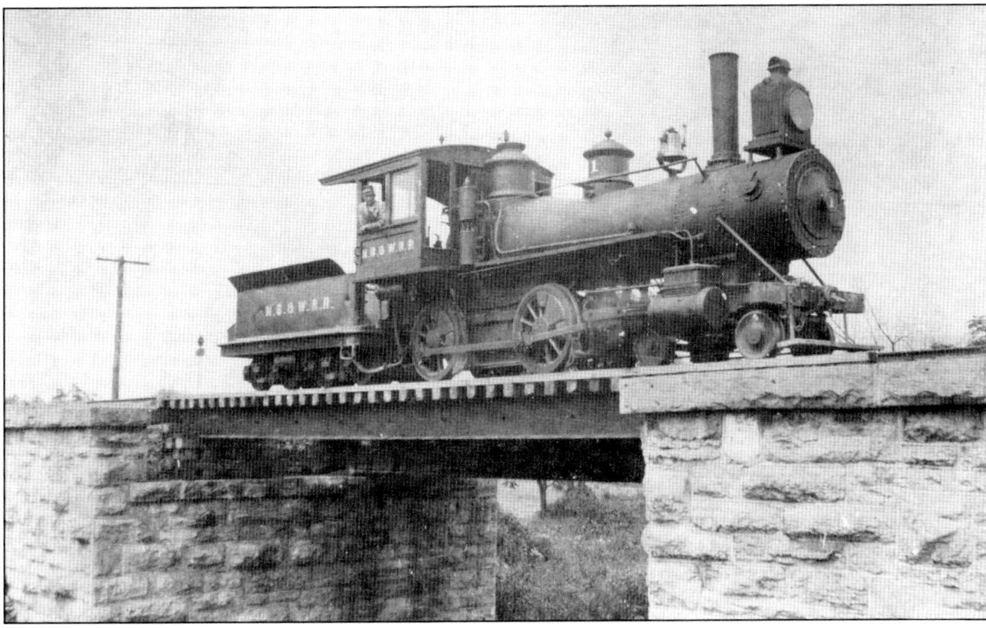

The New Berlin–Winfield narrow-gauge (36 inch) line operated between the towns with some interruptions. Its tracks crossed level farm fields but, outside of Winfield, they were raised at points, as seen in the above photograph. The stone piers are still standing. A severe storm on July 17, 1912, took out these tracks at the Winfield Bridge and part of Dry Valley, resulting in lost ticket and freight sales as well as repair bills that drove the company into receivership on October 2, 1912. The line's maintenance train (below) had a hose around its tender, which was used to get water for the engine from nearby streams. (Above, UCHS 2010.21.180; below, NBHA.)

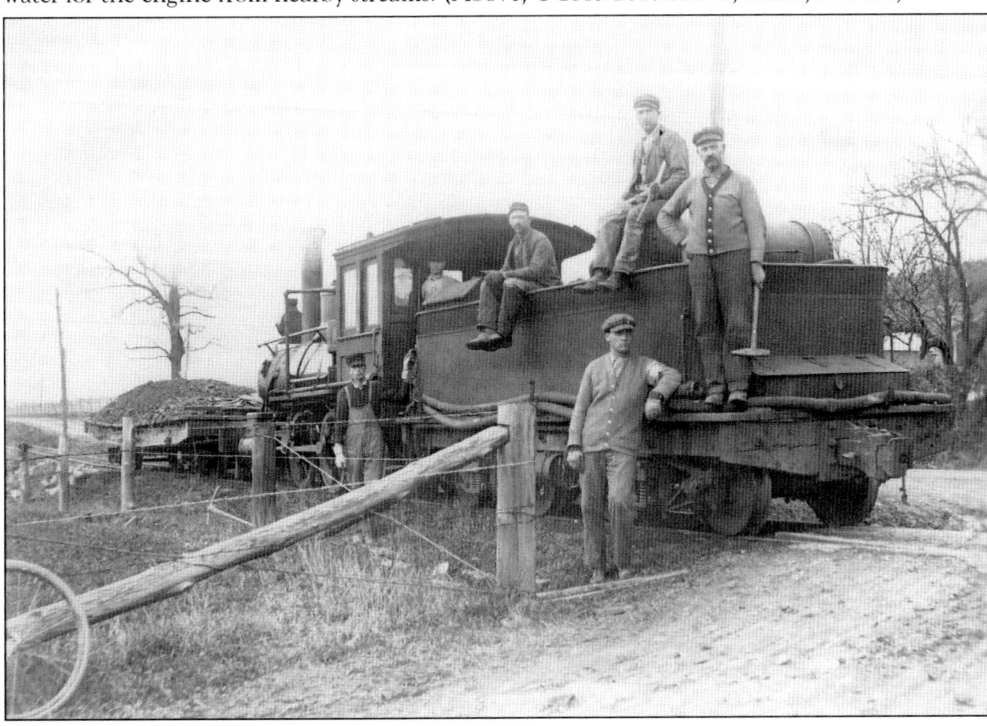

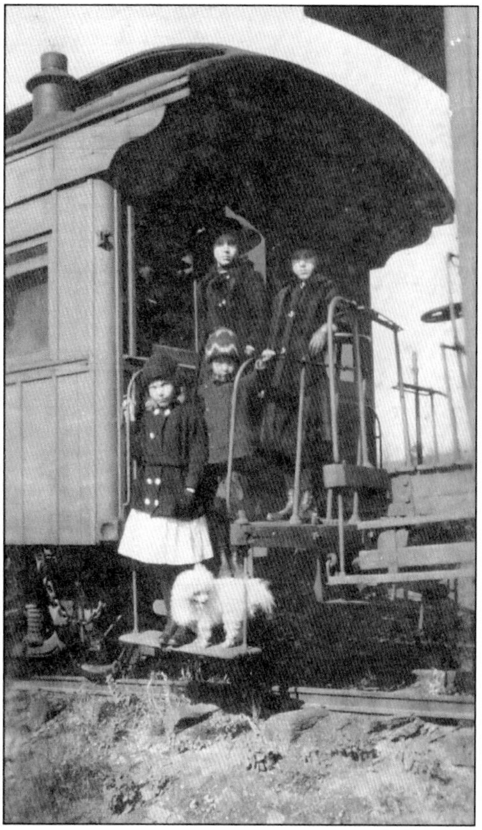

In the left photograph, a family disembarks from the New Berlin train. At the Winfield end, the train connected to the Philadelphia & Reading Railroad station. The Philadelphia & Reading line at Winfield, going south, crossed the river at Sunbury and continued on to Shamokin, Ashland, Tamaqua, and Reading. The northbound Philadelphia & Reading line went through Lewisburg, West Milton, Montgomery, Muncy, Halls, and Williamsport. The line ended at Newberry Junction, where it connected with the New York Central and the Pennsylvania Railroad. After the railroad was abandoned between Winfield and Sunbury, PennDOT used part of the former right-of-way to make Route 11 a four-lane highway. Vehicles from Ammon L. Maurer's Auto Bus Line (below) provided transportation to and from the Winfield train station after the demise of the New Berlin–Winfield train line in 1916. (NBHA.)

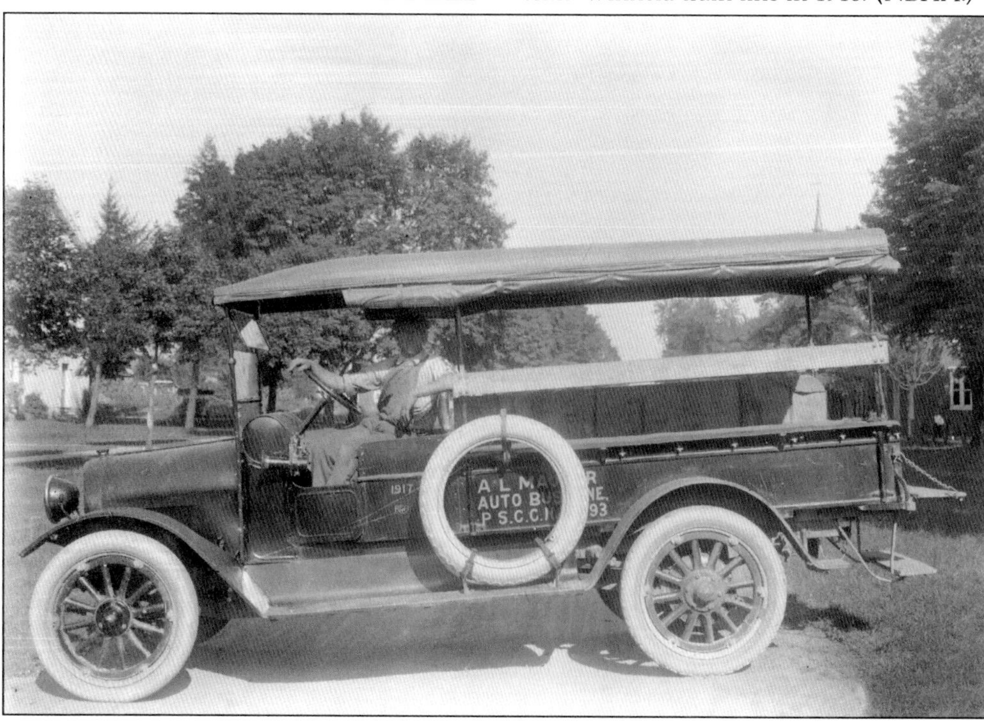

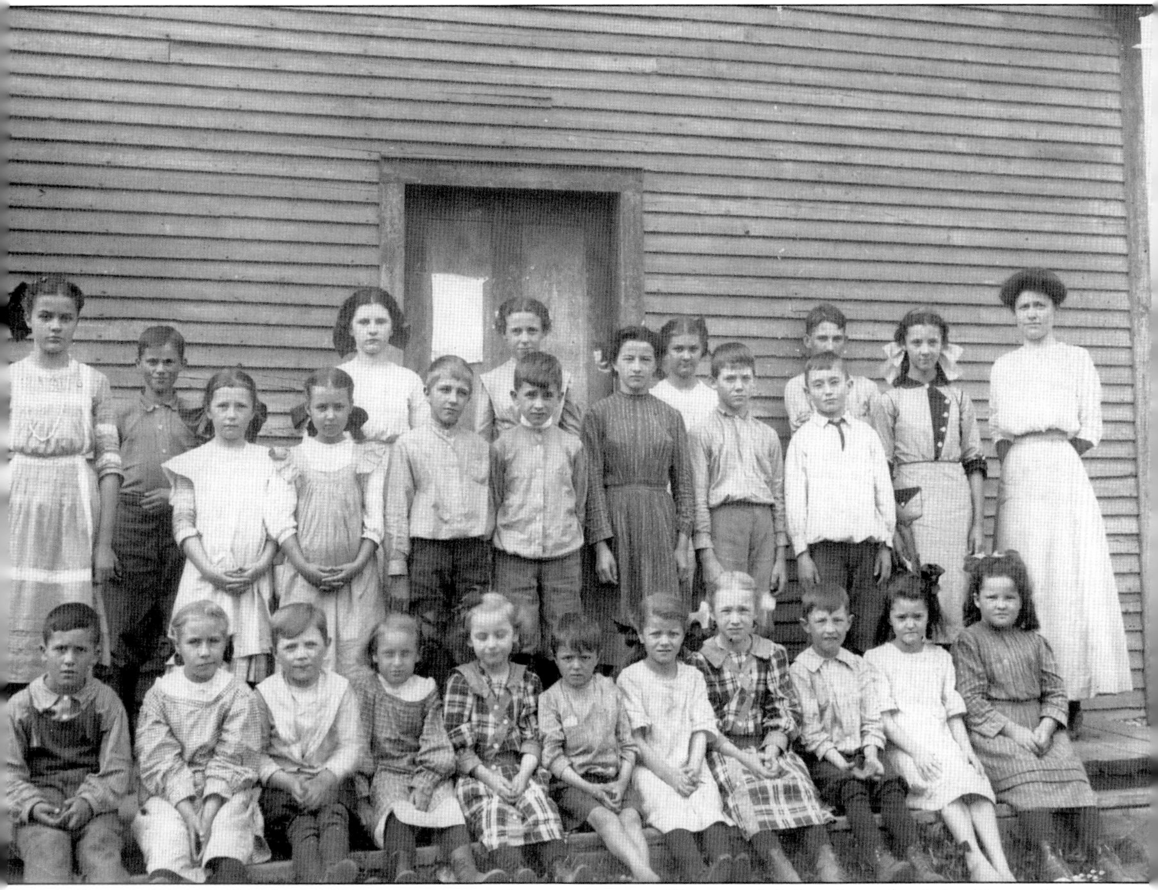

After the Free School Act of 1837 in Pennsylvania, Switzer (Sweitzer) School was built by Samuel Hoover in 1840 on the south bank of Switzer Run, earlier called Lick Run. One of four schools in Limestone Township, it was located on Christopher Seebold III's land on the north side of present Wildwood Road, west of its intersection with Route 304. Most of the one-room schools in Union County were made of brick from local clay, but this one was sheathed with wooden clapboards. It was indicated as a school (SH) in *Pomeroy's Atlas of Union and Snyder Counties of 1868*. (UHCS 94.7.1.)

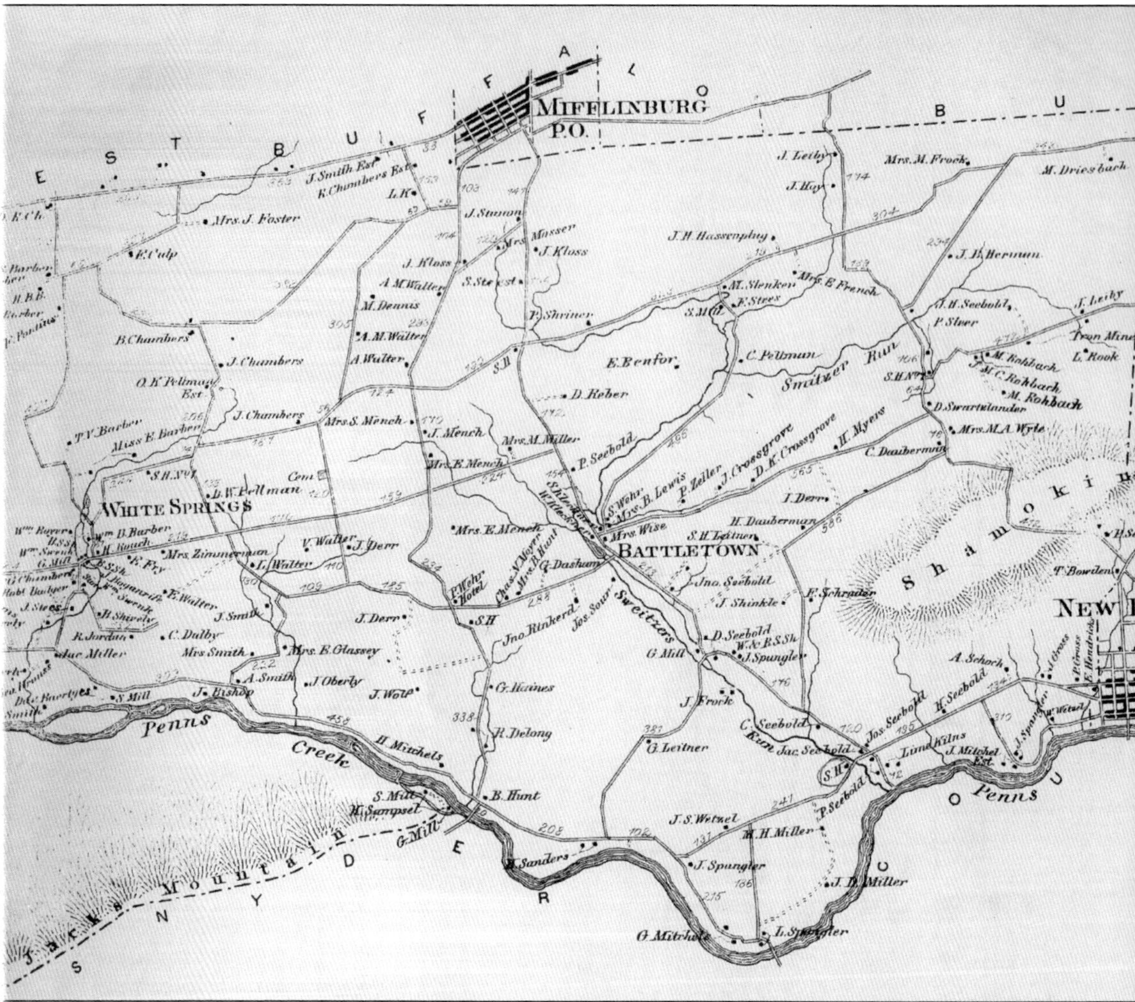

Over time, New Berlin has both filled in and spread north on the slope of Shamokin Mountain. Some residences and a few businesses are tucked into its woodlands near the top and with great views, hence "neighborhoods" are named Teaberry Hill and Seminary Acres. Dirt and, later, paved roads connected New Berlin to Dry Valley and Winfield beside the Susquehanna River—three and one half miles and seven miles due east, respectively. Dice (earlier named Battletown) and White Springs were situated around the west end of Shamokin (also known as New Berlin Mountain) three and five miles away, respectively, with Mifflinburg (formerly Youngstown) another two miles farther north. *Pomeroy's Atlas of Union and Snyder Counties of 1868*, on close examination, shows numerous one-room schools and sawmills, some blacksmith and wheelwright shops, two gristmills, the Wehr Hotel, and the Dunkard Church and cemetery. There was also a cluster of limekilns and iron mines of L. Rook at the base of Shamokin Mountain. (UCHS.)

Two

Dry Valley, White Springs, and Vicksburg

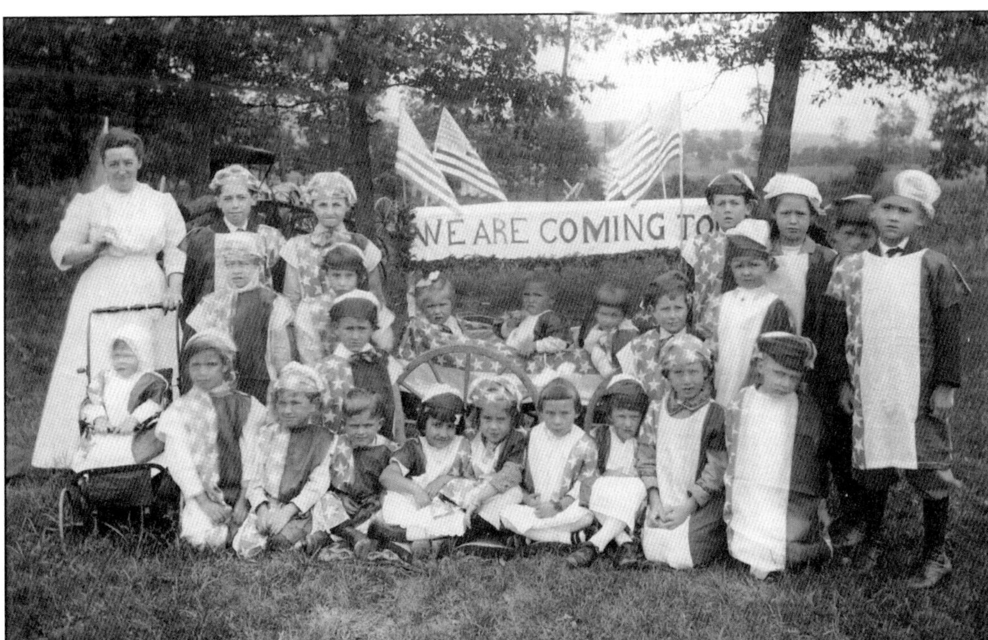

Mary Angeline (Kreisher) Benfer (far left) and her Sunday school class pose in patriotic dress at a picnic at Dry Valley. Mary Kreisher (b. 1873) married farmer Elmer Foster Benfer in 1894, and they lived in Union Township at the time this cabinet photograph was taken in 1912. (UCHS, 2011.42.20.)

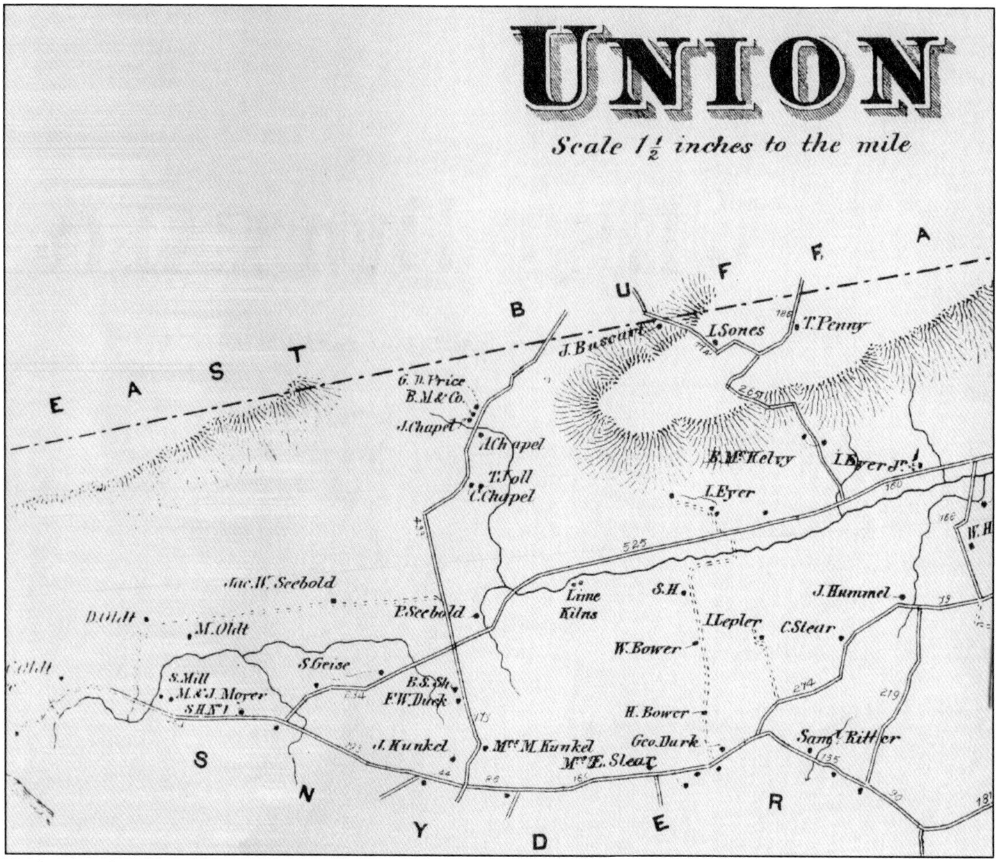

A detail of Union Township from *Pomeroy's Atlas* shows the location of several Oldt family homes just west of the crossroads community of Dry Valley and near the one-room school—called Trutt or Stocker—nearest them. The brick schoolhouse still stands and has been converted into a residence, while the Eyer School, located on the east side of Dry Valley, south of the road and near limekilns, has been razed. Enos D. Oldt's sawmill, located in a field near the Moyers, Penns Creek, and the Snyder County line, was photographed in the winter of 1905, as pictured on page 60. (UCHS atlas.)

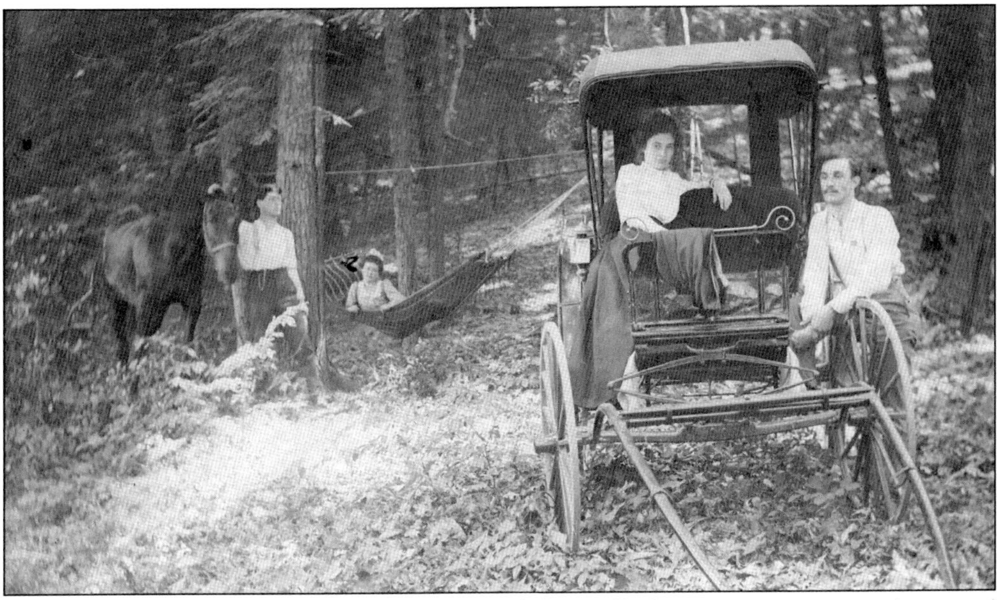

Limestone Township's rural countryside surrounded New Berlin on its western, northern, and eastern sides, while parts of Limestone abutted the western edge of Union Township. It is in the latter area that friends posed for a cabinet photograph (above), taken near M. & J. Moyer's home. Shown are, from left to right, Gerald Oldt, Emily Spangler (in hammock), Bessie Naugle (in buggy), and William Wissinger. The below photograph, taken sometime between 1904 and 1907, was slyly labeled "Marguerite Bingaman and her pony." (UCHS 2012.4.2 and .1)

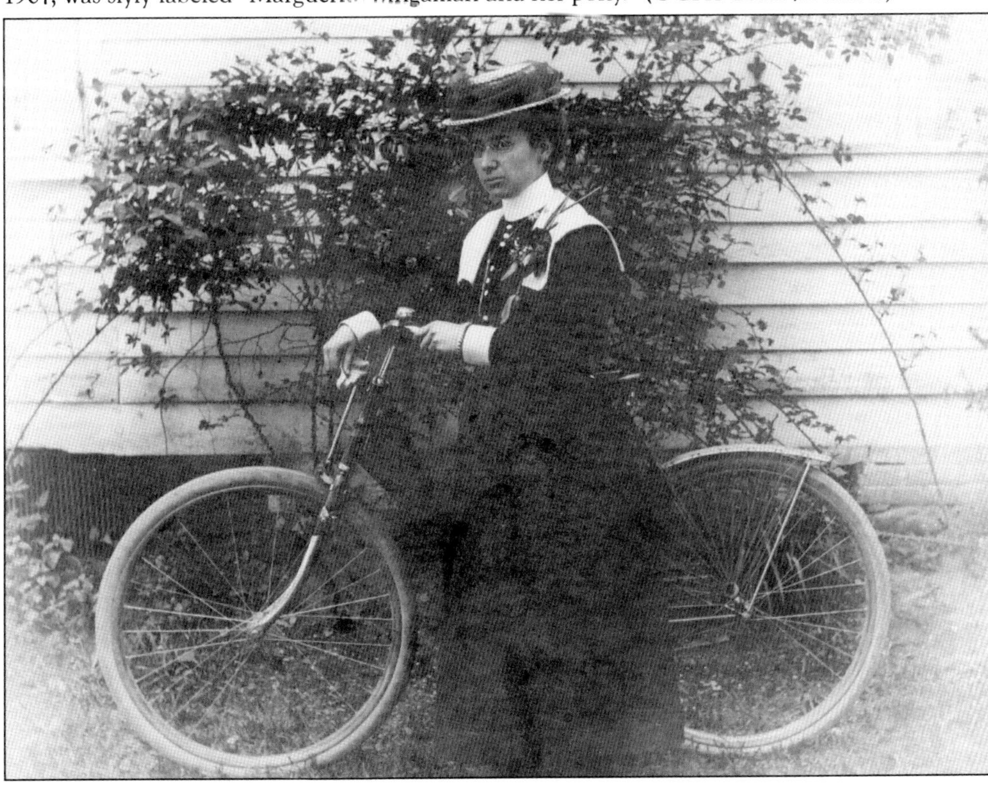

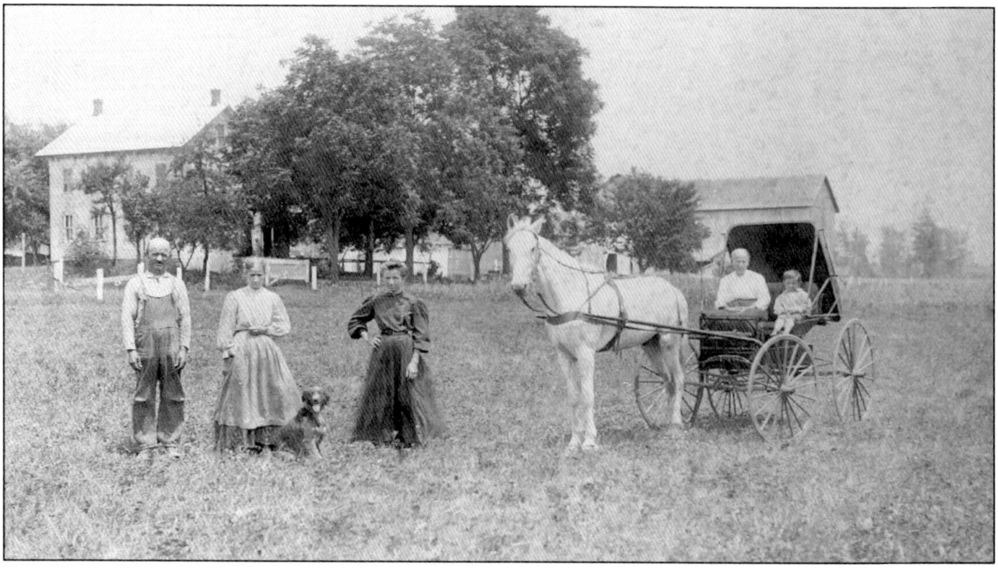

A cabinet photograph (above) of the Oldt farm near Dry Valley was taken by D. Vincent Smith of South Williamsport. Posing from left to right are Charles D. Oldt, Elizabeth Amelia Oldt, their daughter Leva (Oldt) Heintzelman, Leah (Nerhood) Moyer, and Stewart W. Oldt, the younger brother of Leva by 14 years. The Maize farm was also east of New Berlin, on the dirt road that was to become Route 304. That road connected both the Maize and Oldts with Dry Valley and Winfield to the east and New Berlin to the west. Two miles east of New Berlin, the Michael Maize farm in 1810 hosted the third conference and camp meeting of the Evangelical Association. Pictured below 100 years later are, from left to right, Lester Snook, Ellsworth Snook, and Ralph Snook. (Above, UCHS 2010.12.109; below, Deloris and Ellsworth Snook Jr.)

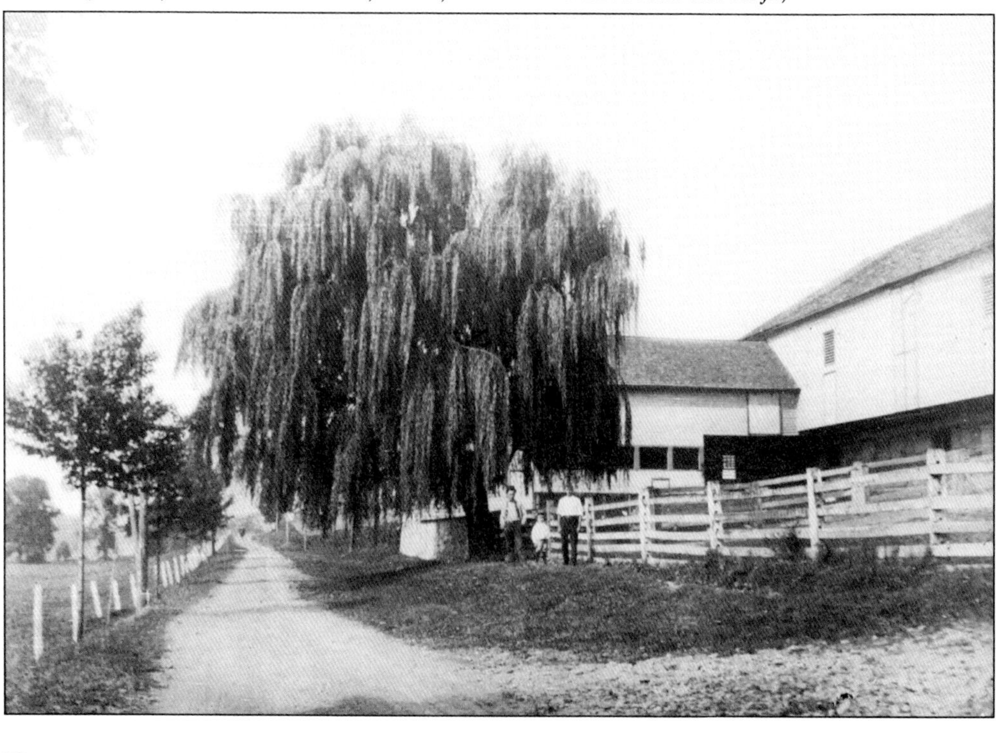

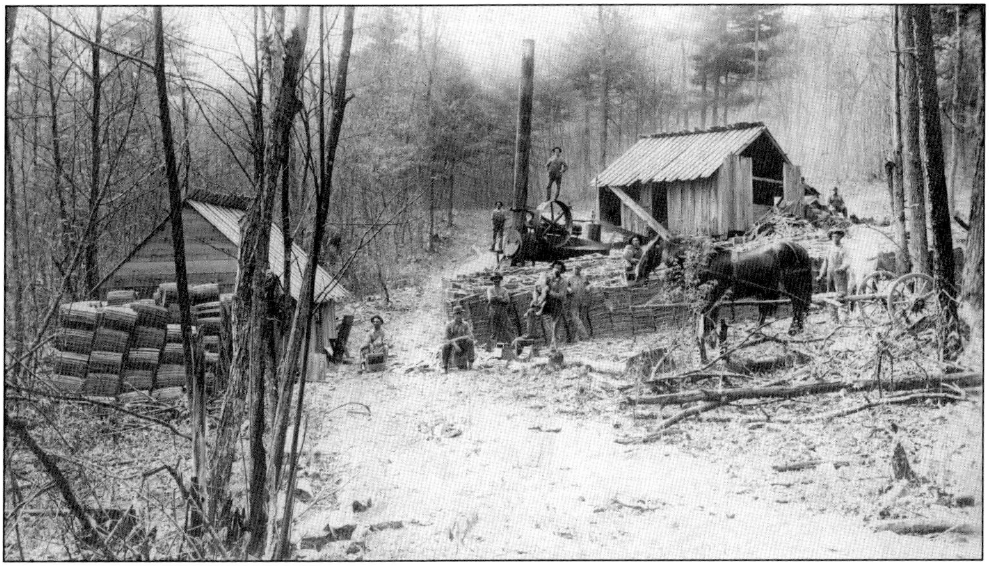

Cabinet photographs from around 1904 show Charles Oldt's stave mill near John A. Klingler's farm, formerly David Oldt's farm, just over the township line separating Union and Limestone. The farm was located on what is now called Whitetail Lane. Posing in the foreground of the above photograph are, from left to right, Enos D. Oldt, Milton Spaid, and Charles Oldt (holding dog). Others shown here include "Nig" Long, ? Ripple, and ? Betsler. In the below photograph, Enos (left) and Charles Oldt are bundling staves. The steam engine in the background was their power source. (UCHS 2011.42.17 and UCHS 2011.42.18.)

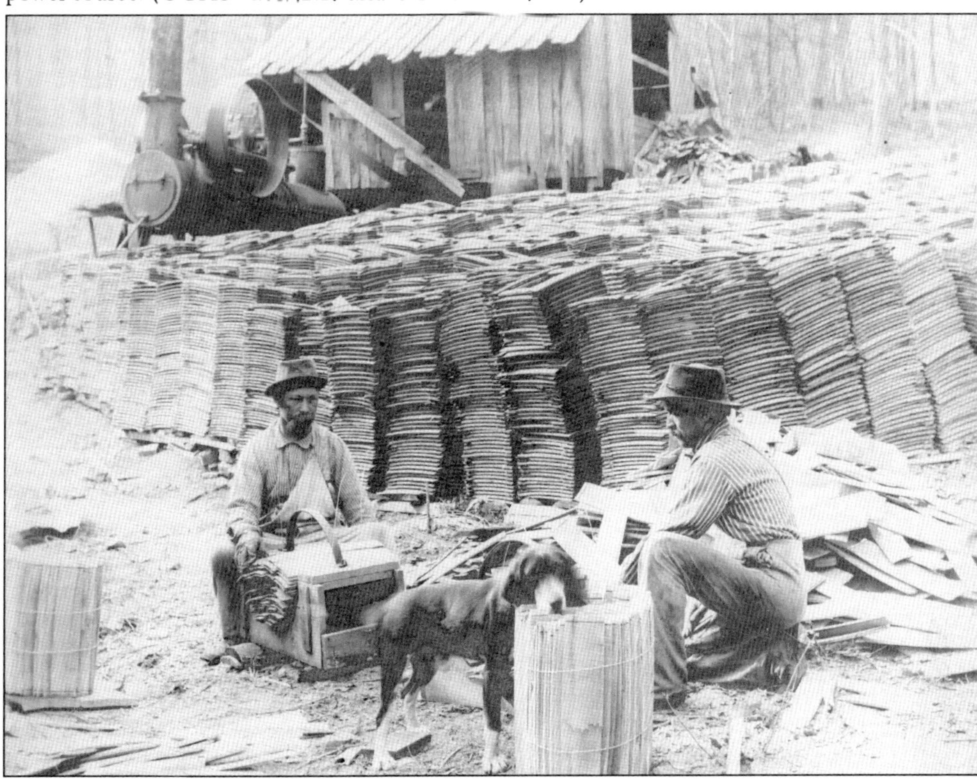

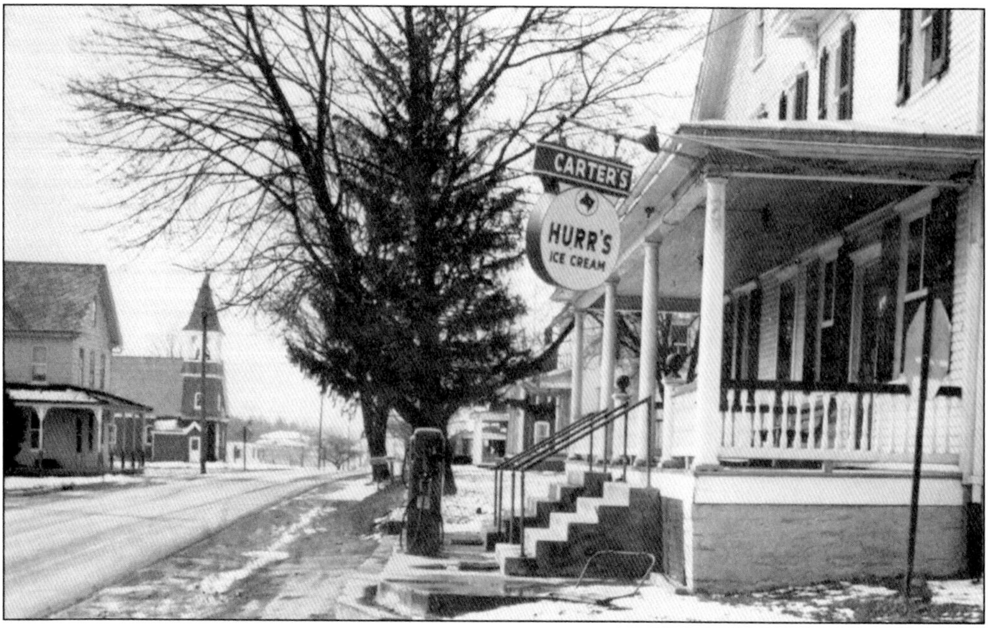

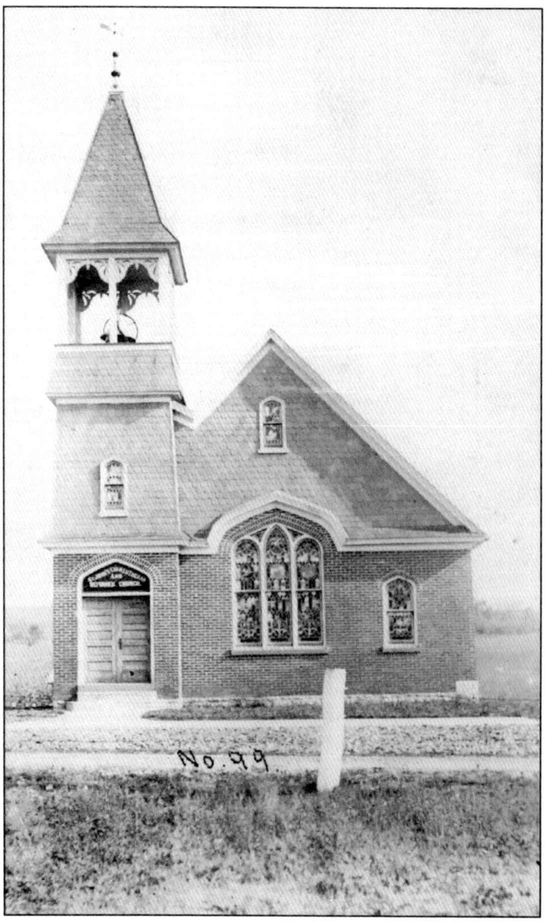

Dry Valley is located at the juncture of Stein Lane and Route 304, about four miles from both New Berlin and Winfield. Prosperous farms surround Dry Valley's small cluster of buildings, which are seen above, in the photolitho postcard from the 1950s: a general store/post office, several houses, and the Lutheran church. Left, the church is seen in a much earlier real-photo postcard. Nearby were a blacksmith shop and limekilns. The house/store was built about 1872 by George Penny, storekeeper and owner until 1904, when George, the first of three Oldts to live there, purchased it. Paul P. Oldt owned it from 1919 to 1935, when it was sold in a bankruptcy proceeding to Charles Renninger. In 1944, Renninger sold the building to David and Grace Oldt, who owned it until 1966. The subsequent owner's estate sold it to Albert and Marie Hause in 1970. (Above, UCHS 2009.2.23; left, Ronald Nornhold.)

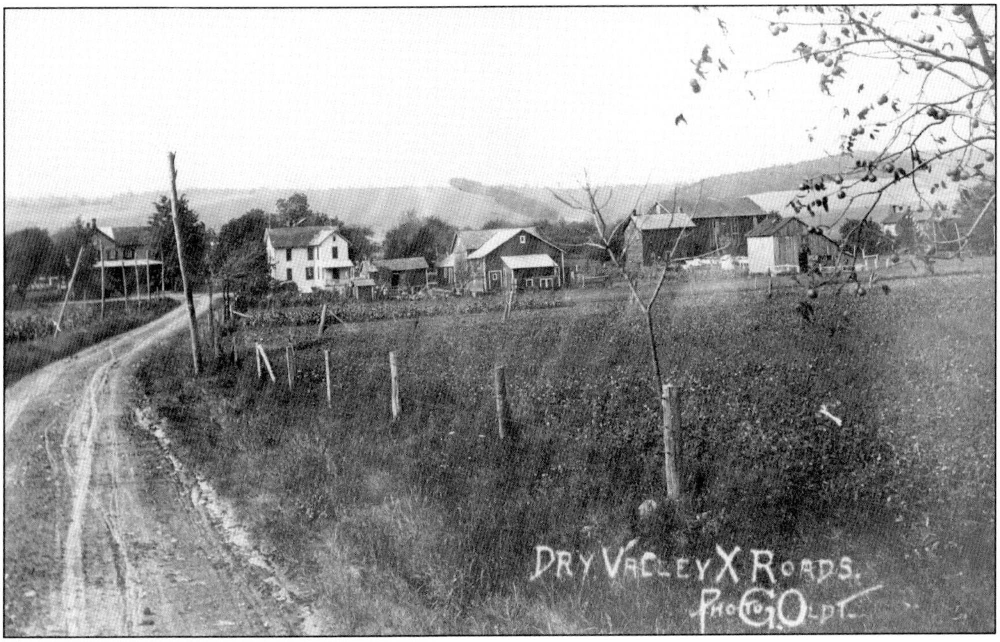

The above view of Dry Valley from a distance was circulated as a real-photo postcard. North and west of New Berlin was White Springs, an early settlement from the mid-to-late 1770s. Like Dry Valley and Dice, the town has not grown appreciably since then. In White Springs (below) are several of the county's earliest log and masonry homes. The town also contains a gristmill, blacksmith shop, two schools, a general store also housing the town's post office, and a Lutheran church. (Above, Carl Catherman; below, Ron Nornhold.)

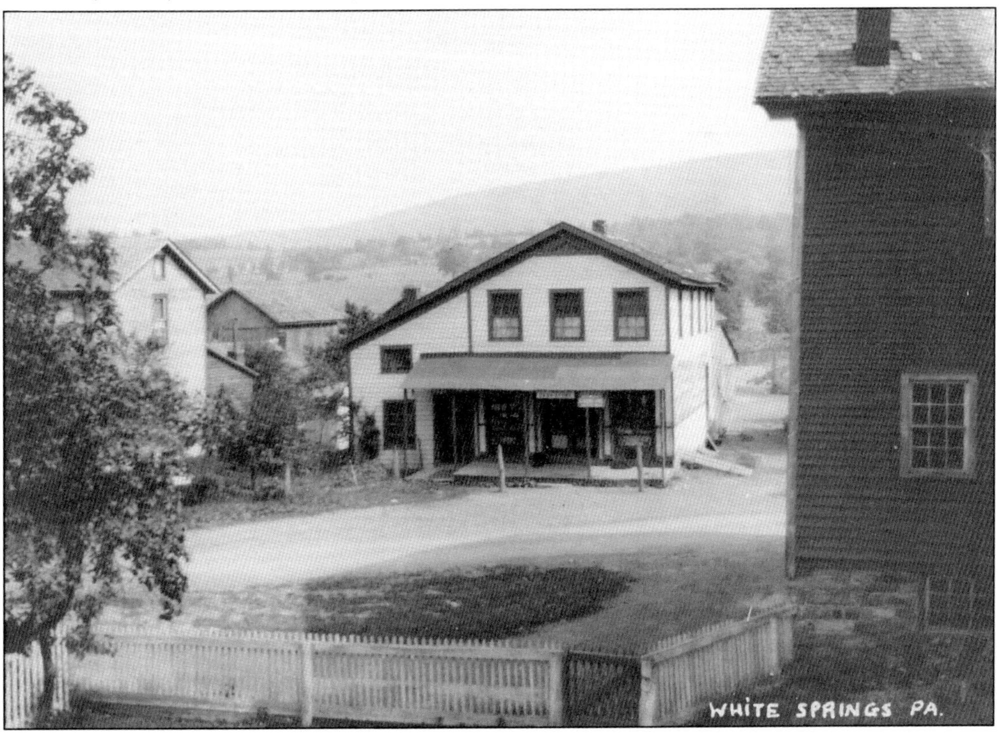

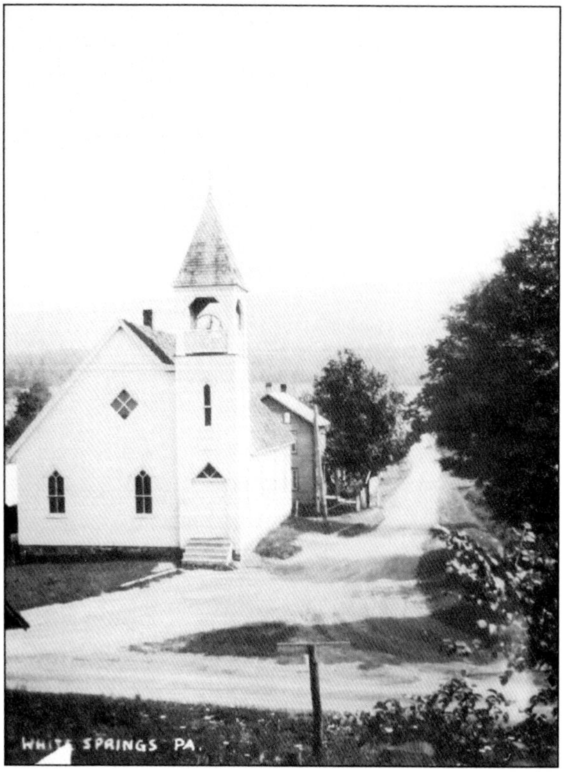

White Springs' Lutheran church was profiled in a real-photo postcard view (left). In the below cabinet photograph, taken in the winter of 1911, the area's schoolchildren pose for a group portrait. The schoolteacher was O.L.B. Thompson. (UCHS 88.6.3 and 92.61.2.)

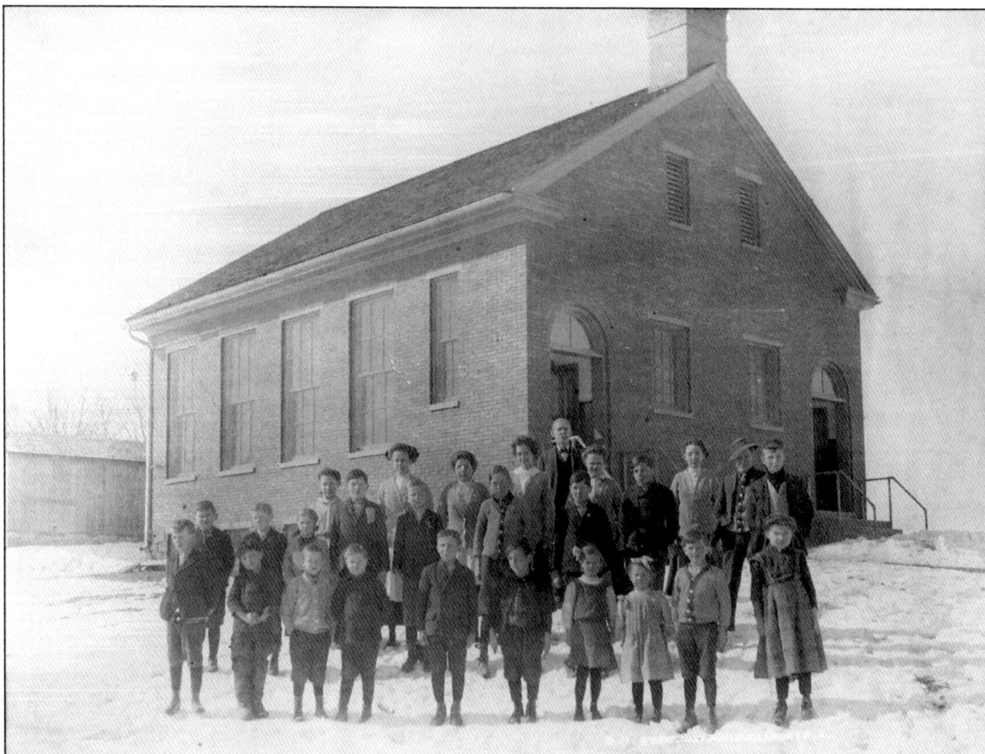

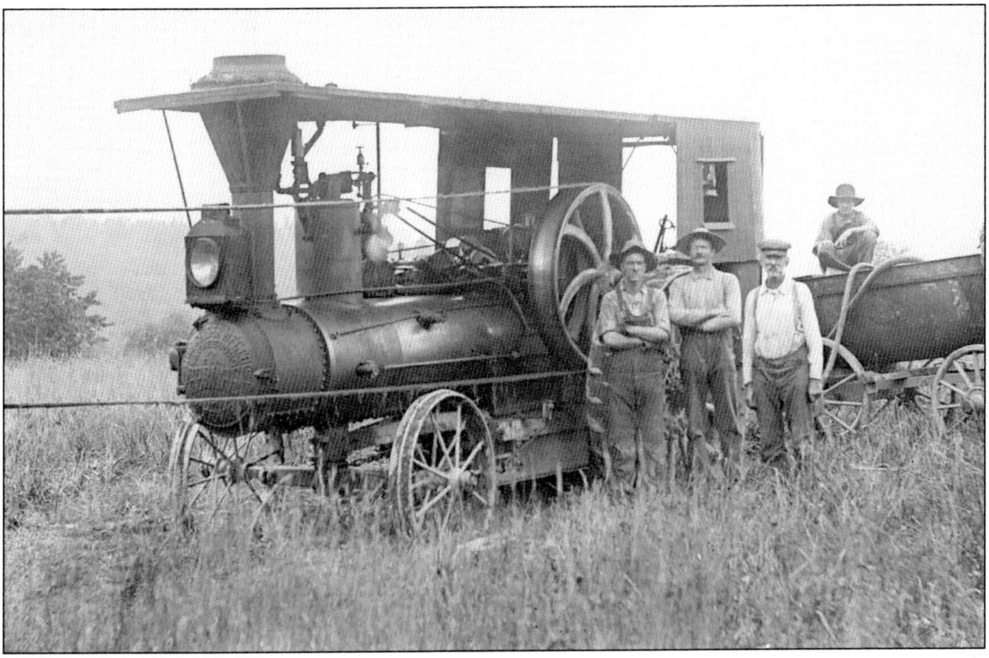

A real-photo postcard, sent as a birthday greeting to Barbara Watson in 1912, shows men with their steam engine. As late as the mid-1950s, New Berlin resident Ollie Hummel brought his steam engine to area farms during the harvesting season. Hummel's engine drove threshing or other machines by belts, as seen here. (Jeffrey L. Mensch.)

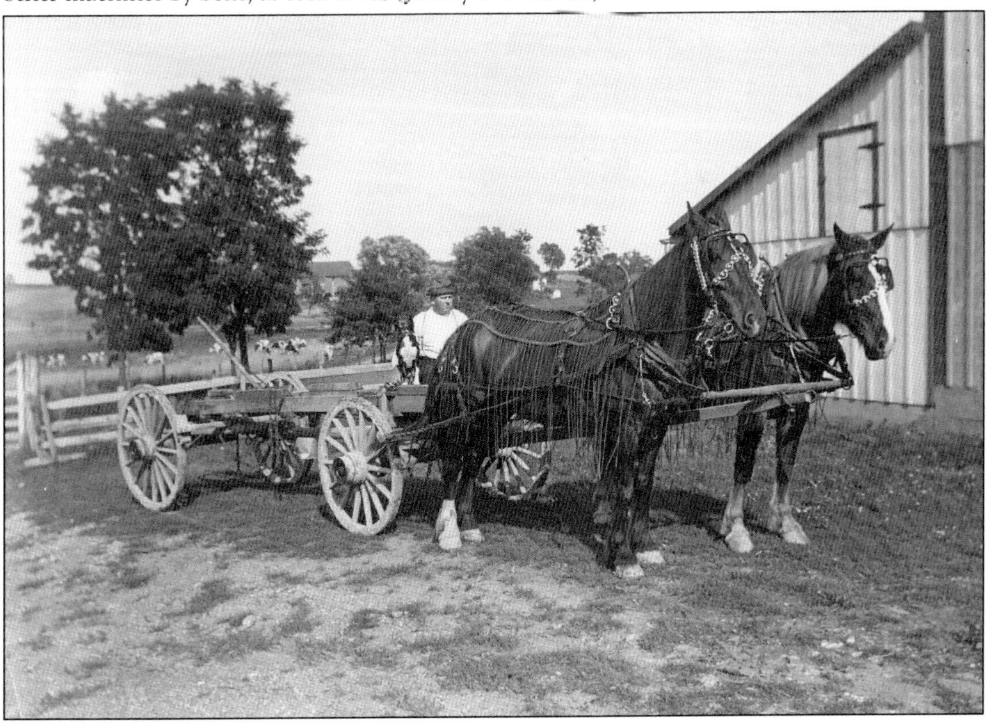

In this c. 1906 photograph, taken at the James Boyer farm near Dreisbach Church in Limestone Township, Boyer sits in a spring wagon. (UCHS 2011.42.21.)

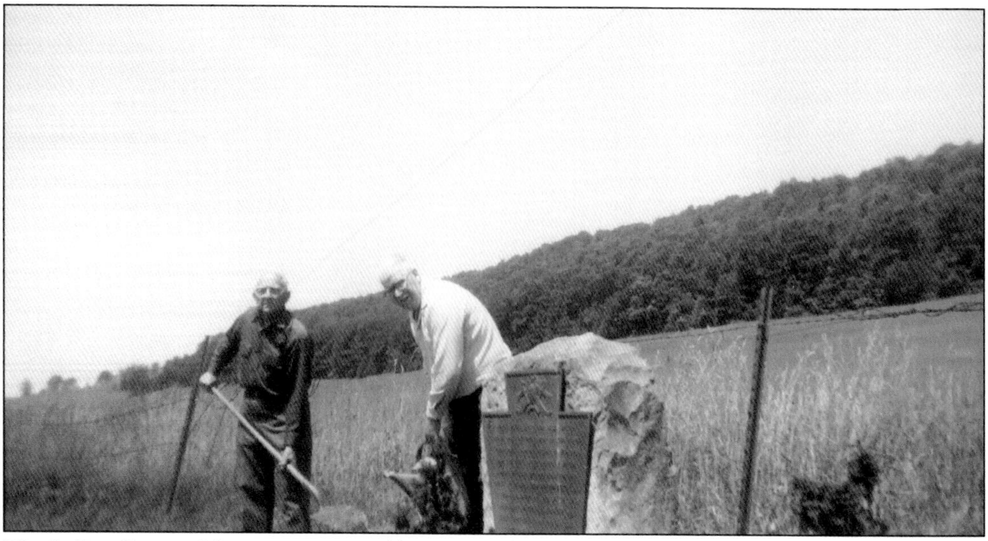

The LeRoy Springs Massacre stone and bronze marker was erected by the Union County Historical Society and the Pennsylvania Historical and Museum Commission in 1919. Above, Sherman Kreisher (left) and John Deans freshen up the site in the mid-1960s. The marker is located across the road from the 1755 LeRoy massacre site on Ridge Road, Limestone Township. In addition to discussing LeRoy Springs to elementary school tours in the 1960s, John Deans and others took students to "Old Buffalo" at Buffalo Crossroads and the Dreisbach cemetery (below). The tours that Deans, former teacher Harold Danowsky, and Lewisburger Lois Kalp developed are still being given by UCHS volunteers and remain a favorite all-day event of area fourth graders. (Above, UCHS 95.6.2; below, Ron Nornhold.)

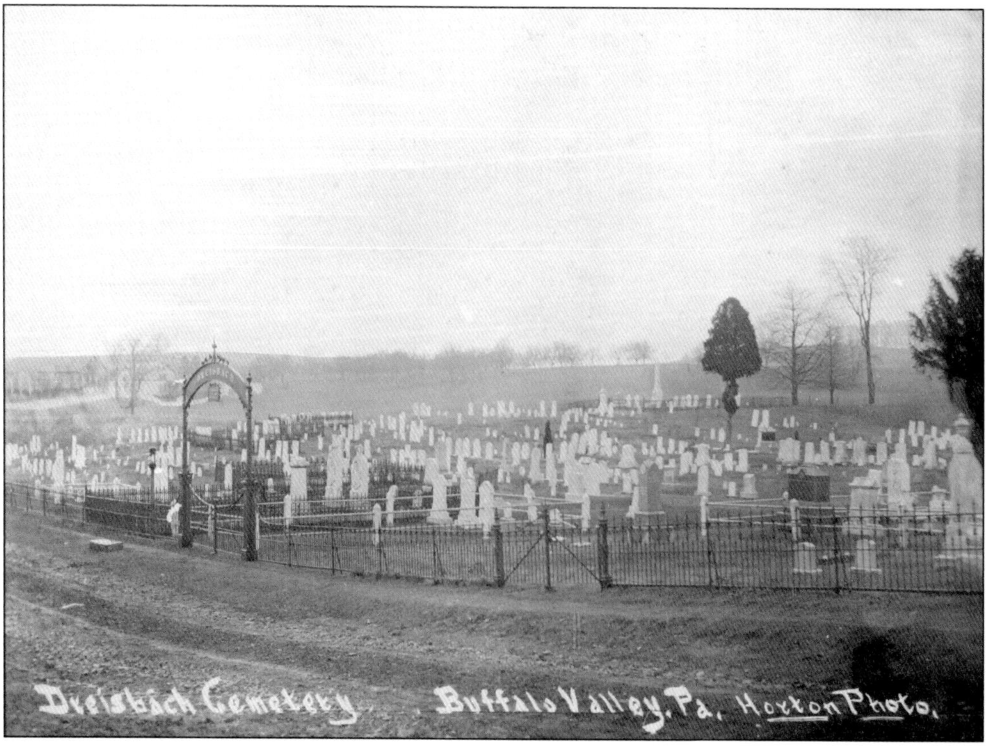

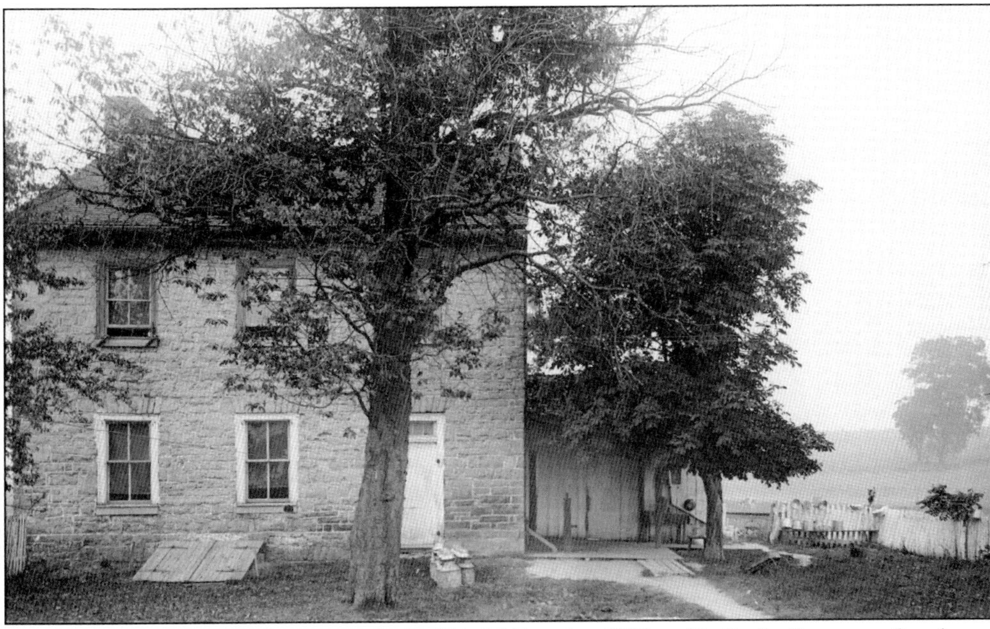

Samuel Maclay (1741–1811) came to the Buffalo Valley after 1770 and built the limestone farmhouse shown in the above photograph. Maclay was an early political figure, surveyor, and farmer in Pennsylvania, as noted on the obelisk honoring him at the nearby Dreisbach Church he helped found. Maclay served in the Pennsylvania General Assembly from 1787 to 1791 and from 1797 to 1802, and in the US Congress from 1794 to 1797. The photo-litho postcard below, printed by a German firm for Lindig's Art Store in Lewisburg, shows the church and the Maclay obelisk, near the church's front facade. This was the second of three churches built on the site. The first was log, and the second was so severely undermined during an excavation that it had to be razed. The present church replaced the damaged building in 1963. (UCHS 92.9.89.44 and 90.20.1.)

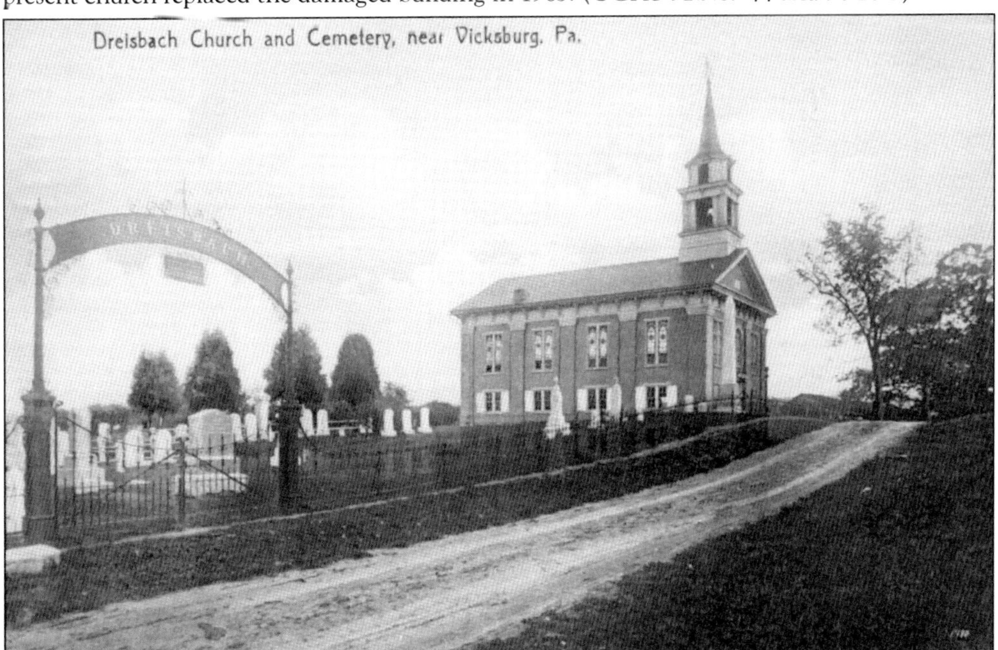

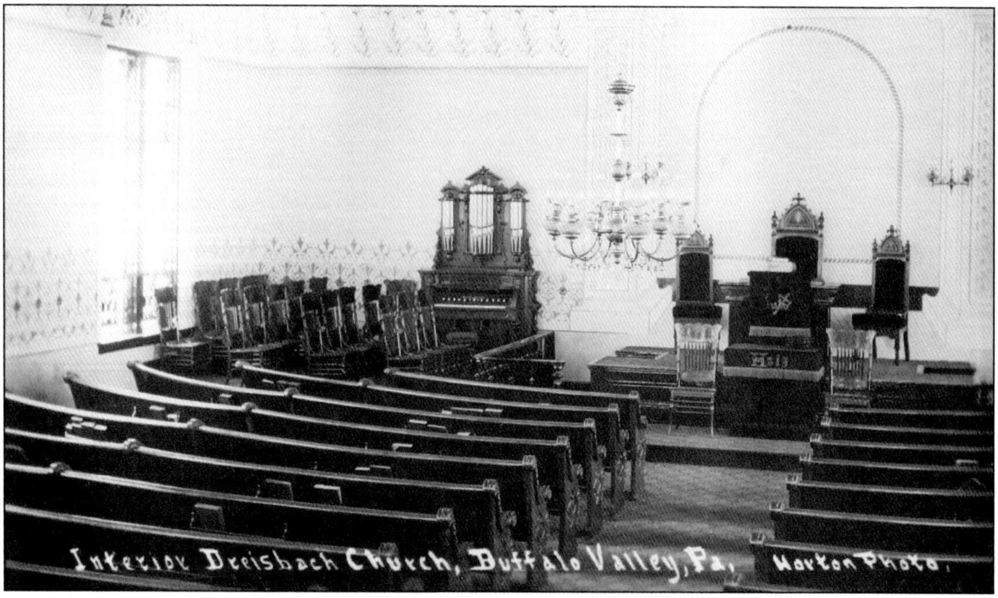

Real-photo postcard views of the interiors of stores, homes, and churches are rare. Interior photographs were taken of the Dreisbach Church sanctuary (above) and the lower-level Sunday school room (below). This brick church was the second for the early Reformed (also known as German Presbyterian) church site, located between Vicksburg and New Berlin. These postcards were produced between 1907 and 1911 by West Milton photographer Stephen Horton, who took numerous photographs in "Buffalo Valley," so named on the cards' fronts, of Vicksburg, Buffalo Crossroads, and Mazeppa. Details of wall stenciling, framed items, and furniture, including a shelf clock, kerosene lights, and a chandelier, bring life to the images. (UCHS 97.1.12 and 2006.41.10.)

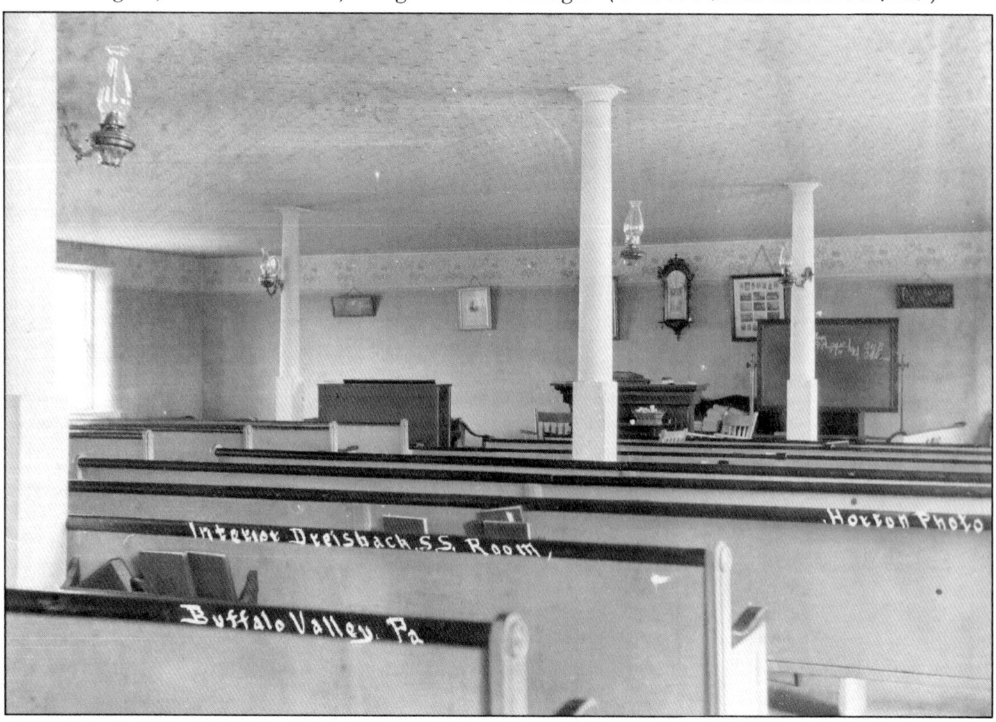

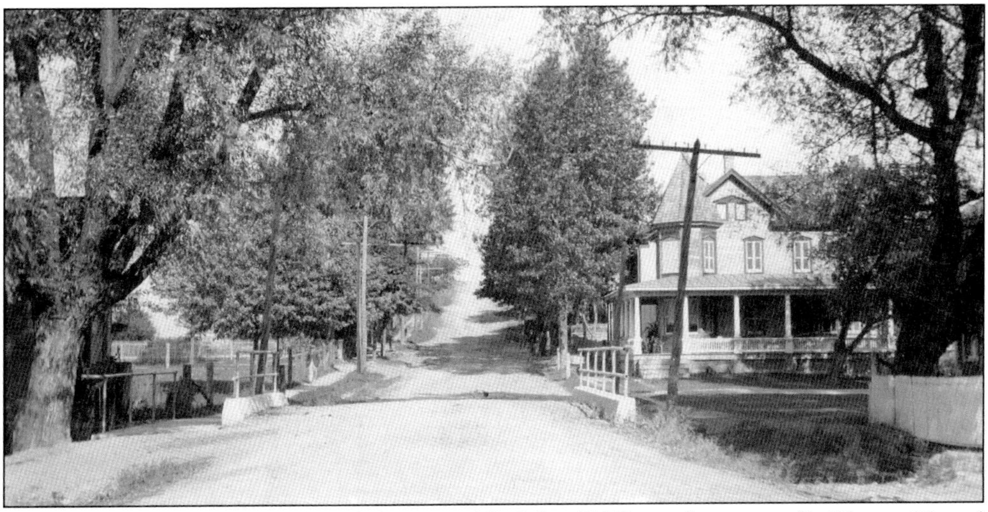

Surrounded by good farmland, Vicksburg straddled the Old Turnpike, now called Route 15, and was nearly equidistant from Lewisburg to the east and Mifflinburg to the west. In the 1880s, trains brought visitors to Charles Dreisbach's three-storied Great Western Hotel. Eventually, it had a ballroom, croquet green, tennis court, and a liquor license. When business declined, it was razed in 1971. In Vicksburg, there was also a church, blacksmith shop, Burrey's store, and Roudebush's store and mansion. One-room schools were located on both the east and west sides of town. Sone's, shown below on April 5, 1967, was among the last businesses established there. In 1971, the Groffdale Mennonites built their second meetinghouse in the county nearby, and member Isaac Reiff had a buggy-making shop close at hand. (Above, Joseph Prah; below, 82.4.C61.4 YY.)

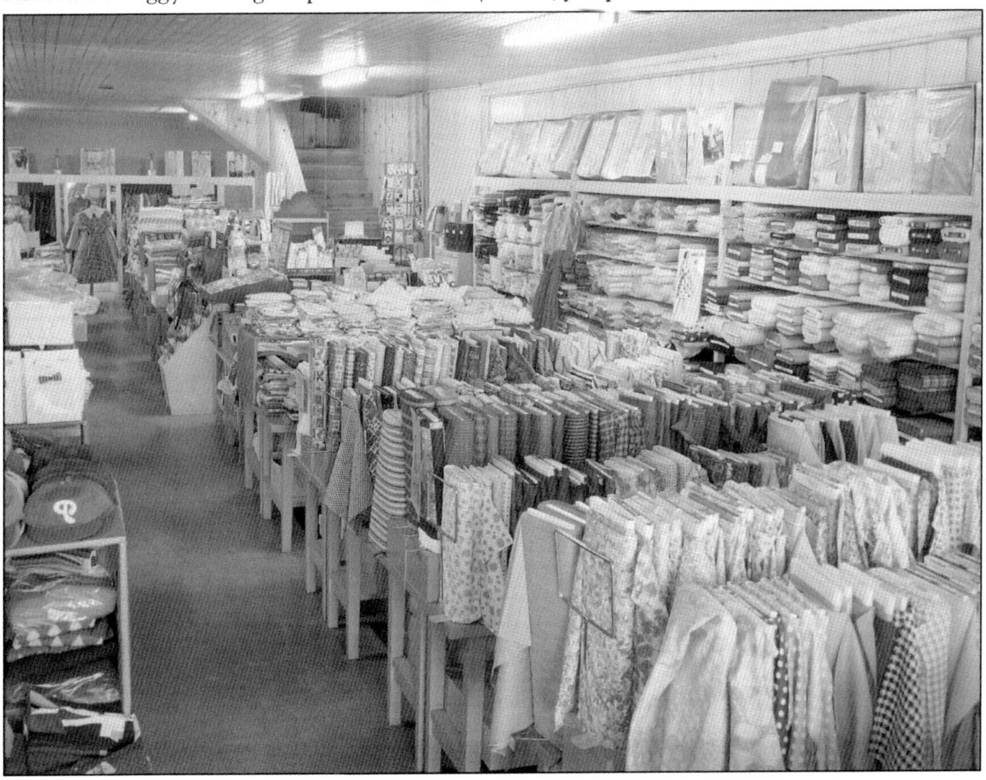

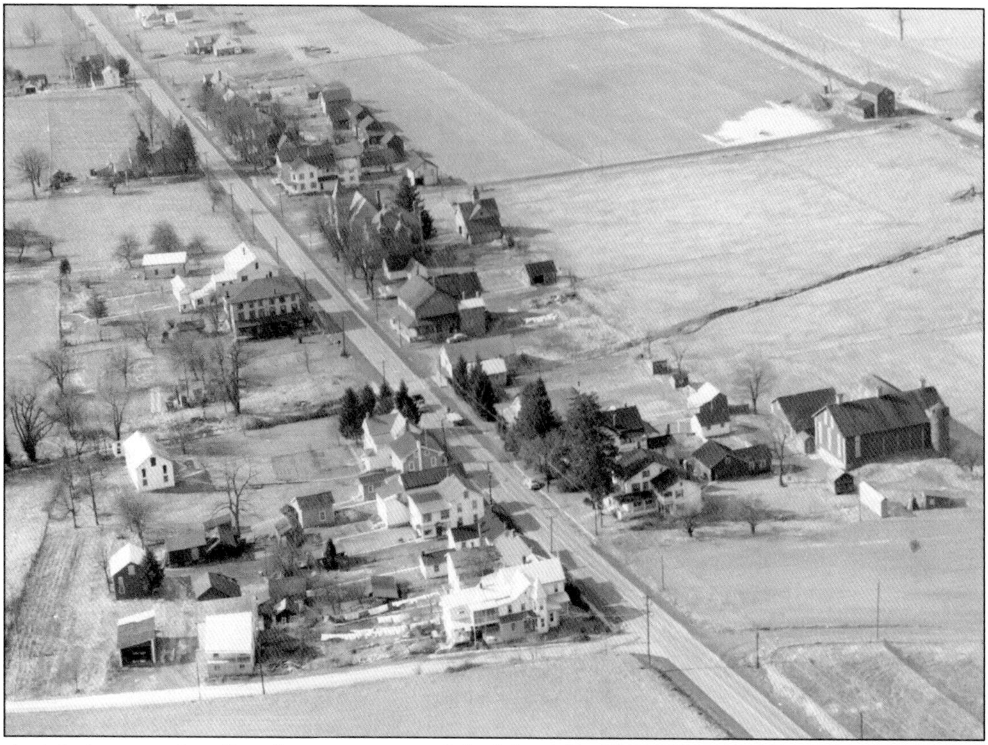

Aerial photographs of local towns were made by Henry De Wolf of Rochester, who also produced real-photo postcards in the 1950s. The back of the above photograph, of Vicksburg, reads, "Copies of this photo may be ordered at any time by mentioning this photo marked #208.88." Buildings on the south side included the Great Western Hotel, which was owned for many years by John E. Everitt (1861–1951). He also owned an adjacent livery stable, which was famous for its horse auctions. Below, in a c. 1940 cabinet photograph by the Slear Studio in Mifflinburg, John Everitt is selling an early wool wheel and other antiques on the porch of the hotel. The Great Western Hotel appeared in one of a series of six printed postcards that were reissued as stationery in the 1970s. (Above, UCHS 2007.6.13; below, John Bower.)

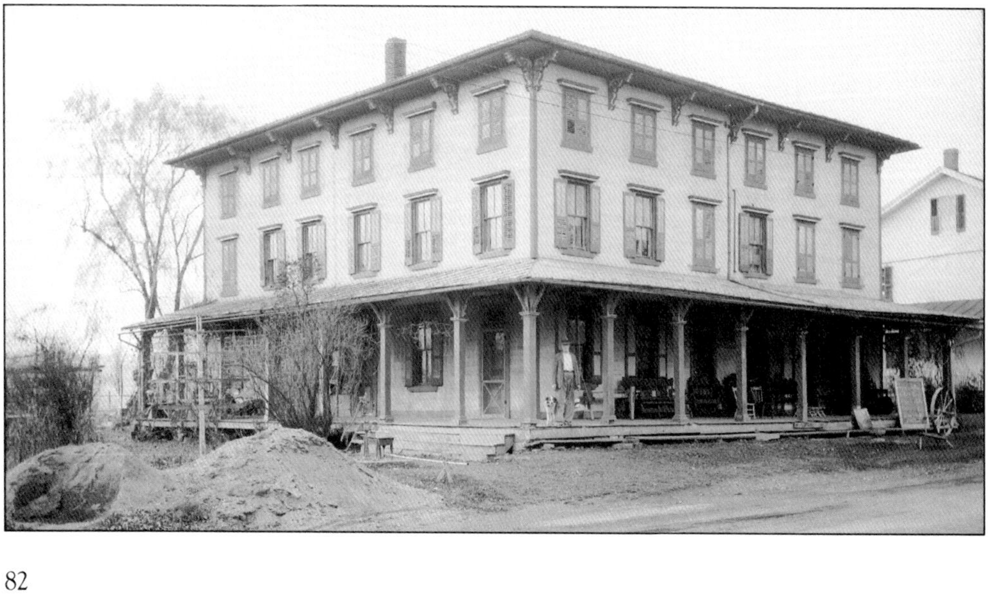

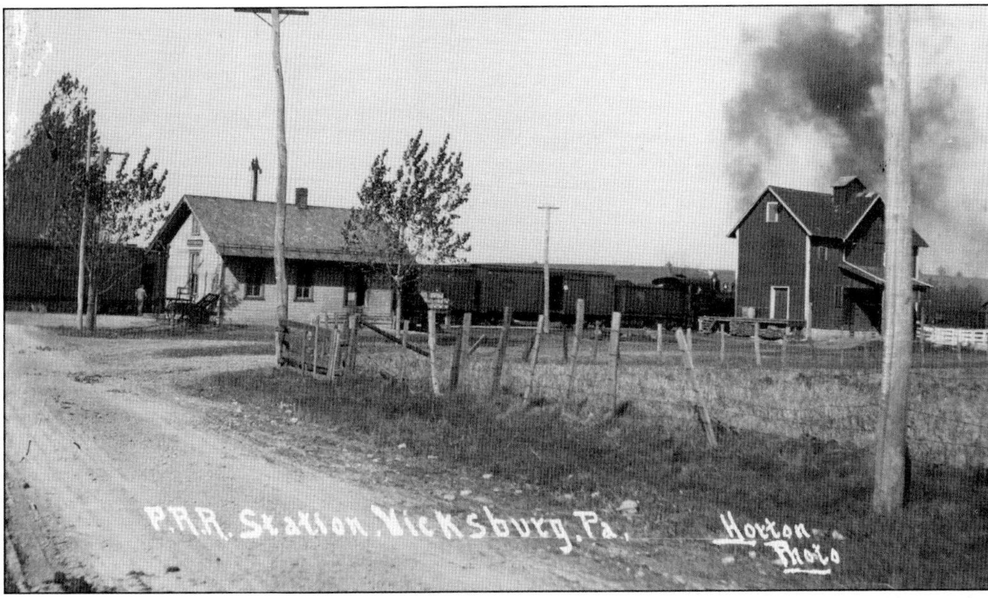

Above, the train station at Vicksburg and a train headed west to Mifflinburg and beyond is shown in a Horton real-photo postcard from between 1907 and 1911. From this station, many of the county's Amish left for Kansas in the 1880s. They found, however, that the farmland in the Midwest did not compare to what they had worked in Buffalo Valley, and many lost their savings in the venture. The tarring of the first poured road (below) was photographed in Vicksburg around 1910 and released as a postcard. Road construction in Winfield, Lewisburg, Vicksburg, and Mifflinburg must have been of particular interest, as it was photographed in this, the initial era of road improvement under Pennsylvania governor Gifford Pinchot. (Joseph Prah.)

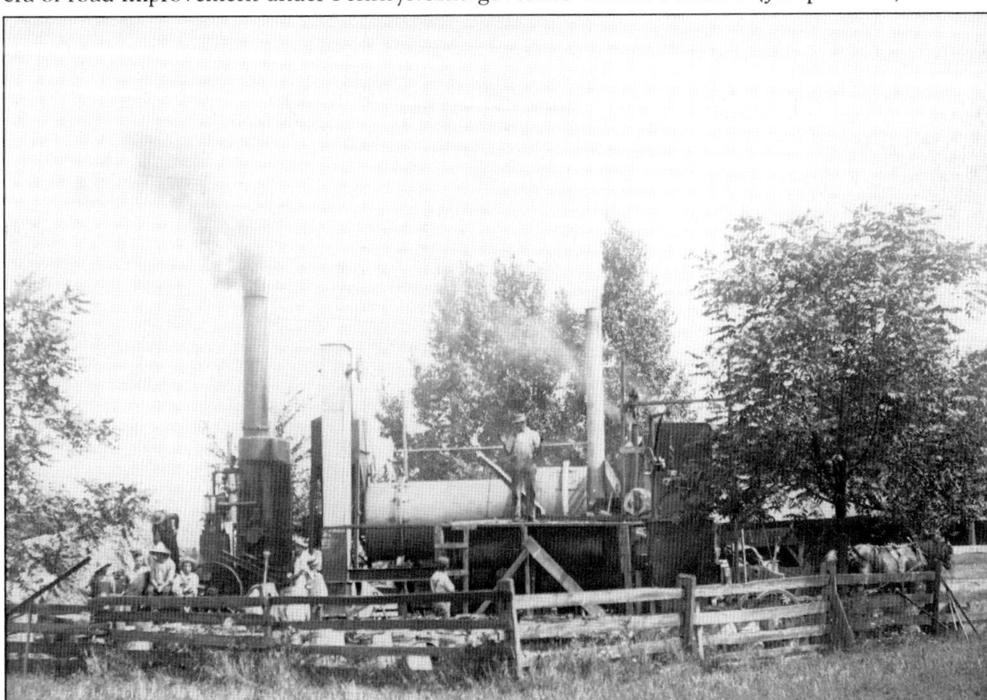

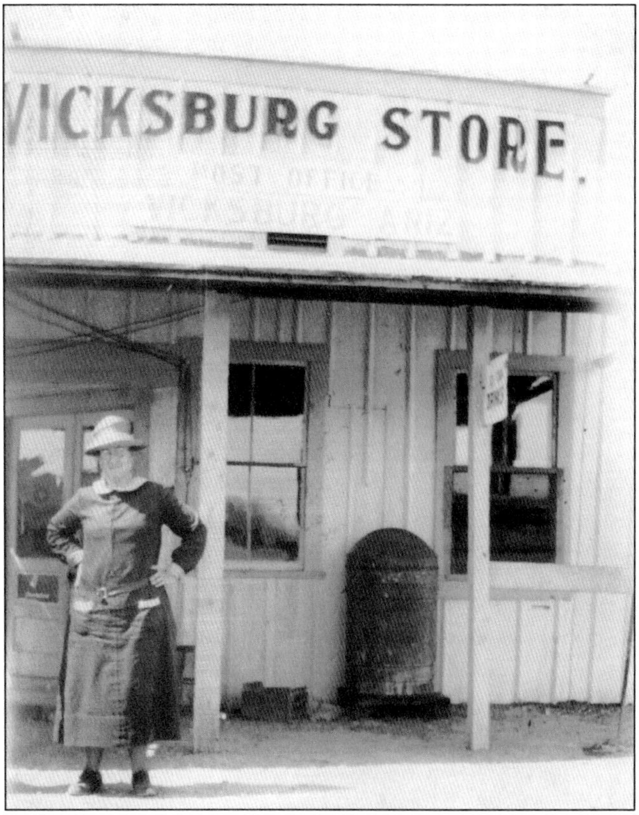

Mary Barber Hagey (1891–1967) stands in front of the Vicksburg post office. (Bill and Sharon Herald.)

Apples were a major crop in the area. Red Astricans, Gravenstines, Sweet Boughs, and Starks are some of the apple varieties grown here. Many area farms had orchards. Families traditionally made cider and apple butter and kept their apple harvests in the cellar or in an "apple cave" dug in their gardens. In this Stephen Horton real-photo postcard from between 1907 and 1911, barreled apples ready for transport stand beside Beaver Run in Vicksburg. (Joseph Prah.)

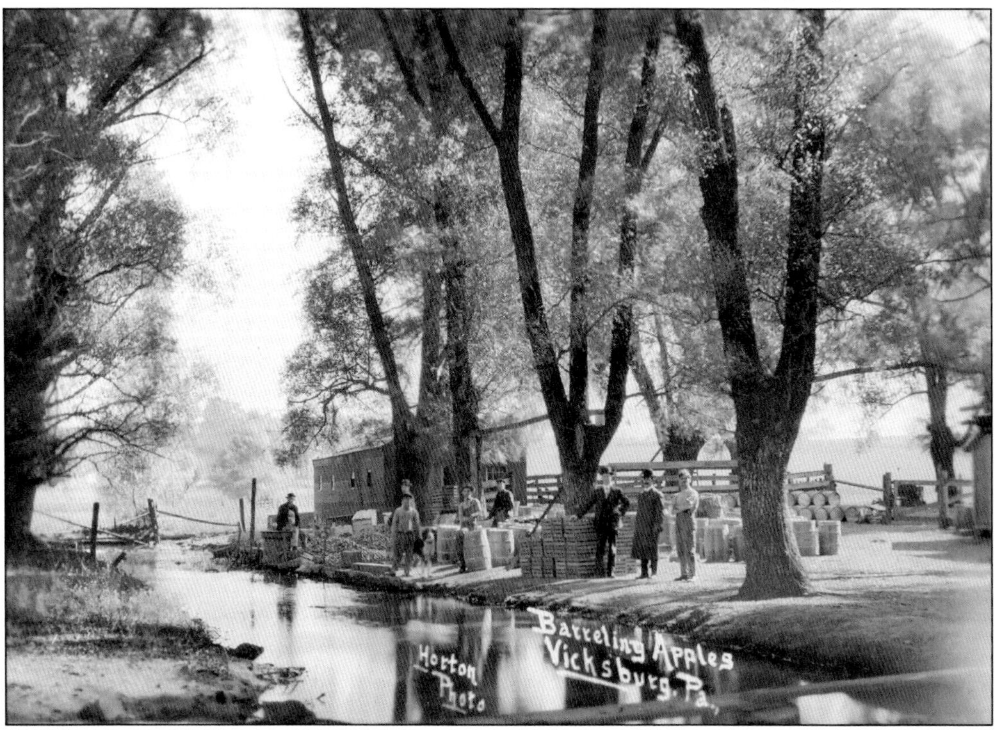

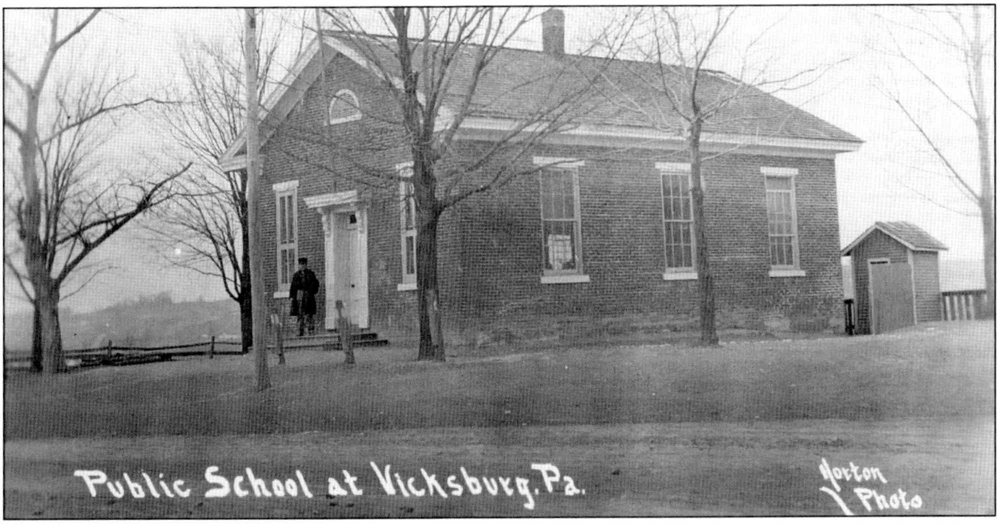

The above photograph, taken by Stephen Horton, shows the exterior of Vicksburg's brick one-room school (also called the Pike School, because it was on the Old Turnpike), located east of the small community. The interior photograph below captures the scholars at their desks; their teacher is in the rear. Some of the pupils moved while the photograph was being taken, resulting in the blurred effect. The schoolhouse was built in 1871 and, like many one-room schools of that era, replaced an earlier log building. This school, now a private residence, was closed in 1948 when the newly built Buffalo Crossroads Elementary School on Johnson Mill Road opened. The consolidated Buffalo Crossroads School closed in 2011, when the Mifflinburg School District consolidated its outlying elementary schools in New Berlin, Laurelton, and Mazeppa. (Above, Joseph Prah; below, Ronald Nornhold.)

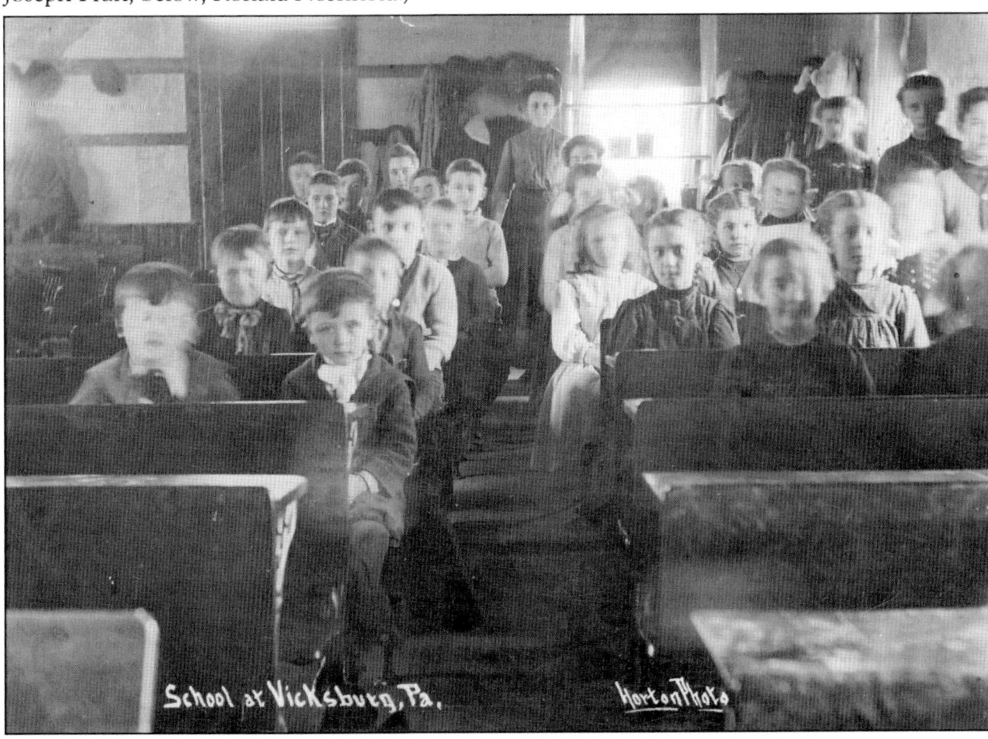

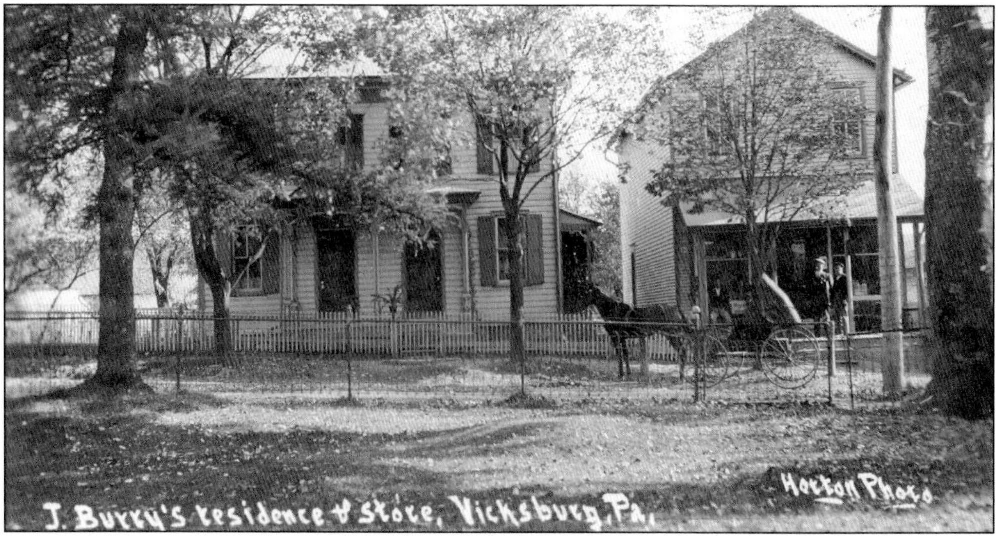

J. and Hazel M. Burrey's residence and store in Vicksburg (above) were photographed by Stephen B. Horton. The Burrey store sold groceries, coal, lumber, roofing, shoes, drugs, and fertilizer until it closed in 1958. The Burreys had another establishment in Lewisburg. Anderson's "Big Store" in Buffalo Crossroads (below), also photographed by Horton, offered Buffalo Crossroads postcards in both real-photo and black-and-white photolithographic versions. The Anderson store was built by William Linn in 1863 and remained a general store until 1974, when it was converted into apartments. An early limestone house from 1817 built by a Linn forebear is on the opposite corner and still stands. (Above, Joseph Prah and bottom, UCHS, 89.5.15.22.)

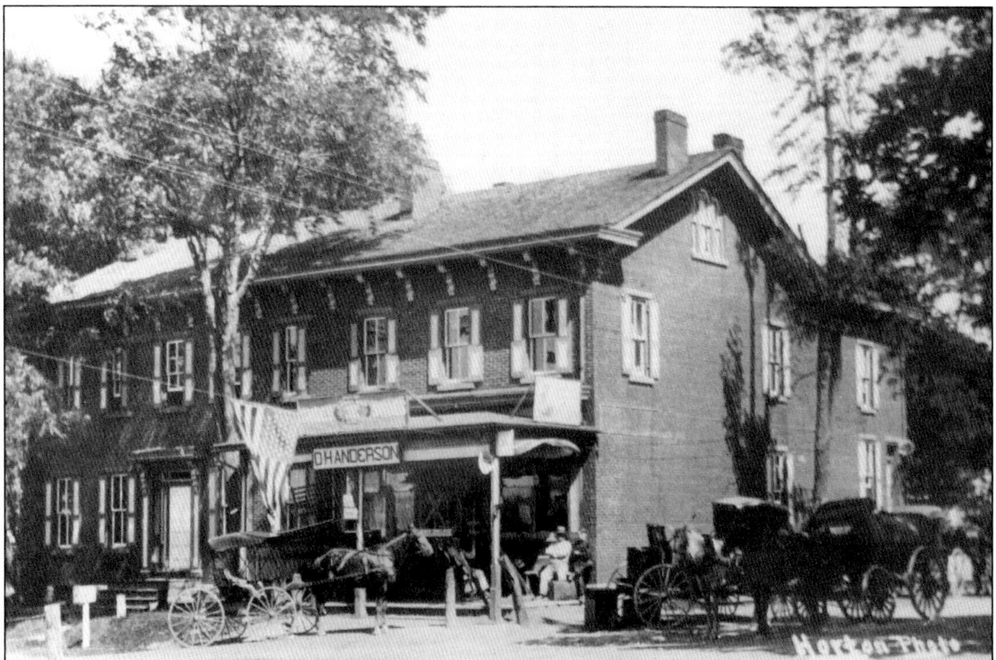

Three

Dale's Ridge, Buffalo Crossroads, and Mazeppa

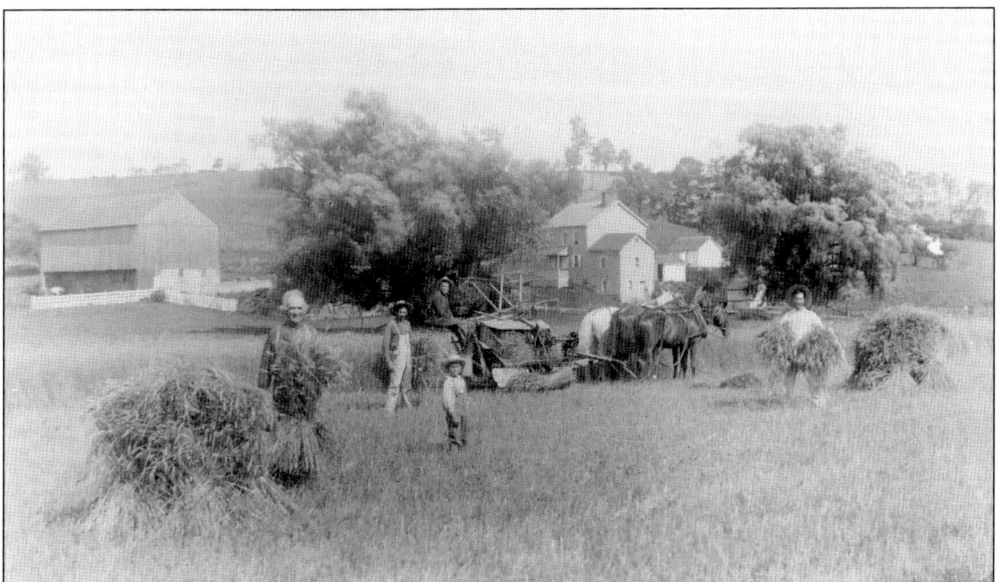

D. Vincent Smith of Williamsport photographed a wheat harvest on the Heiser farm outside of Buffalo Crossroads around 1905. Shown here are, from left to right, Charles Heiser, William Heiser, Robert Heiser (young boy), Jasper Ross (on binder), and William Neiss. The clapboard-covered log house was the site of an Indian party passing through the family's land, which was commemorated in a carving on the east gable end of the Sierer house. (Cherry Reigle Will.)

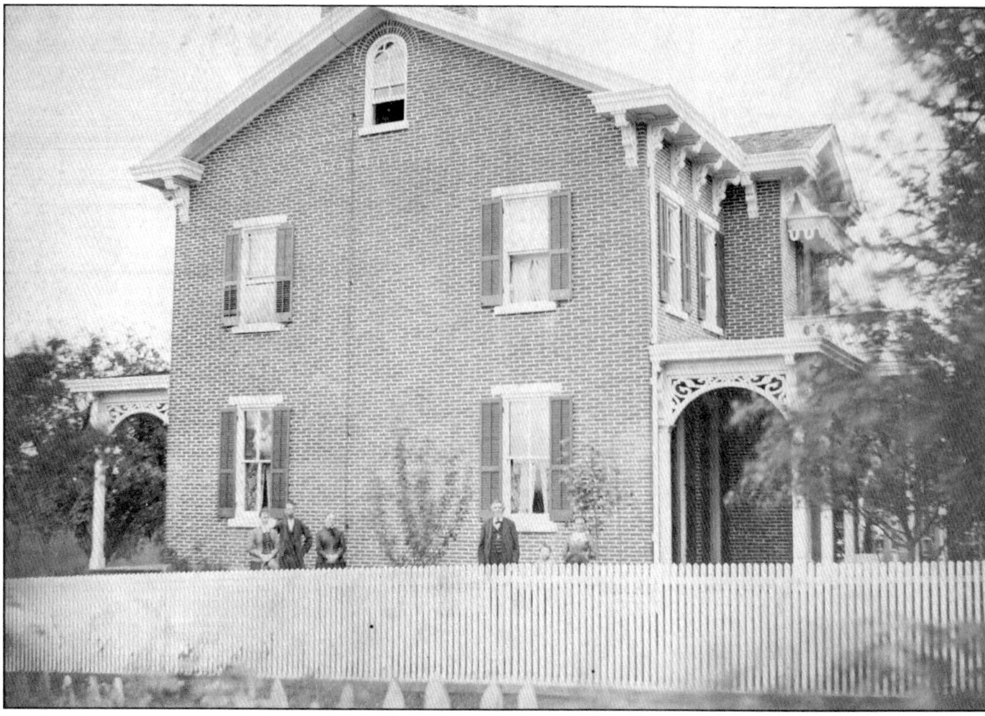

In the above photograph, Joseph W. Shriner, a partner in the foundry business of Geddes, Marsh & Co., poses with his family on his back porch in the late 1880s. The house was built for them in 1867. The foundry, later renamed Slifer, Walls, Shriner & Co., manufactured farm equipment. In the 1870s, Joseph Shriner purchased and operated the Wolfe Mill on Buffalo Creek, renamed Campbell's Mill, which was destroyed by fire on December 7, 1979. Also beside Buffalo Creek is Wolfland, a secluded spot off Hoffa Mill Road. It looks much the same today, more than 100 years from when the Stephen Horton real-photo postcard below was sent in 1908. (Above, Michael and Carol Manbeck; below, UCHS 2006.61.1.)

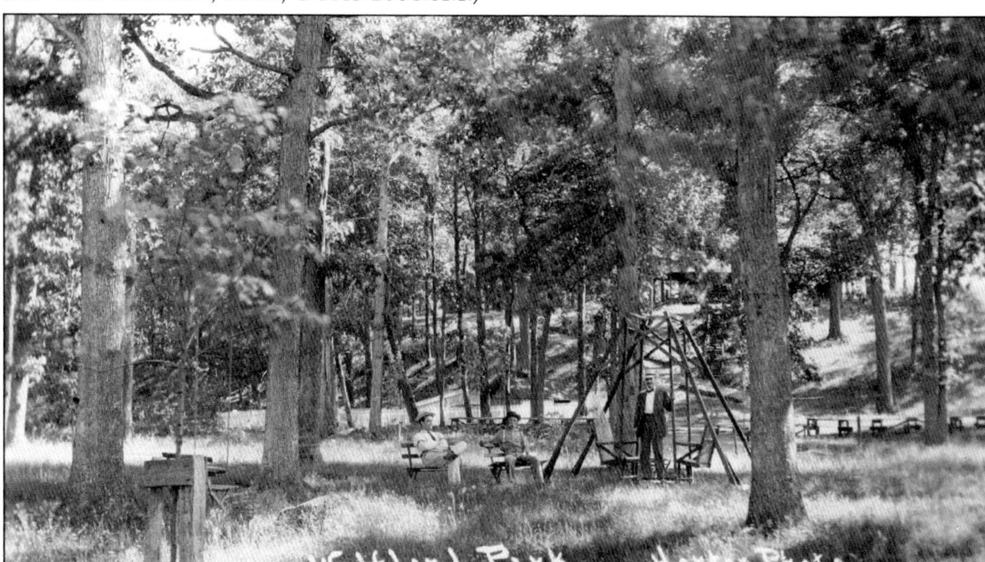

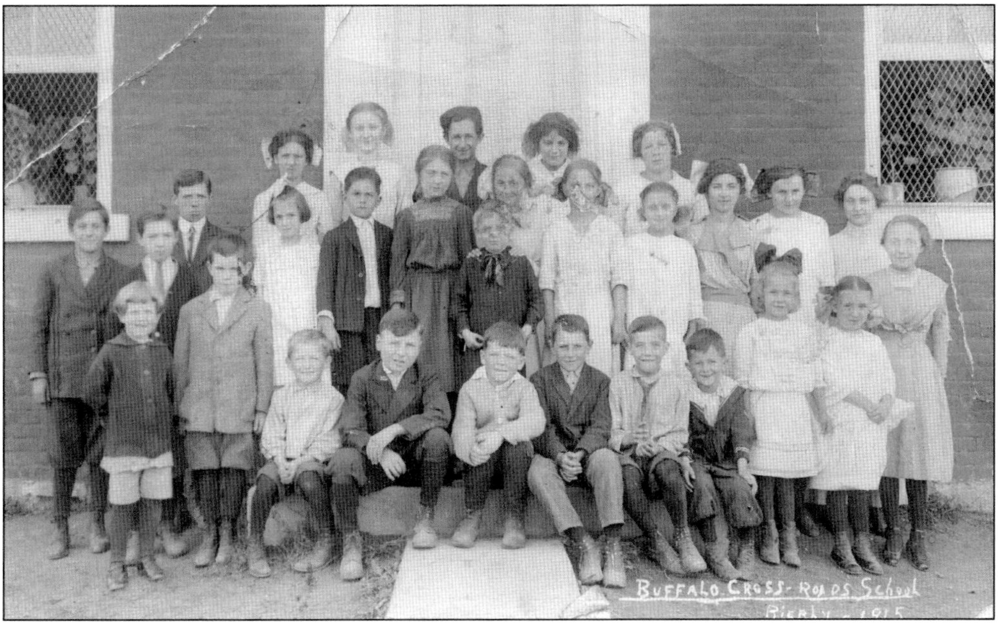

A real-photo postcard of Buffalo Crossroads School students (above) was taken between 1914 and 1920 by Grover Bierly of Mifflinburg. (Eleanor Maher Rawitz.)

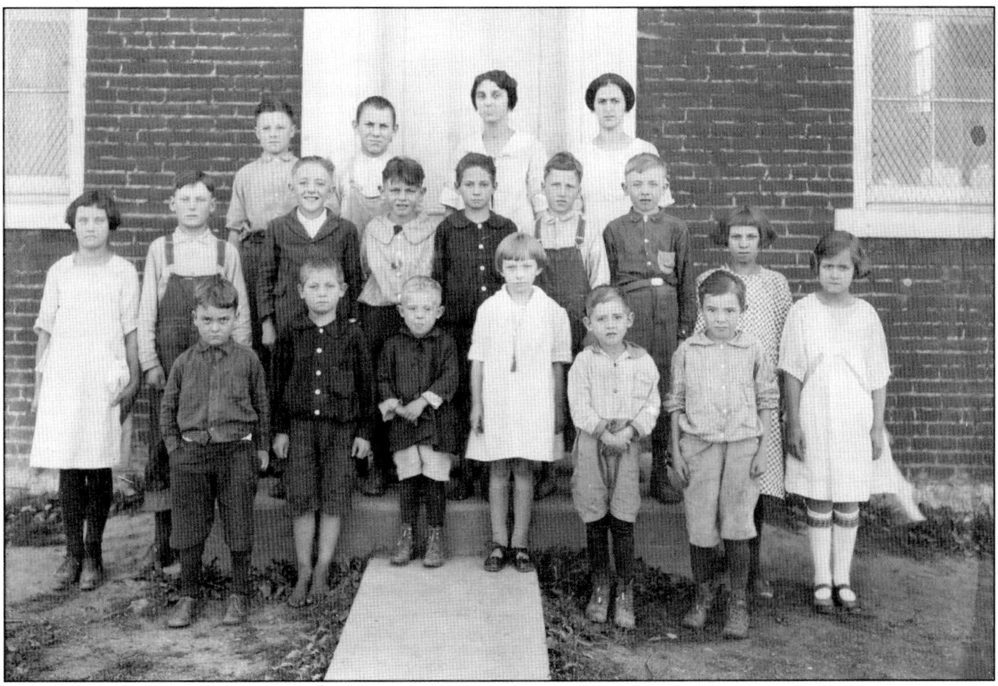

A cabinet photograph taken in 1926 by Bierly when he lived in Ludlow, Pennsylvania, identifies on its reverse side, from left to right, (first row) Jack Patton, Ernest Loss, Marlyn Beaver, Mary Ruhl (Maher), Larue Beaver, and Eugene Beaver; (second row) Dora Troup (Kline), Lloyd Troup, Charles Beaver, Harold Walter, Norman Loss, Lee Troup, Elwood Beaver, Beulah Loss, and Raylene Stuck; (third row) Lee Walter, Ernest Snyder, teacher Irma Lohr, and Ruth Wehr. (Eleanor Maher Rawitz.)

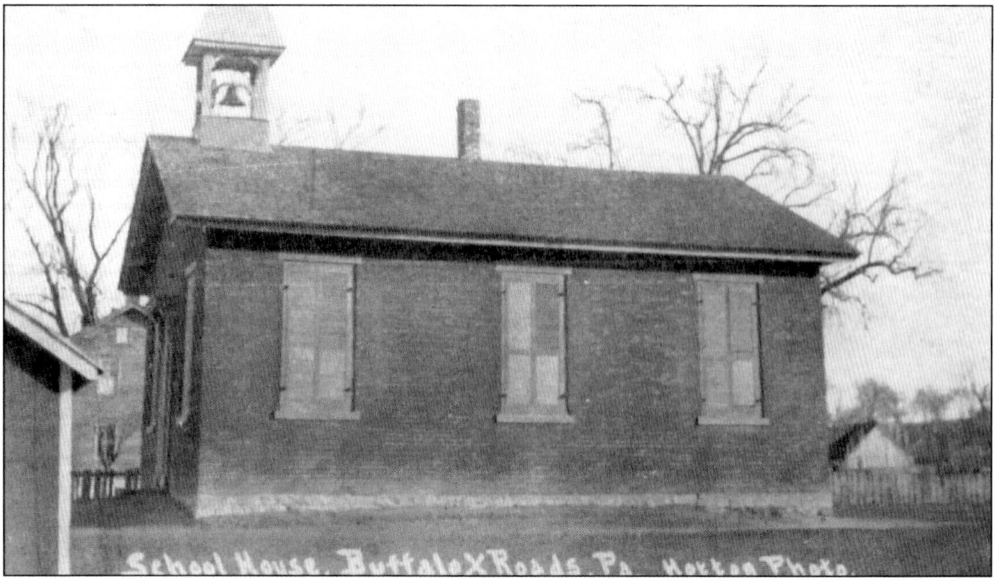

In 1807, John and Susanna Sierer and Christopher and Susanna Baldy were paid $6 for more than two acres by the trustees for a High German school, similar to the Dreisbach German School. The new building featured two rooms: a classroom in the front and a room in the rear for the schoolmaster. In 1869, the original tract was divided into four lots. Lot No. 2 was sold by the trustees of the High German School House to the Buffalo Township School District. There, the one-room brick schoolhouse in the above real-photo postcard was built. Eventually, it was closed, and in 1953 it was sold to Cloyd A. and Anna A. Kistler for $1,640. Below, the Buffalo Crossroads School's scholars, some seated on school furniture, are seen in a c. 1914 cabinet photograph by professional photographer Nelson Caulkins of Watsontown. (Above, Ron Nornhold; below, UCHS 2010.16.12.)

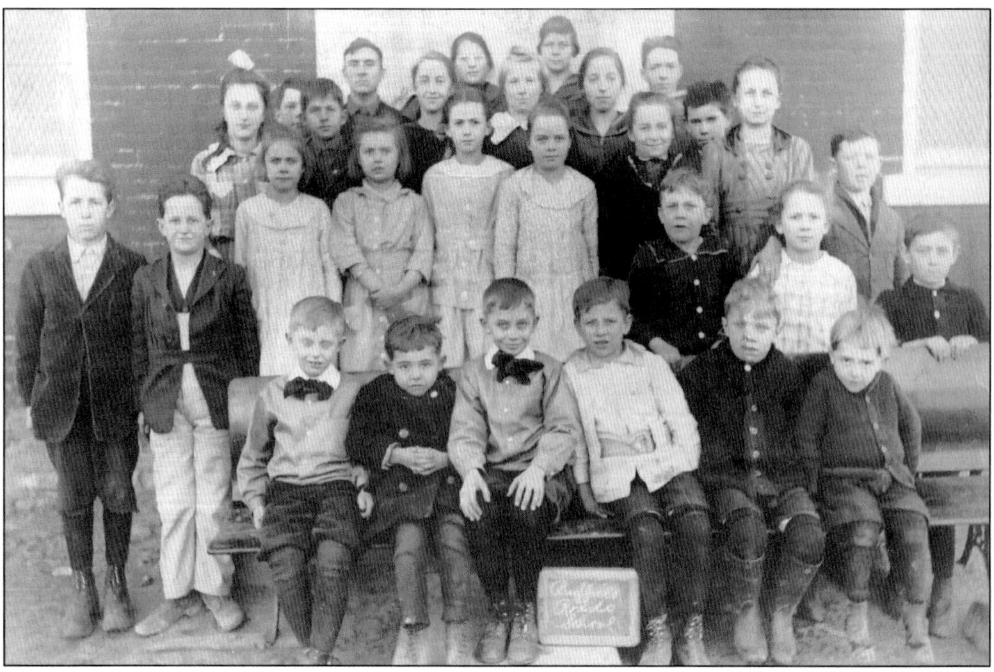

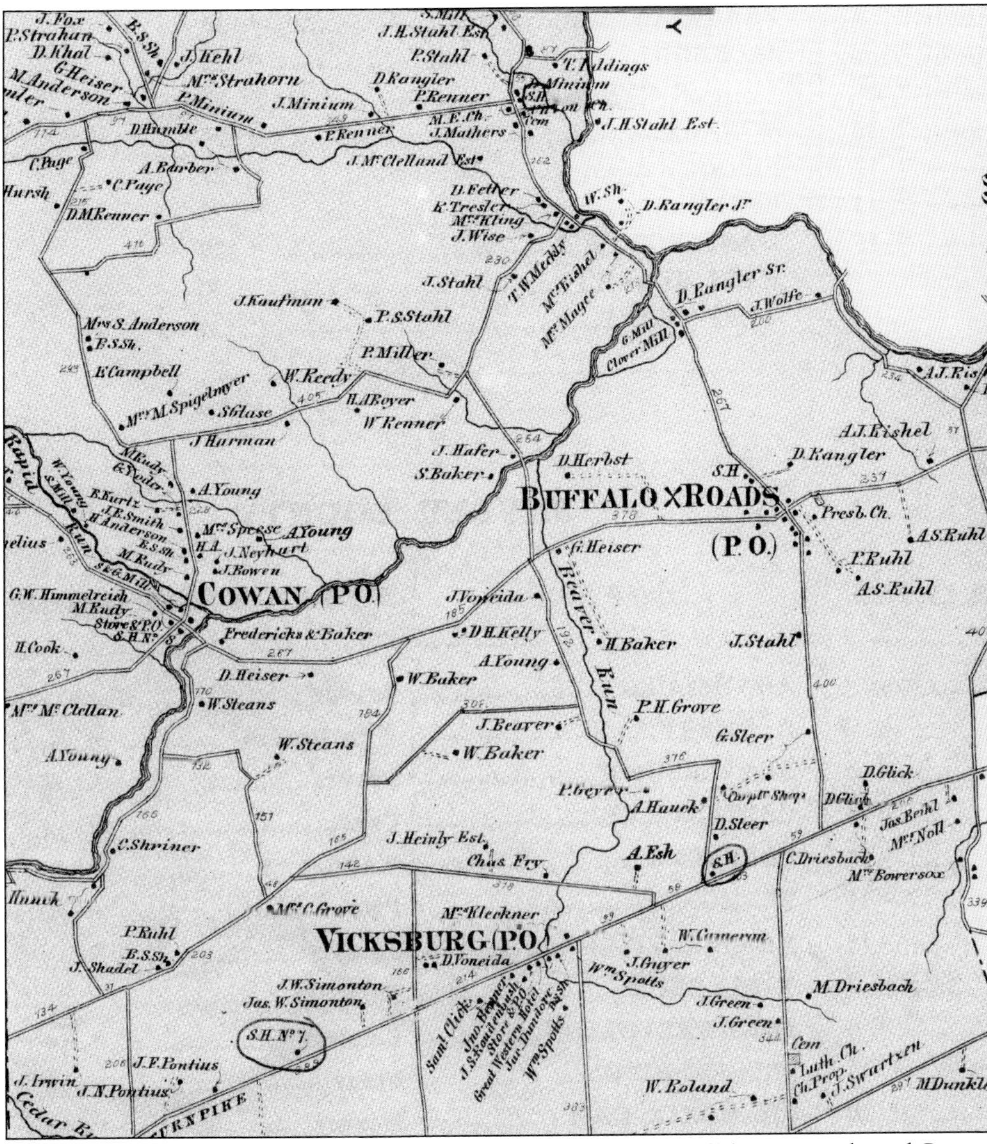

A detail of Buffalo Township in *Pomeroy's Atlas* shows Vicksburg, Buffalo Crossroads, and Cowan. Note that Boyertown (later called Mazeppa) is not yet indicated as a distinct community with its own post office, as Vicksburg, Buffalo Crossroads, and Cowan had at that time. On the atlas page is the confluence of Spruce Run/Black Run and Buffalo Creek, near which a clover mill and gristmill were located. Also seen on the north end of what would become the newest town in Buffalo Township is the Methodist Evangelical church, opposite the Union Church, schoolhouse, and cemetery. In 1916, a devastating fire went through Mazeppa, taking seven houses, four barns, a store, and the meat market. To the southeast of Vicksburg, located on the Old Turnpike, is the area settled by the Dreisbachs. In 1868, Martin Dreisbach's home was located by the end of Beaver Run and above the German Presbyterian, later known as the Lutheran Reformed church and cemetery, which his family founded. (UCHS.)

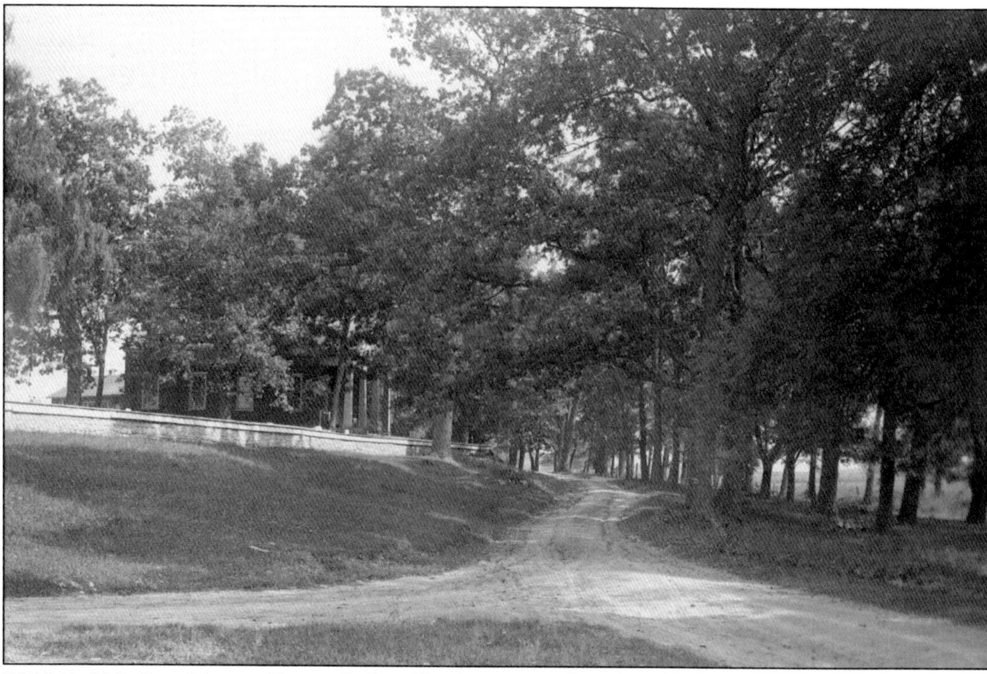

"Old Buffalo," as Union County's first Presbyterian church is known, is nestled in a grove of trees in the real-photo postcard above. Ellen Shields, a professional photographer who lived in Taylorville and Lewisburg, produced photographic work from around 1909 to 1921. For decades, the church was a pilgrimage site, along with LeRoy Springs, for those interested in local history, because it was the earliest congregation west of the Susquehanna River. The third building on the site, it has been preserved and is still available for school tours, programs, and wedding services. Below, West Milton photographer Stephen Horton approached the Buffalo Crossroads general store (in the center-left background) from the larger town of Mazeppa. The commercial buildings in the distant background still stand and are in close proximity to "Old Buffalo." (UCHS 98.44.75 and 79.469.1.)

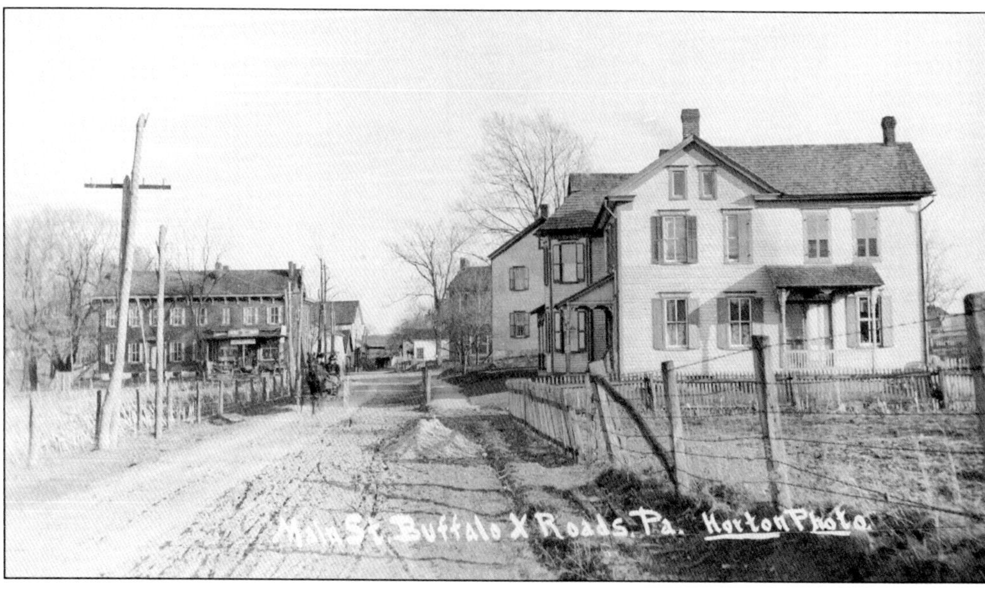

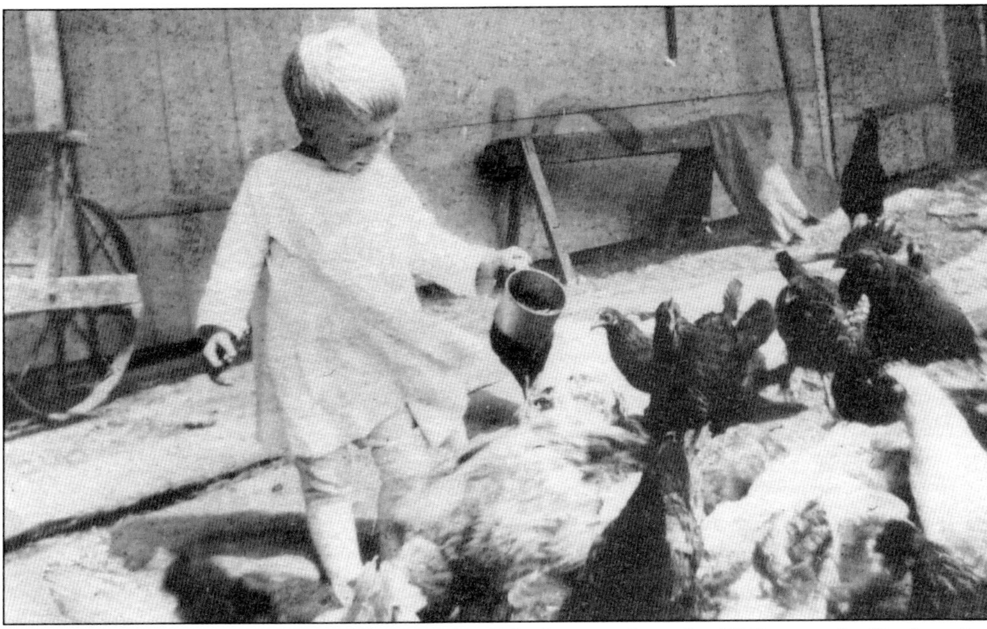

Philip and A.S. Ruhl owned several homes at Buffalo Crossroads in the 1860s, near the Presbyterian church that family members have overseen since 1975, when it was purchased by the 1773 Buffalo Church Association. A candid photograph from around 1912 shows George A. Ruhl (above) attending to the needs of the barnyard chickens at the home of his parents, Frank and Eleanor Shaeffer Ruhl. In the below photograph, also from around 1912, Frances Shriner Ruhl (left), a Mifflinburg schoolteacher, stands with her daughter-in-law Eleanor Shaffer Ruhl and Eleanor's two sons, George A. Ruhl (on swing) and John H. Ruhl. (Eleanor Maher Rawitz.)

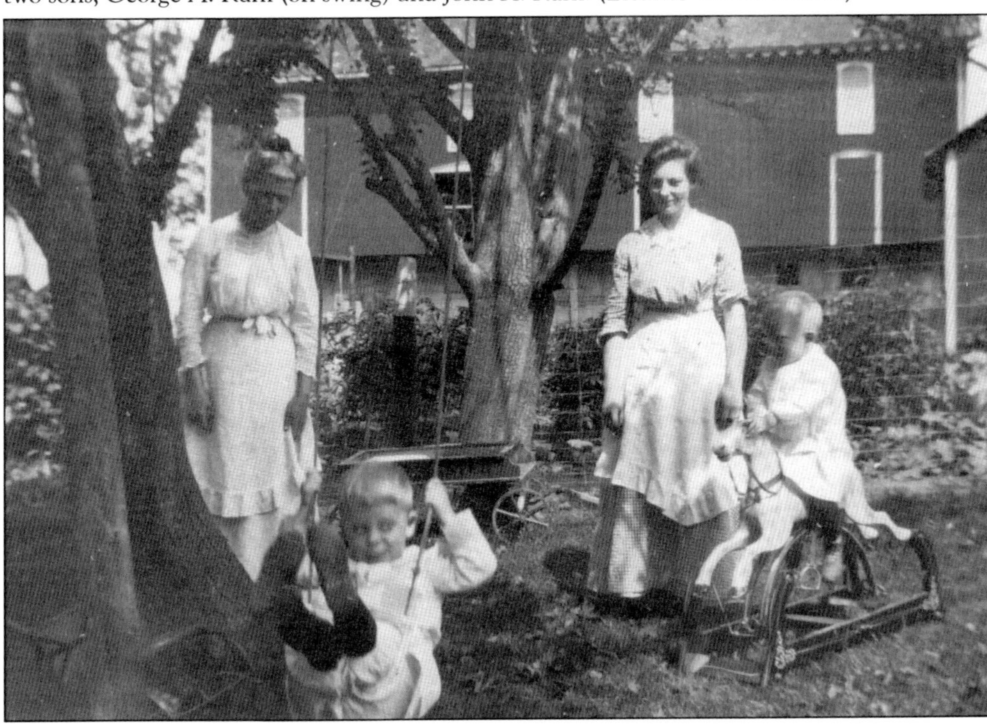

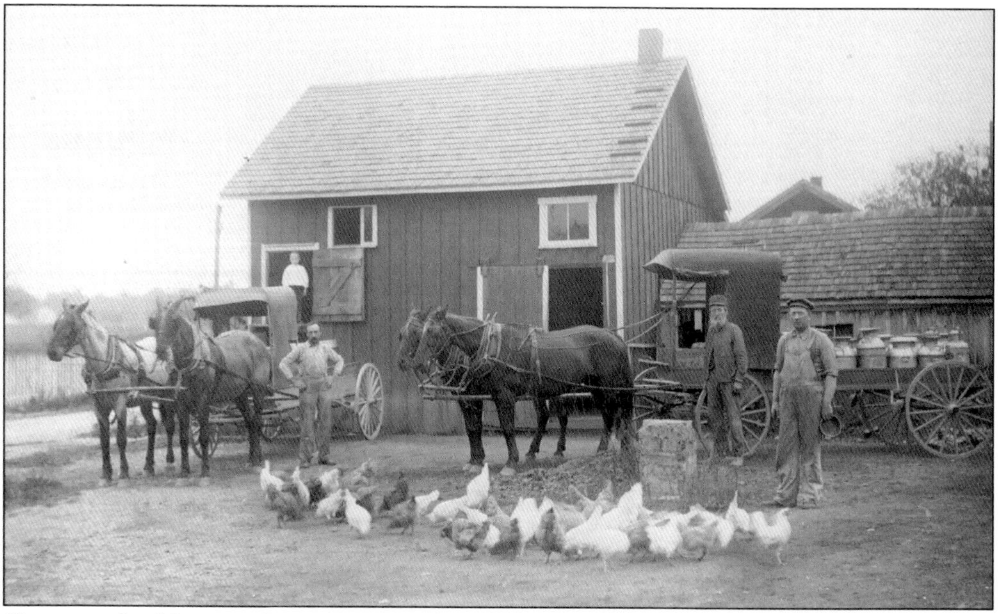

Shown at the Mazeppa Creamery around 1910 are, from left to right, an unidentified boy in mown hay, Henry Shannon (1860–1932), John Swartzlander, and Tom Pierce. Pierce operated the creamery and lived in the house seen in the background. Henry Shannon was a later owner of the house, which is now owned by Albert Delcamp. (Shannon family.)

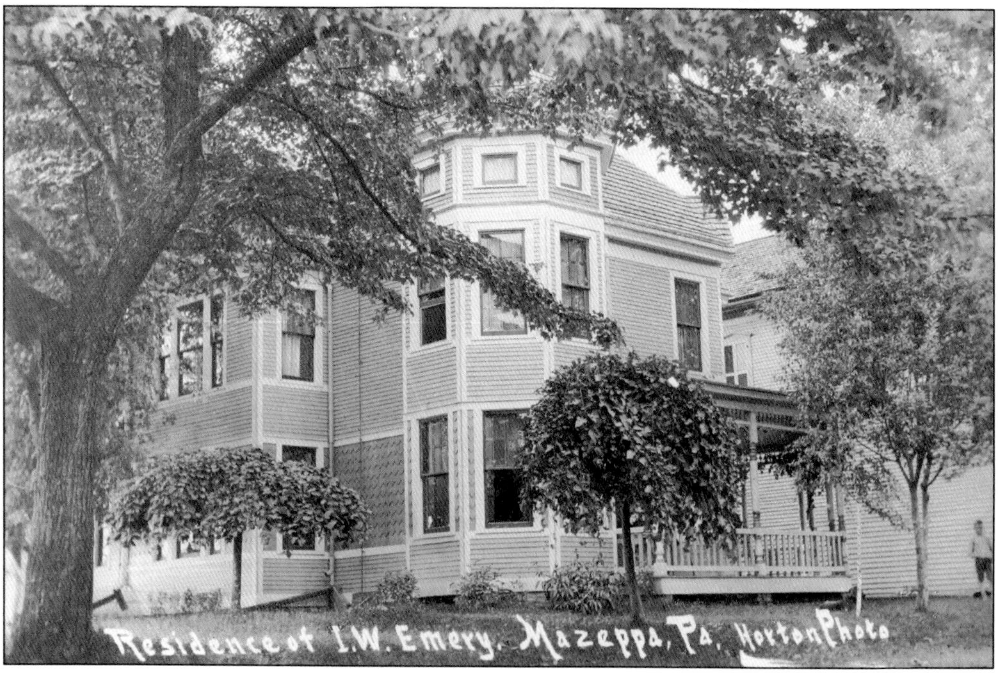

Stephen Horton's real-photo postcard showcases the I.W. Emery residence in Mazeppa. Maggie Emery sent the card to her cousin Jane Gunsall in Osage, Iowa, noting that Mrs. Deiffenderfer was sick again with jaundice in her lungs, Aunt Lizzie was still in bed, Aunt J. had a bad cold, while John Young had a daughter born on March 26. Diaries of the era often include many entries for sicknesses and funerals in addition to mention of the weather. (UCHS 2005.28.7.)

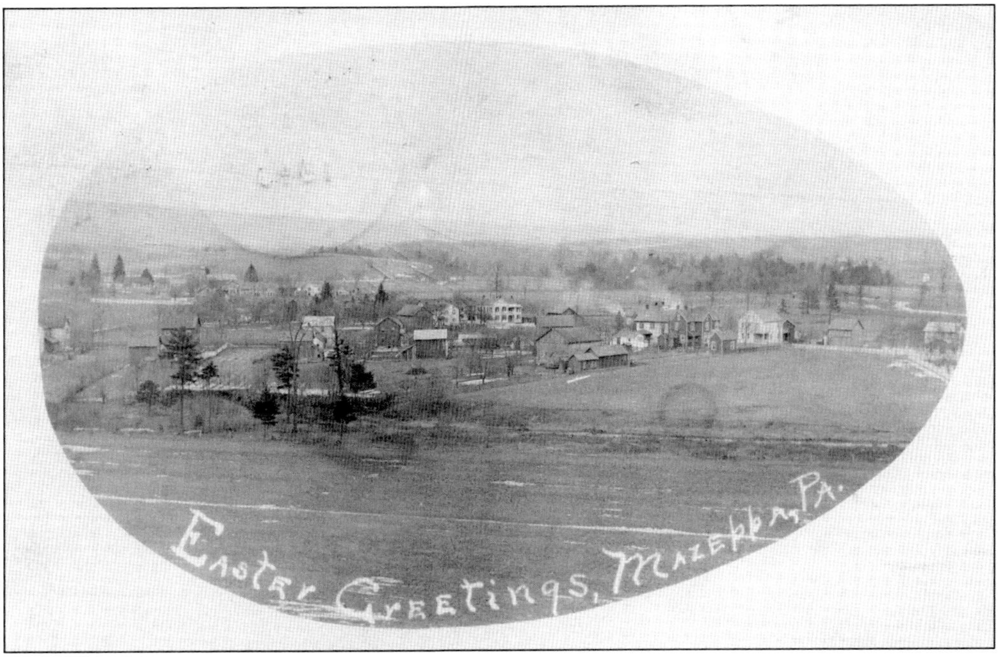

The real-photo postcard above, featuring a distant view of Mazeppa, is shaped like an egg and was sent at Easter in March 1910. Its message to Sallie Edmunds reads: "Dear Kid, Isn't this a lovely little town. But a few more days and I must leave. Many, many thanks for the flower. Its fragrance shall *never* pass away. Must go home this morning. Truely yours, F.P.B." Almost 50 years later, an aerial view of Mazeppa (below) presented a much larger village, with Buffalo Creek in the right foreground. Lester Mook wrote Ralph Kohler in St. Petersburg, Florida, in 1958: "We had quite a snow storm up here! Roads were drifted shut for a while. Heard the oranges got nipped down there. We had eight below zero one morning. That's too cold." (UCHS 2001.62.7 and 2009.2.31.)

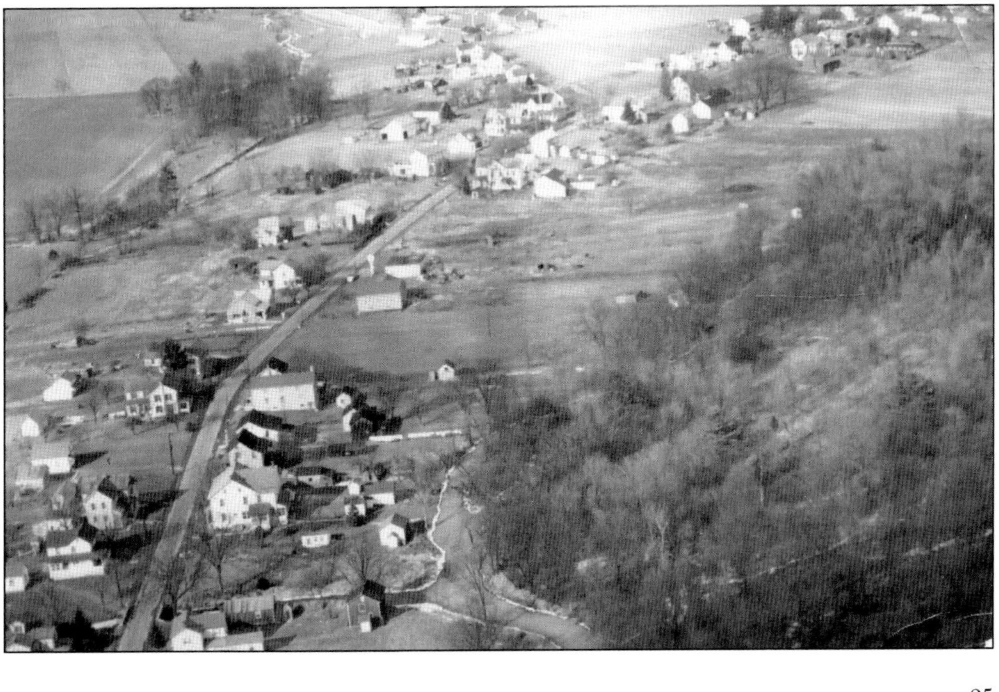

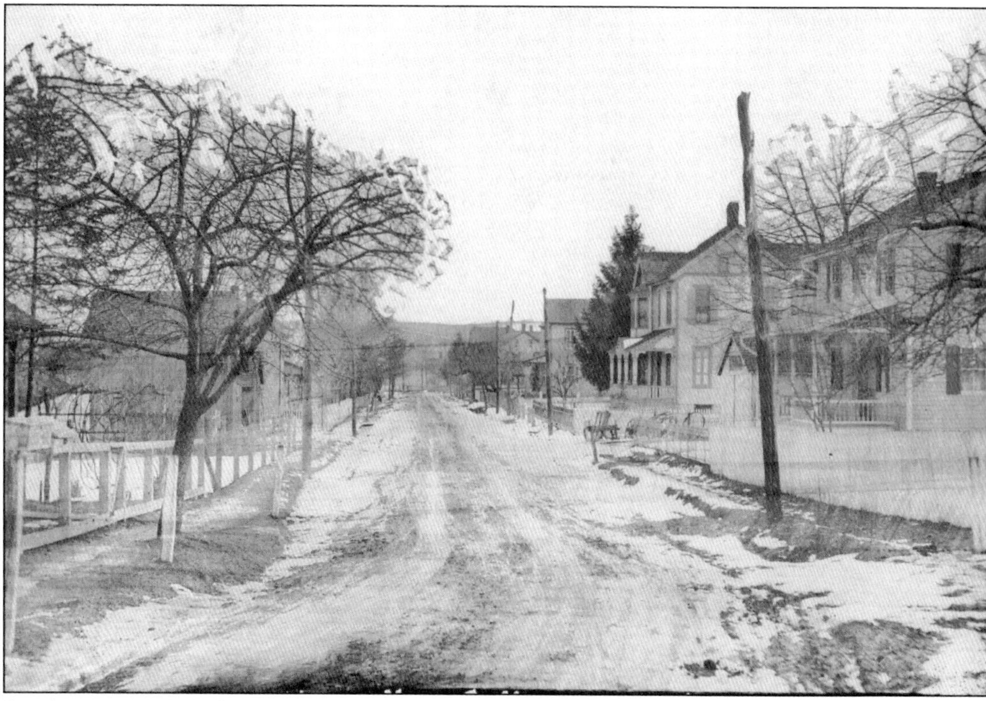

Stephen Horton's real-photo postcard above captures Mazeppa's Main Street, looking north. The George H. Brown residence (below) in Mazeppa burned in 1916, not long after this card was made. Real-photo postcards of an individual's home were often commissioned by the homeowner from a visiting photographer, like Stephen Horton. (Above, Beth Johnson Hackenberg; below, UCHS 2009.25.35.)

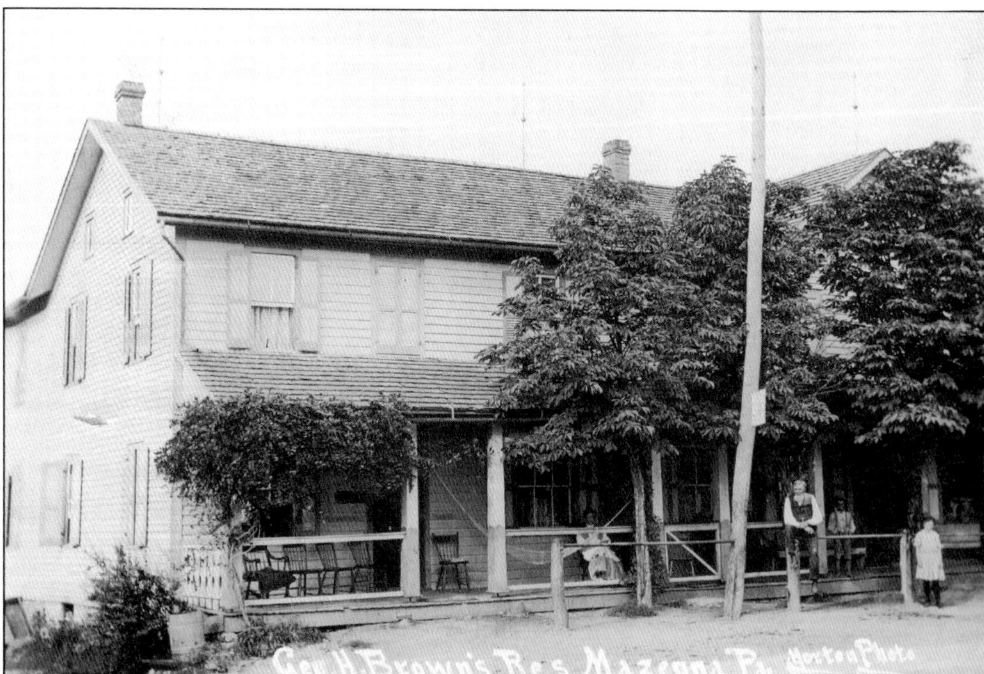

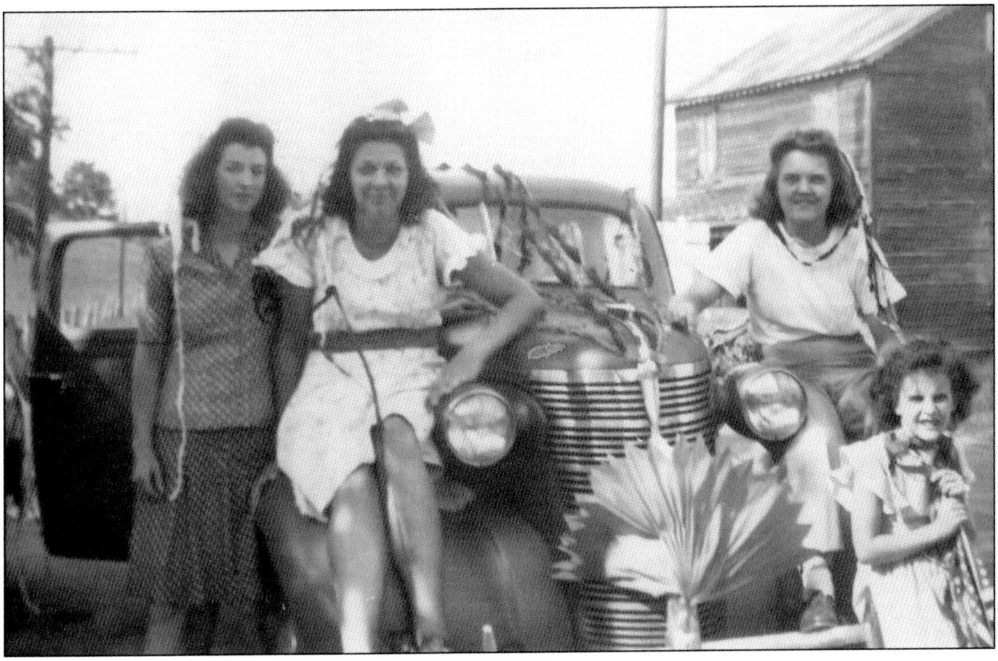

Parades featured prominently in Mazeppa's activities. The parade seen in these photographs was a V-J Day or a World War II victory parade in 1945. (Beth Johnson Hackenberg.)

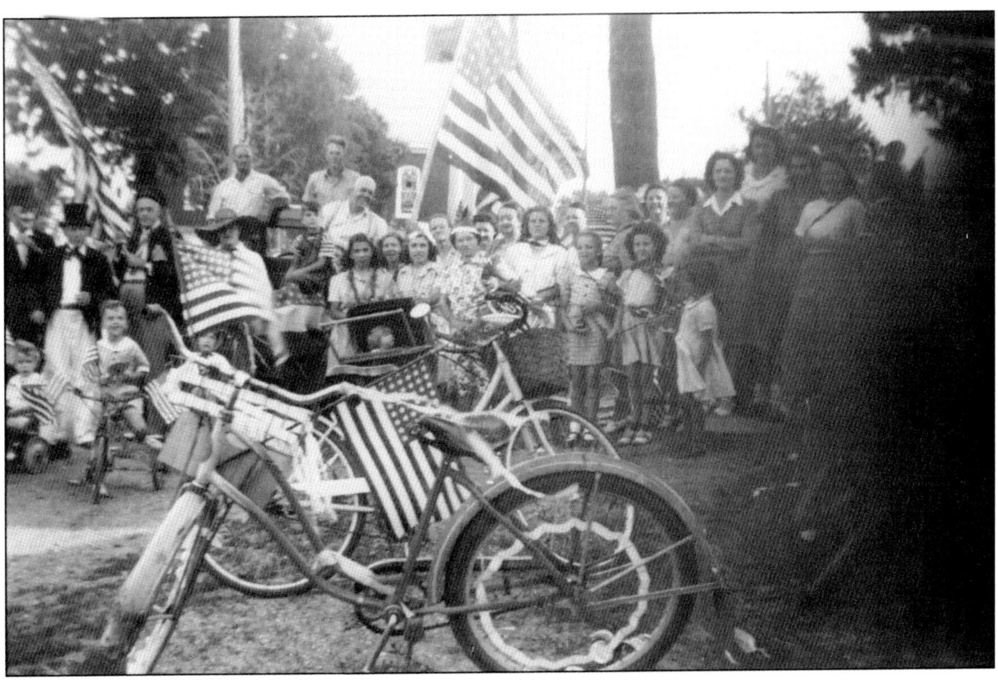

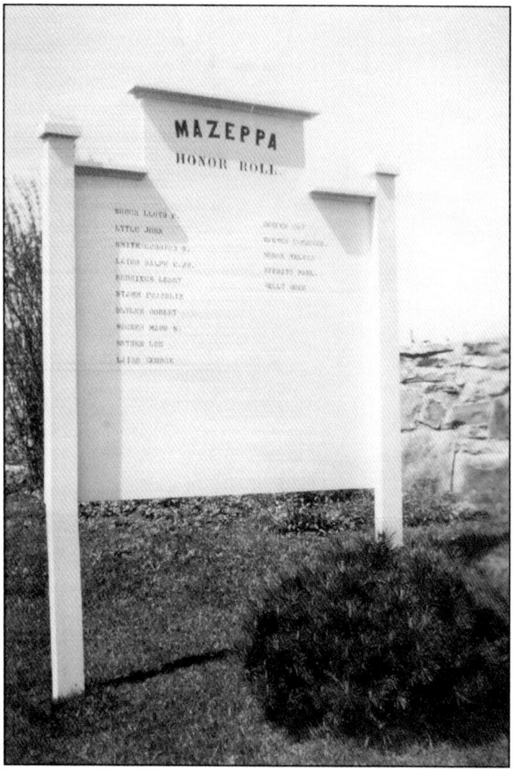

Paul Everett made a wooden sign commemorating Mazeppa's men who served in World War II: Lee Snyder, Paul Everett, Robert Blyler, Mark Wagner, Franklin Stamm, Leroy Heddings, George Laird, Ralph E. Laird Jr., Groover Smith, John Lytle, Guy Benfer, G. Marlin Baumer, Lloyd Shuck, Melvin Shuck, and Oren Kelly. The sign was erected on Paul Everett's farm. (Judy Reed.)

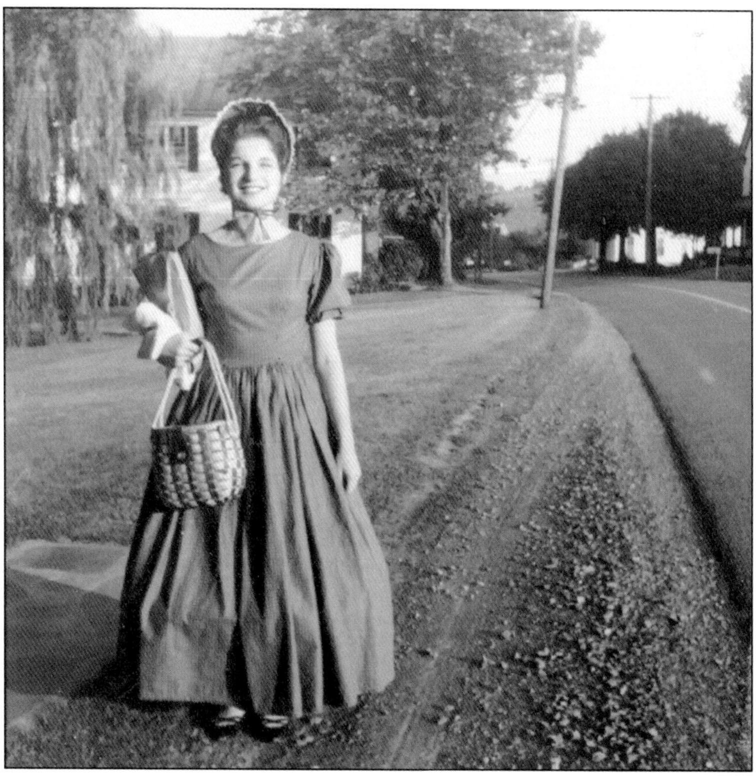

Judy Everitt Reed of Mazeppa poses in her Union County sesquicentennial dress in July 1963. Women in towns and crossroad communities throughout the county made such dresses, bonnets, and, sometimes, parasols, while the men donned bowlers and grew beards as "Brothers of the Brush." (Judy Reed.)

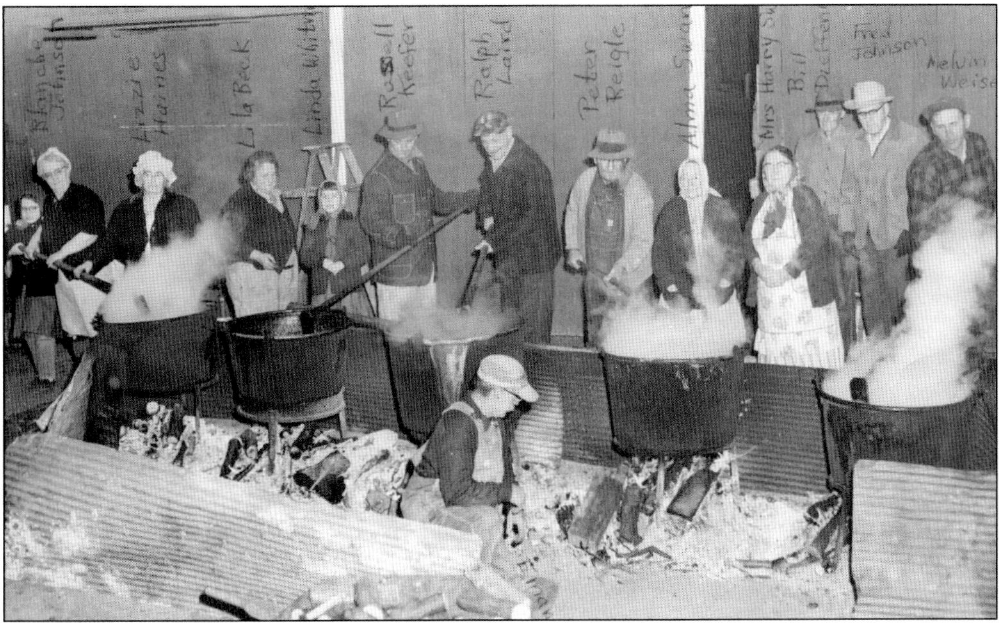

A community apple-butter boil to benefit the Mazeppa Union Church was held in 1953 on the property of Emanuel Beck (seen kneeling at the fires). Shown here are, from left to right, unidentified girl, Blanche Johnson, Lizzie Haines, Lila Beck, Linda Whitmeyer, Russell Keefer, Ralph Laird, Peter Reigle, Alma Swank, Mrs. Harry Swank, Bill Dieffenderfer, Fred Johnson, and Melvin Weiser. (Beth Johnson Hackenberg.)

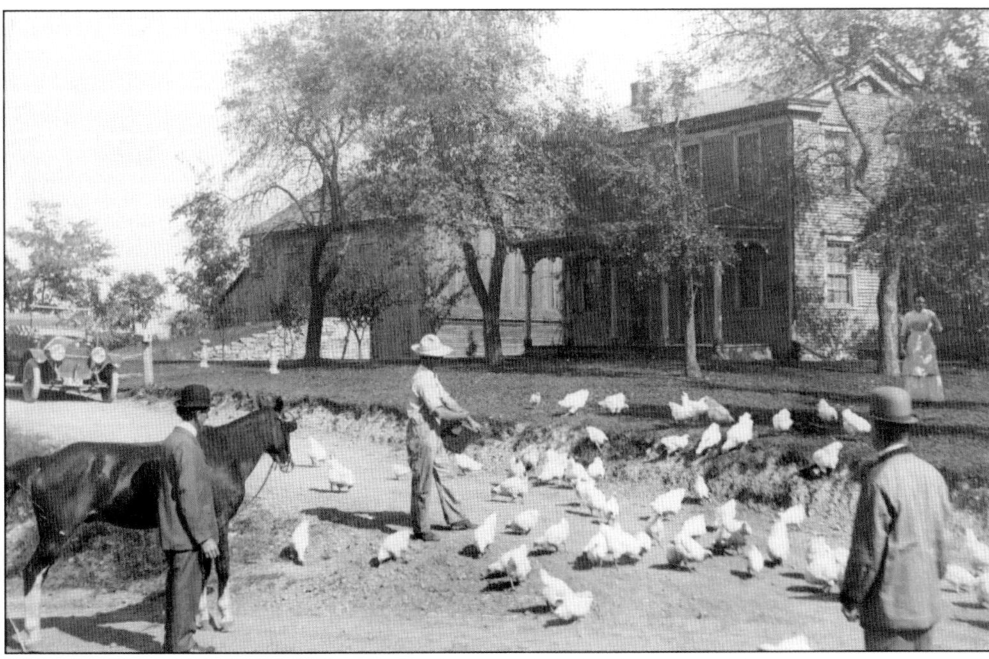

This photograph of the Bergenstock residence at Muddy Run, near Mazeppa, includes people, livestock, home, and a vehicle. An embossed stamp, "HALLMAN," was on the card, which dates from 1907 or later. (Joseph Prah.)

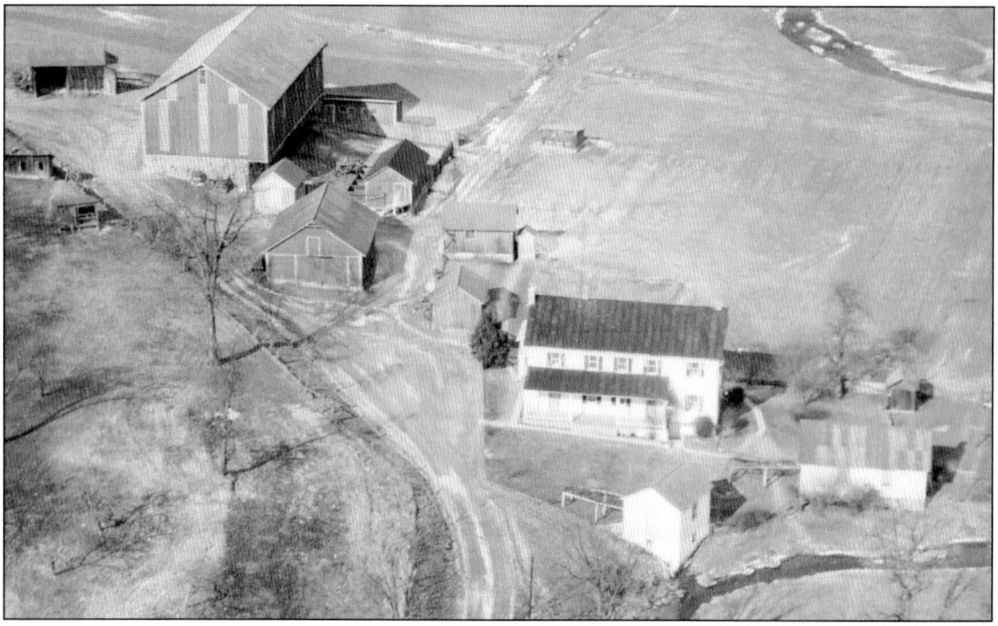

Above, a real-photo postcard provides an aerial view of the Stahl farm outside of the town of Mazeppa. Such farms, including Noll's and Snyder's, hosted the annual farm festivals organized by Bob and Dean McNettt until around 1960. Starting in the 1950s, annual ham-and-egg suppers were held the Saturday after Easter, first at the Buffalo Crossroads Grange Hall, then at Mazeppa's old schoolhouse. In the below photograph are, from left to right, Katheryn (Hause) Everitt, store owner Ralph Lytle, and his wife, Cloyce (Lindenmuth) Lytle. They are presiding over a ham-and-egg breakfast at the Sand Bridge, located on Route 192 between Forest Hill and Half Way Run. (Above, Janice and Donald Snyder; below, Judy Reed.)

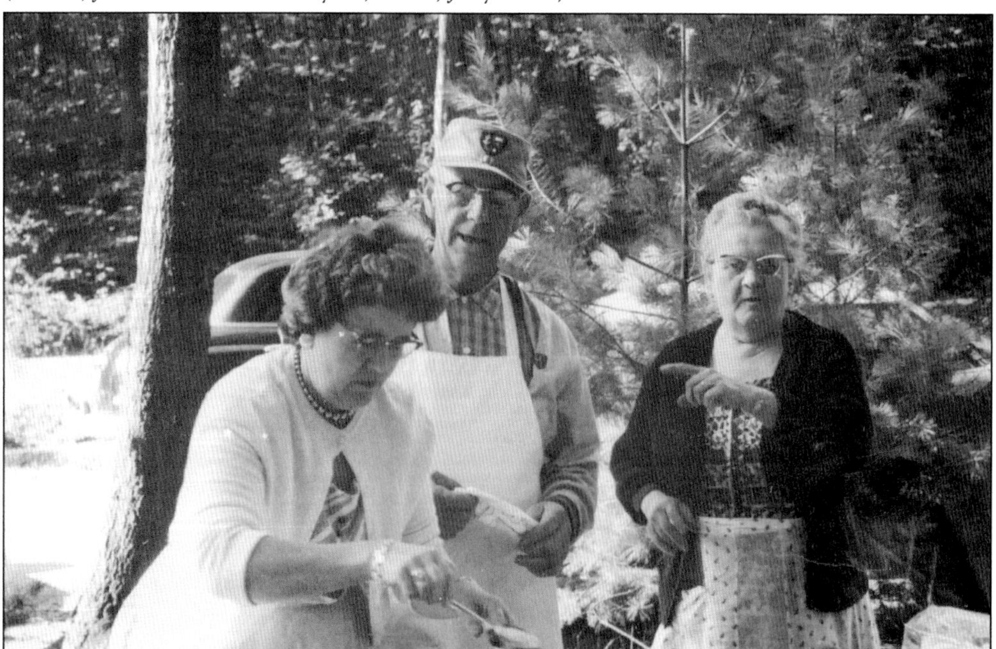

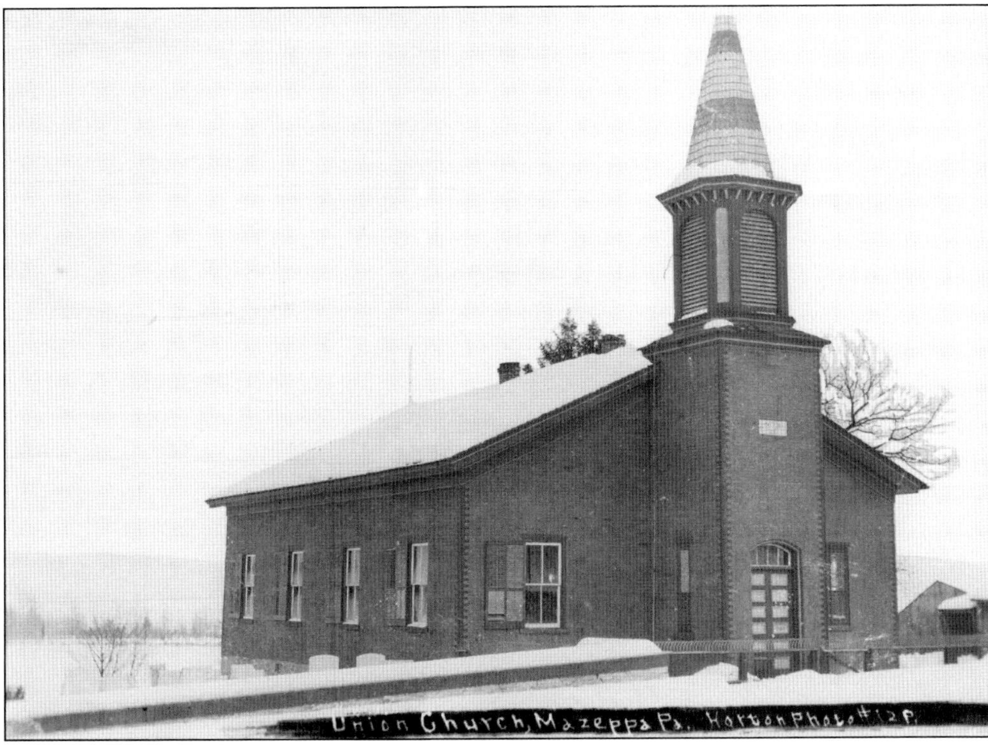

The Mazeppa Union Church, built in 1841, is the oldest church in Union County to hold continuous services in the same building. Across the street is the United Methodist Church, initially named Union Immanuel Evangelical and built in 1859 (right). Both buildings were damaged when a tornado hit Mazeppa on June 22, 1926. The Evangelical church's steeple was hurled into the street, and much of its roof was torn off. The building was substantially rebuilt. Along with the Sun Rise Church near Kelly Crossroads and churches in Forest Hill and Pleasant Grove, the Mazeppa Methodists are selling their church and plan to join in purchasing the former Buffalo Crossroads Elementary School on Johnson Mill Road. This consolidation and move represents significant change in the respective communities. (UCHS 92.9.89.39-.39.)

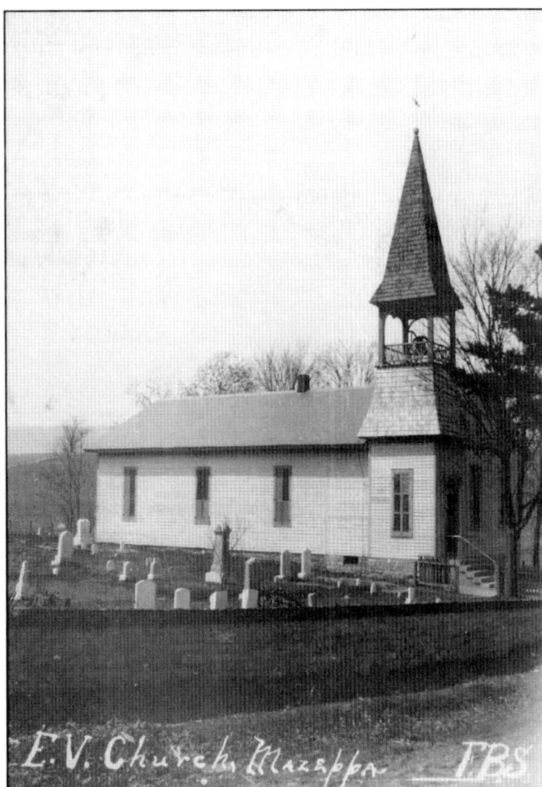

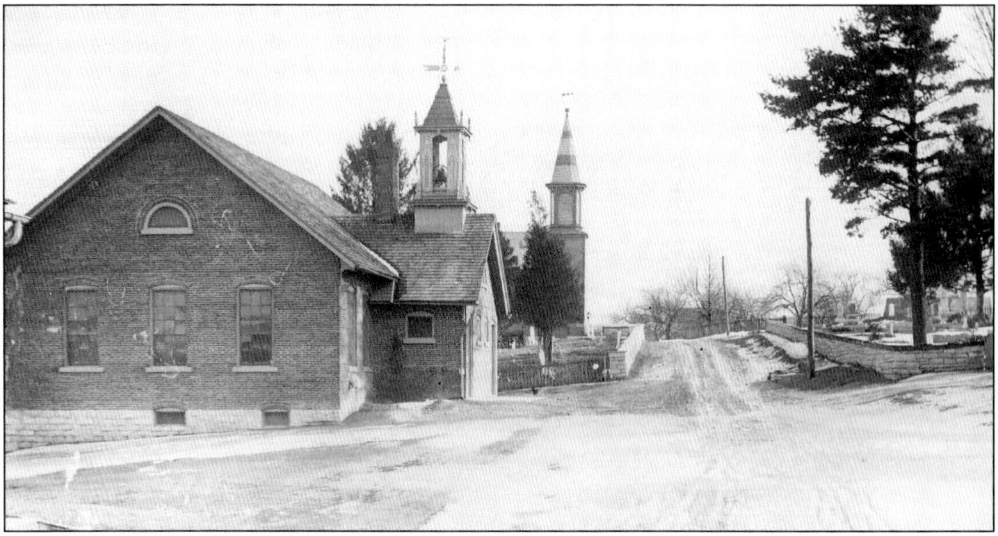

A real-photo postcard (above) shows the Mazeppa School (foreground) and the Union Church in the background, across from the cemetery. Below, a cabinet photograph shows the Union Church's Sunshine Class. From left to right are (first row) unidentified, Mable Witmer, Helen Wagner, Lauren Hoffman, unidentified, and Katherine Koch; (second row) Lloyd Stahl, Vera Wagner, Raymond Snyder, Ethel Wolfe, Sara Heiser, Ted Shuck, Myrtle Snyder, and Clark Erdley; (third row) Miriam Emery, Thelma Shuck, Miriam Miller, Helen Fisher, and Bob Heiser; (fourth row) Foster Emery, Merrill Kelly, two unidentified men, Myron Kleckner, and unidentified. (Cherry Reigle Will.)

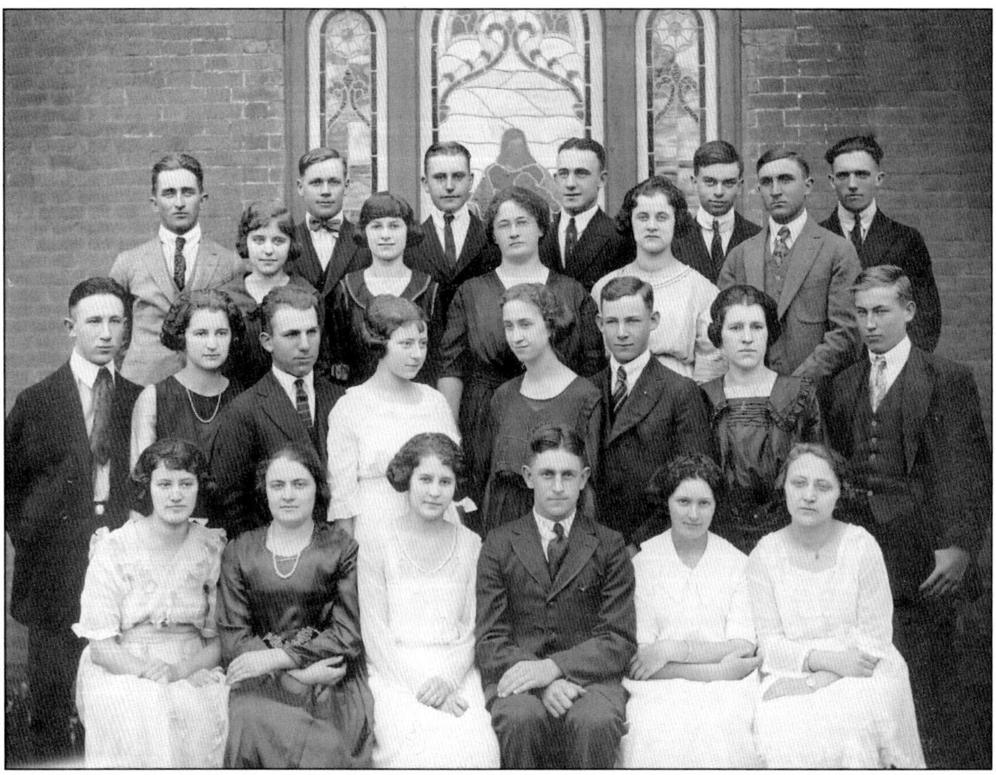

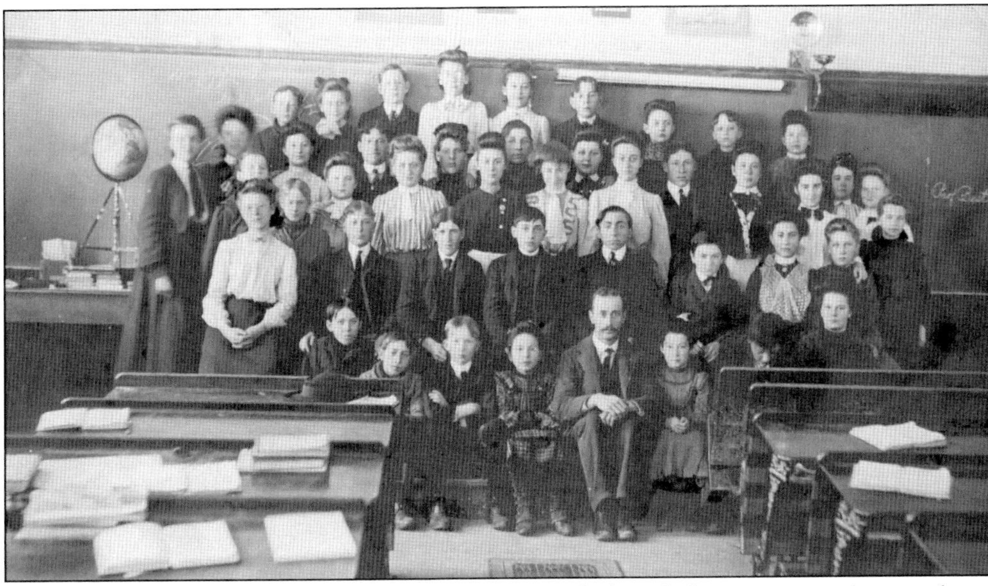

Milton E. Best's grammar school classes in 1905 pose with their desks, instructional material, and furnishings, including kerosene lights. The two-room brick schoolhouse, built in 1895, was located near the intersection of Johnson Mill Road and Colonel John Kelly Road. It was the third school built in that immediate area. Its south room was for the primary grades, and the north room served grammar grades. Sliding doors—when opened—produced an auditorium seating approximately 200 people. The Mazeppa School was sold in 1953 to the Union Church for $1,300. An earlier school was a log structure located just south of the Union Church. The second school, built of brick in 1838 and known as the Union School, was located just north of this school. (Above, Janice and Donald Snyder; below, UCHS 2004.22.9.)

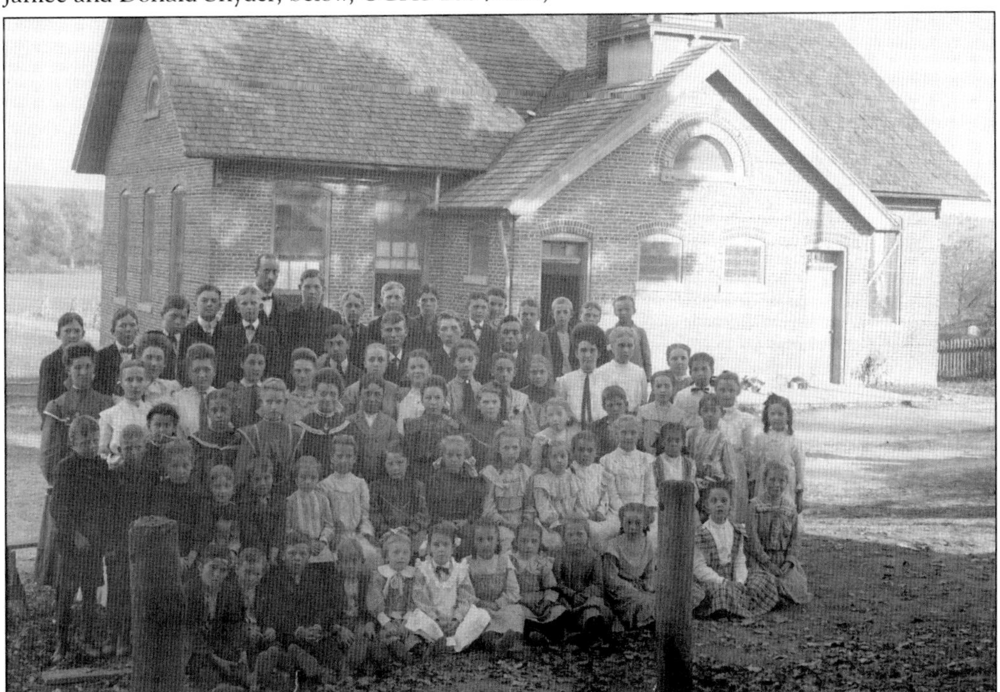

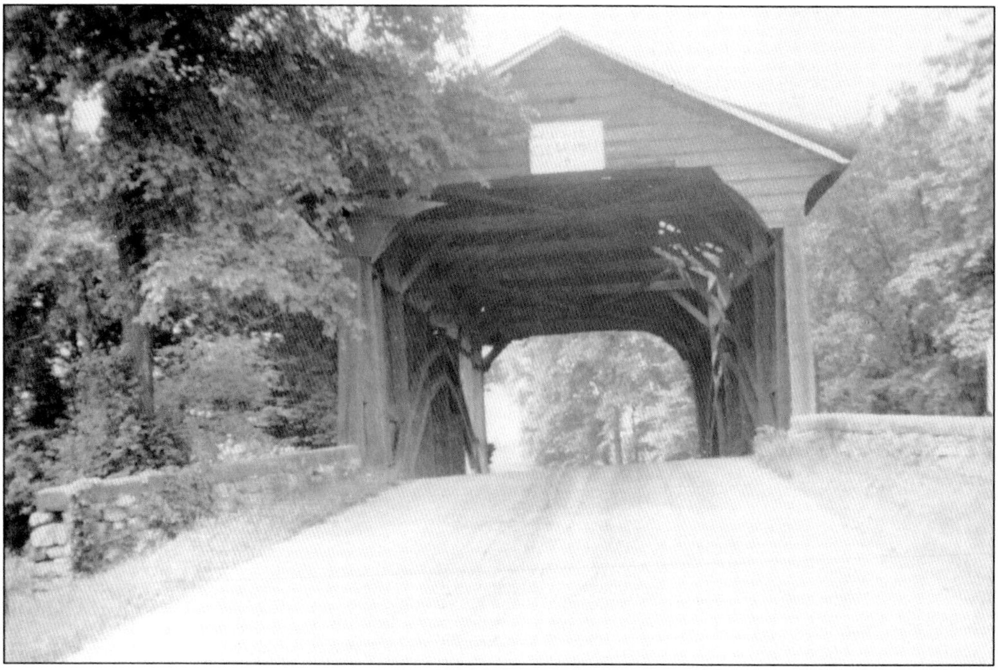

The covered bridge over Spruce Creek/Run is seen in the above photograph in 1949. It was located west of Wagner's and east of Mazeppa, bounding the east side of Buffalo Township and the west side of Kelly Township. The Spruce Run Reservoir, located below Nittany Mountain in White Deer Township and adjoining Buffalo Township, still provides a gravity-fed water supply to Lewisburg. The intake on Buffalo Creek supplies Mifflinburg, while White Deer Reservoir supplies Milton. The digging of waterline trenches in 1916 from the Spruce Run Reservoir traversed open land in parts of Buffalo Township. The below photograph, one in a series, is labeled "Going up Bowersox Hill November 22, 1916." (Above, Vicki Garinger; below, UCHS 88.19.32.)

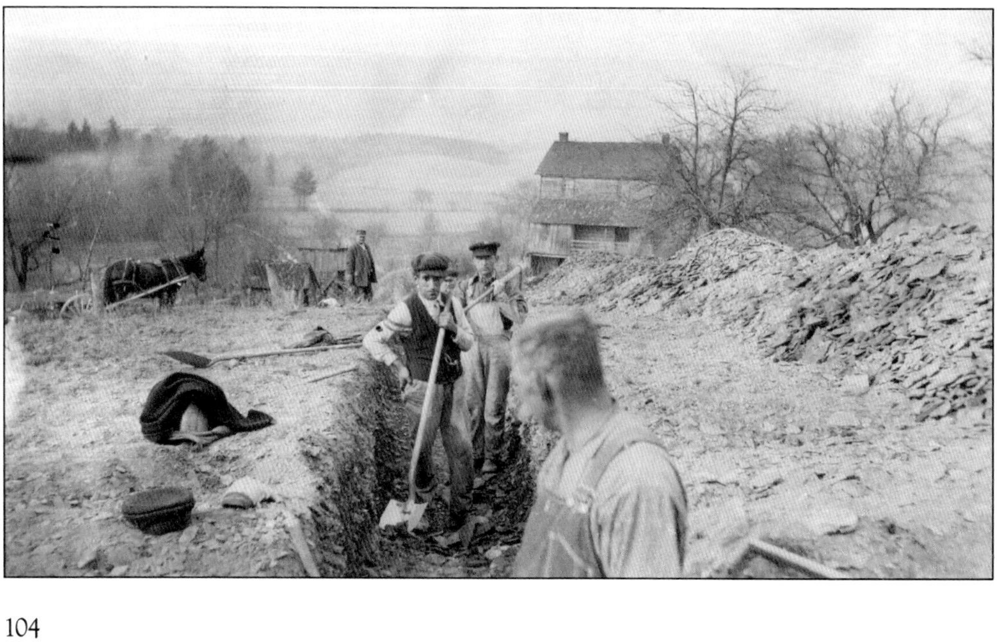

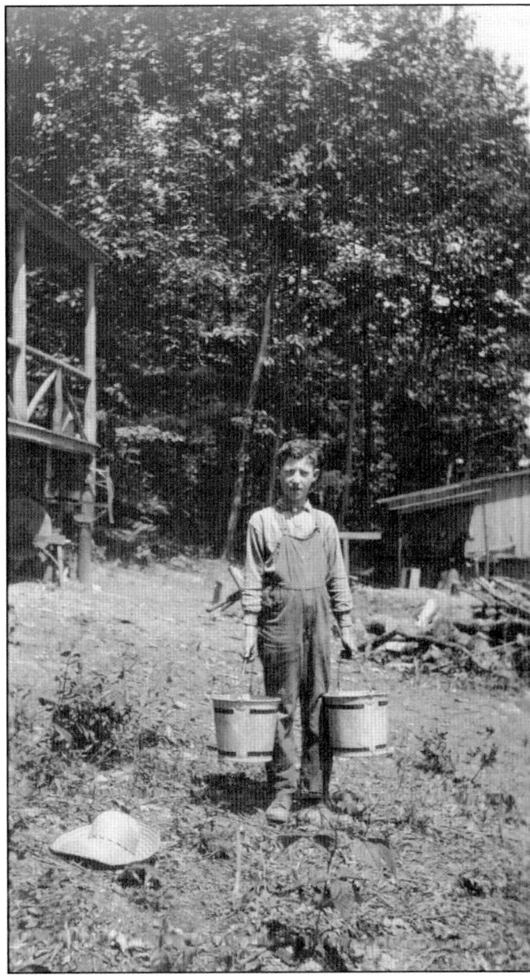

Photographs from the Spruce Run series show a "house boy" at the laborers' quarters (right) and water pipes readied for transport on July 6, 1916 (below). (Above, UCHS 88.19.10; below, UCHS 88.19.11.)

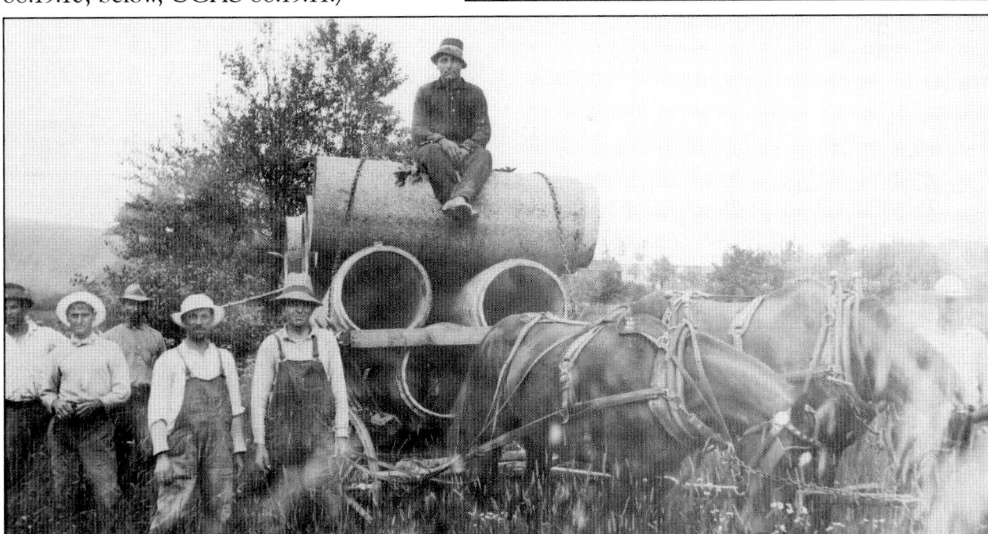

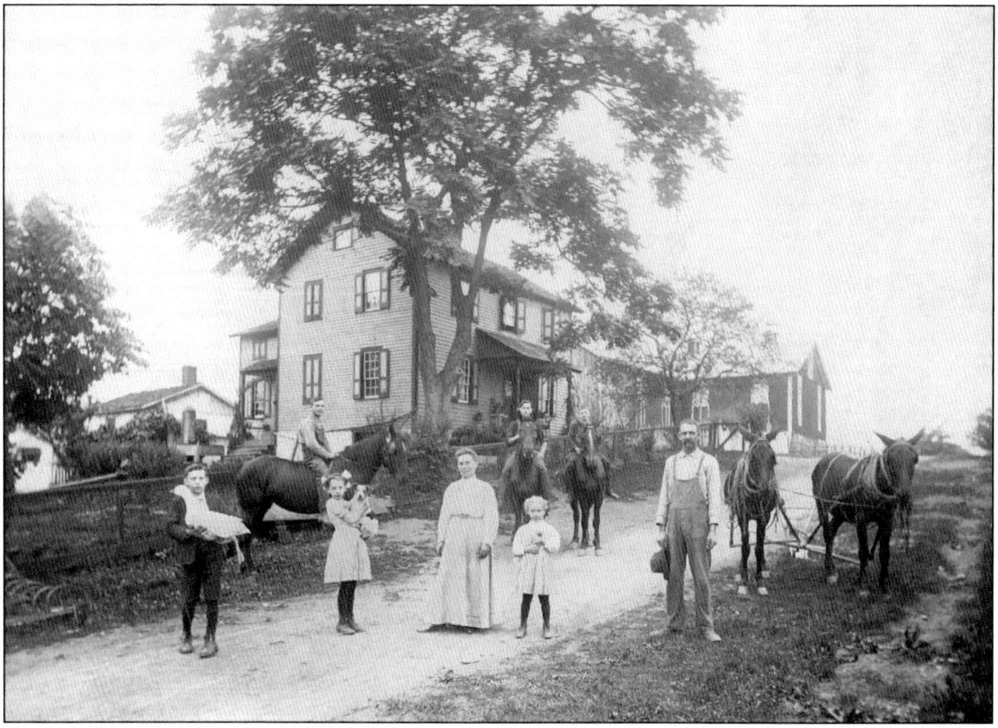

Above, the Miller family poses around 1910 for a group portrait on their farm, located between Mazeppa and Forest Hill. Pictured are Lake Miller, Bland E. Miller, Miriam Miller, Nora Wagner Miller, Loren Miller, Tranie Miller Witmer, Logan D. and Daniel E. Miller, along with their family pets and farm animals. The below photograph shows the Miller family working out in the field. (Evelyn and Donald Miller.)

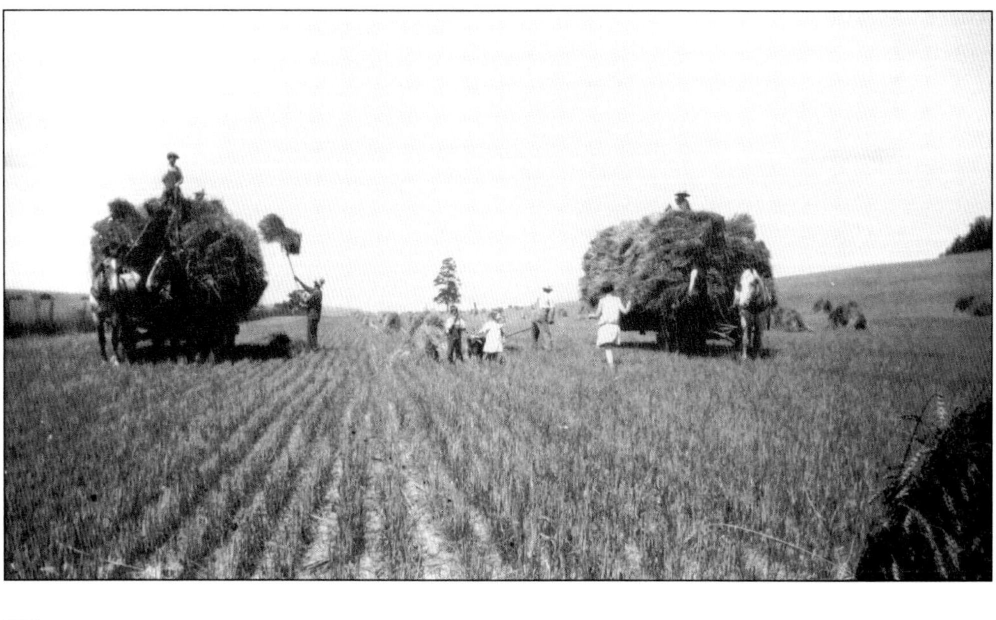

Four

Cowan, Red Bank, Rand, and Forest Hill

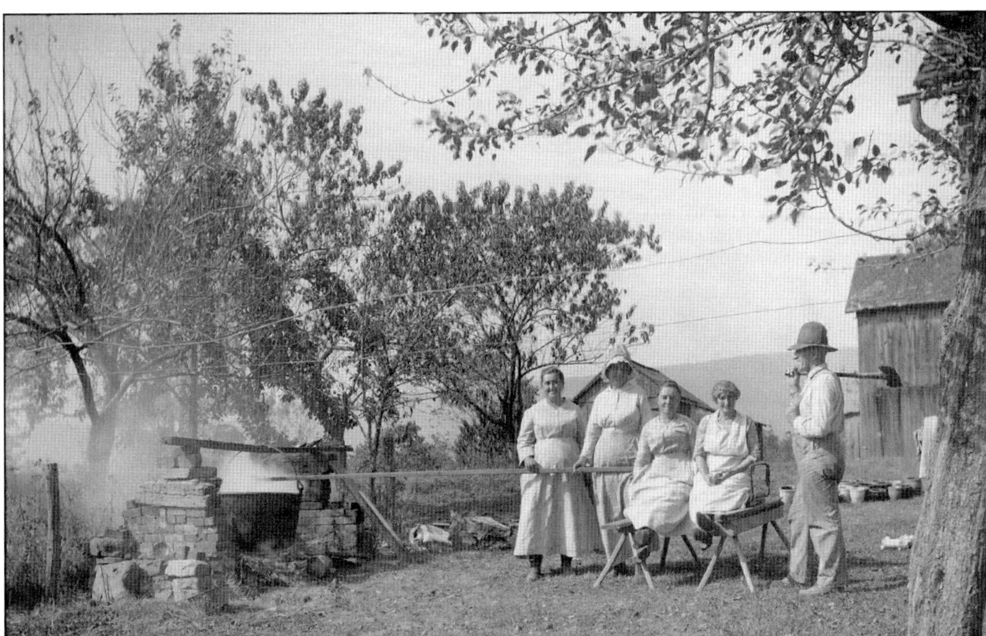

In the above photograph, apple butter is being boiled at the Jodon home near Forest Hill around 1922. The traditional fall event was held on area farms and is still done for the public in New Columbia, Union County, every mid-October. The apple butter was put up in crocks, with the hopes that enough had been collected to last a year. Shown here are, from left to right, Susan Jodon Heiser, Flora Jodon, Eva Jodon Cromley, Mrs. Mader, and Edgar Cromley. (Cherry Reigle Will.)

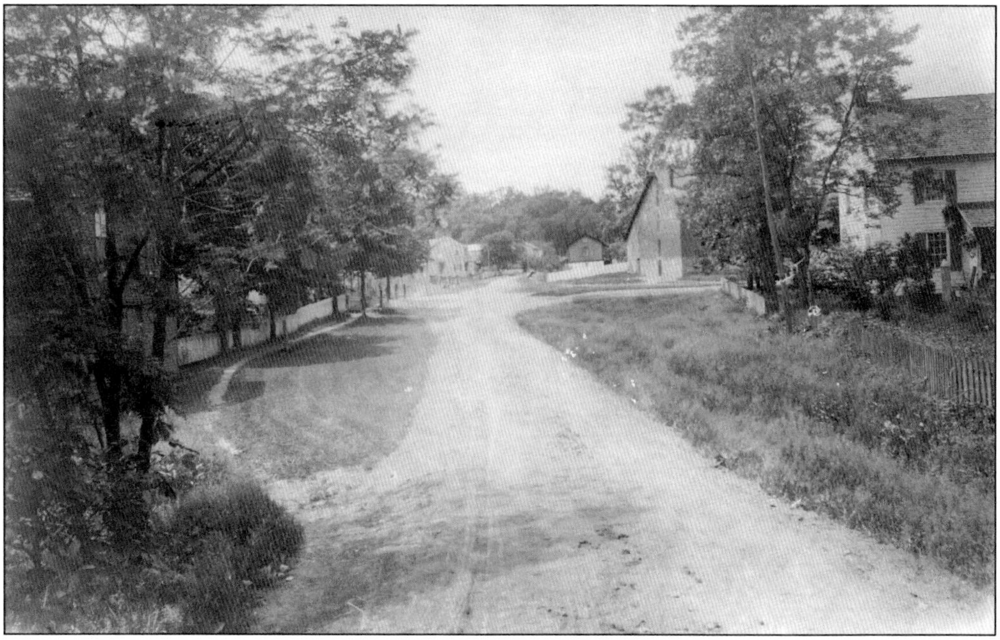

Above, a real-photo postcard focuses on Cowan's unpaved main street, with its gristmill at right in the distance. Another card, below, from 1909, offers a full view of the mill. In the late 1790s, Adam Wagoner built a gristmill on this site, where Rapid Run joins Buffalo Creek. Fires destroyed that first mill, as well as a second one built around 1830. In 1836, Daniel Guldin purchased the mill, which he then operated until 1850. A small town developed, first called Guldy's Mill, later called Farmersville, and finally named Cowan. A fire struck what had been renamed the J.D. Johnson Mill, and on February 19, 1942, the mill's interior was destroyed. (UCHS 97.1.20 and 97.1.21.)

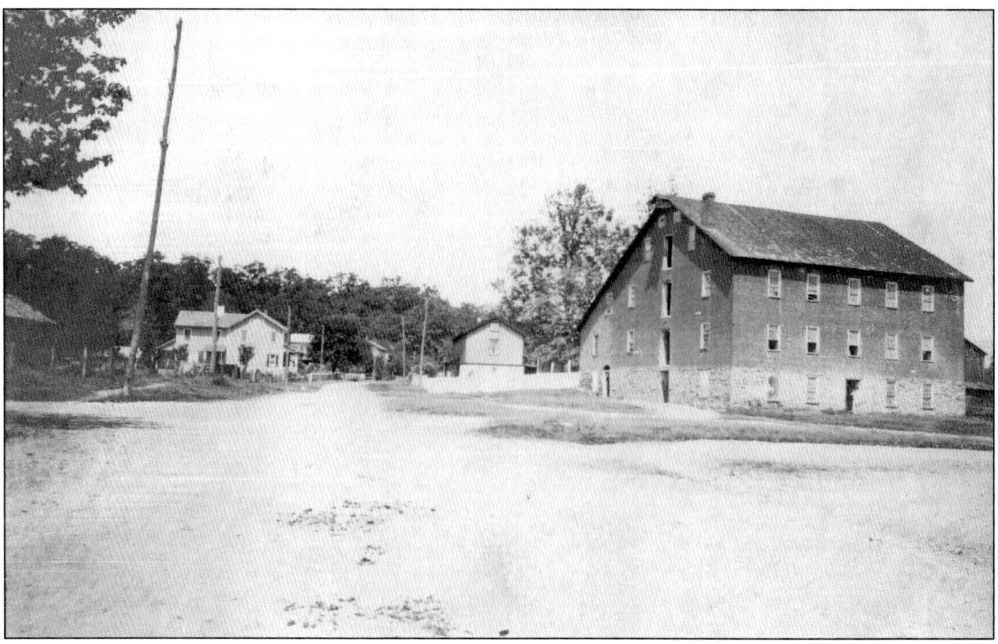

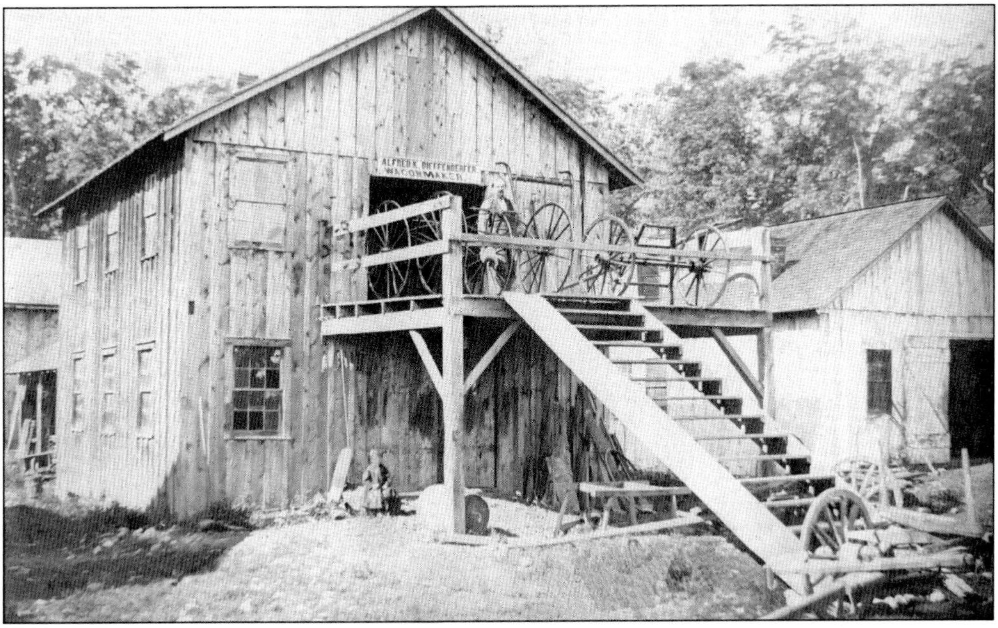

The Alfred K. Dieffenderfer coachworks in Cowan was typical of small buggy-making enterprises scattered throughout Union County between the 1860s and the 1910s. Buggy shops were located in Cowan, New Berlin, New Columbia, Laurelton, and Lewisburg. Mifflinburg was distinct in having nearly 80 coachworks, ranging from small to large enterprises. The child in this c. 1880 photograph at Dieffenderfer's coachworks is Alfred's son Frank (b. 1876). (Fred Blyler.)

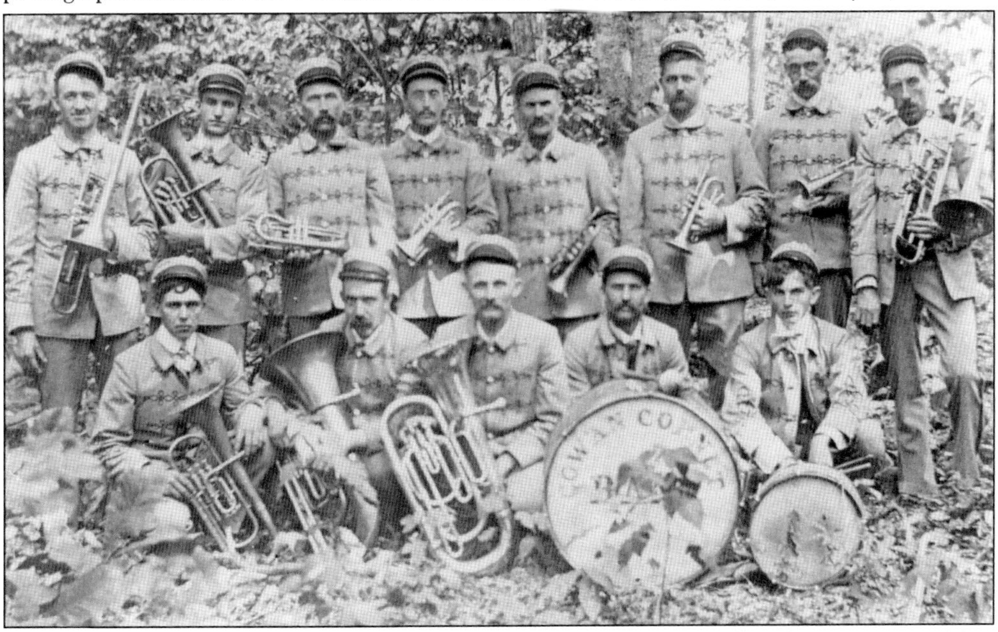

Many small towns in the county had bands and, in some cases, a small orchestra. Cowan, New Berlin, Swengle, Laurelton, and West Milton all had bands. The Cowan band members, shown here in 1905, are, from left to right, (first row) George Miller, John Young, George Bottinger, Thomas Musser, and Clive Rowe; (second row) George Dietrich, Lee Miller, James Dietrich, Milton Best, Harvey Rowe, William Yoder, Henry Kimple, and David Boyer. (UCHS, 89.5.22.1.)

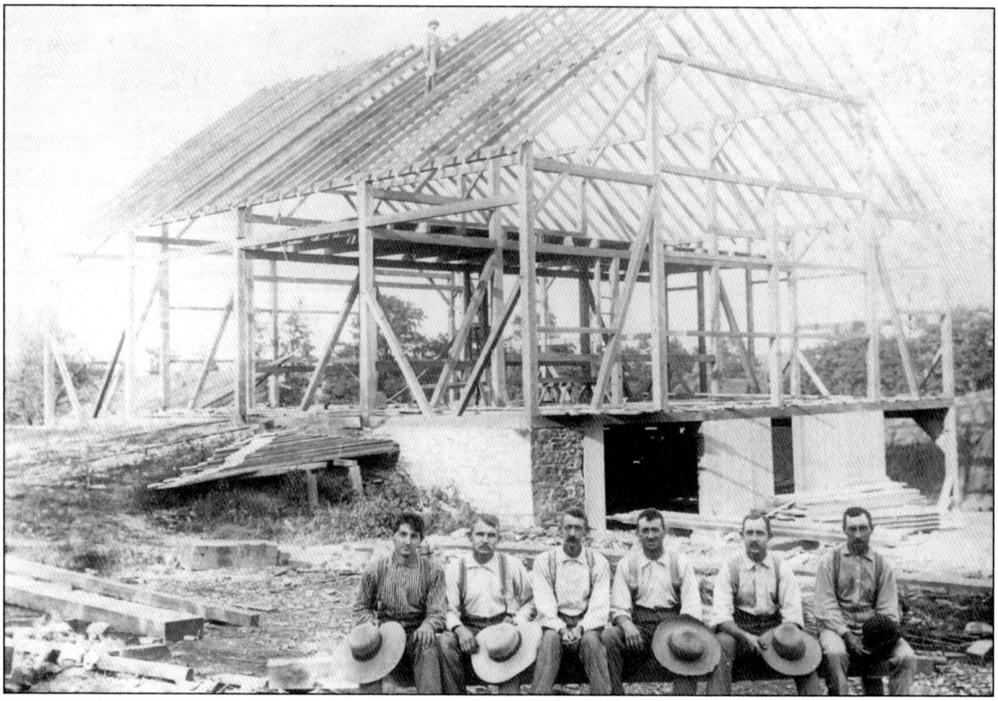

Cowan's barn-raising crew, shown in the above photograph, are, from left to right, David J. Boyer, George Bottinger, William Reber, George Dietrich, R. Willard, and William Klingman. They were photographed at two of their Union County barn-raising projects, sometime between 1900 and 1915. The framing is exposed in the above photograph, and the sheathing is featured in a photograph of the later stage of construction (below). Barn raising is a tradition still maintained by some Amish and Mennonite groups in the area. In the fall of 1969, a barn raising at the Glen and Ann Miller farm outside Dice, headed by Groffdale Conference Mennonite Daniel Zimmerman, was conducted to replace a barn destroyed by fire that August. Zimmerman raised the barn with the help of 193 Mennonites who arrived by bus from as far away as Lancaster County. (UCHS 89.5.9.11 and .12.)

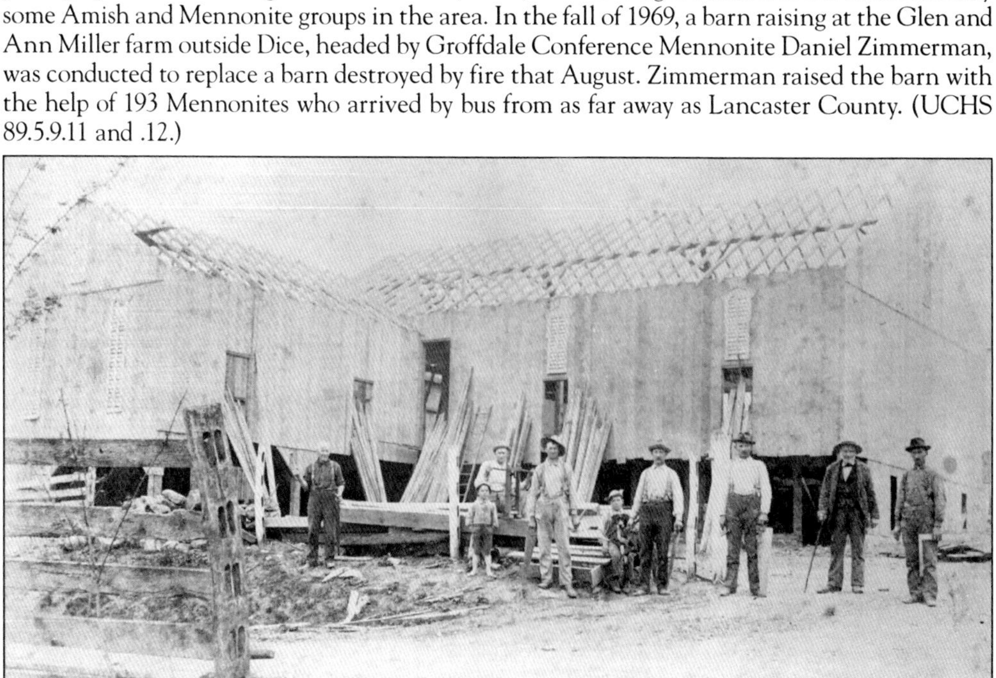

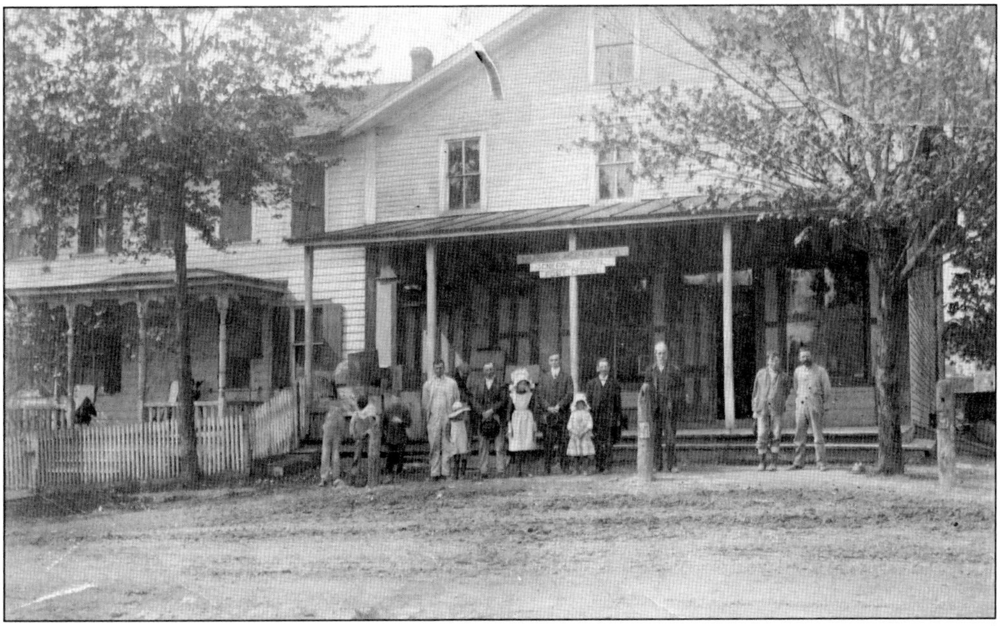

The combined general store and post office in Cowan was first owned in 1848 by Samuel Shoemaker. The establishment was later called Messina, Heiser & Co., as seen in the store's sign in this real-photo postcard from around 1910. (Ron Nornhold.)

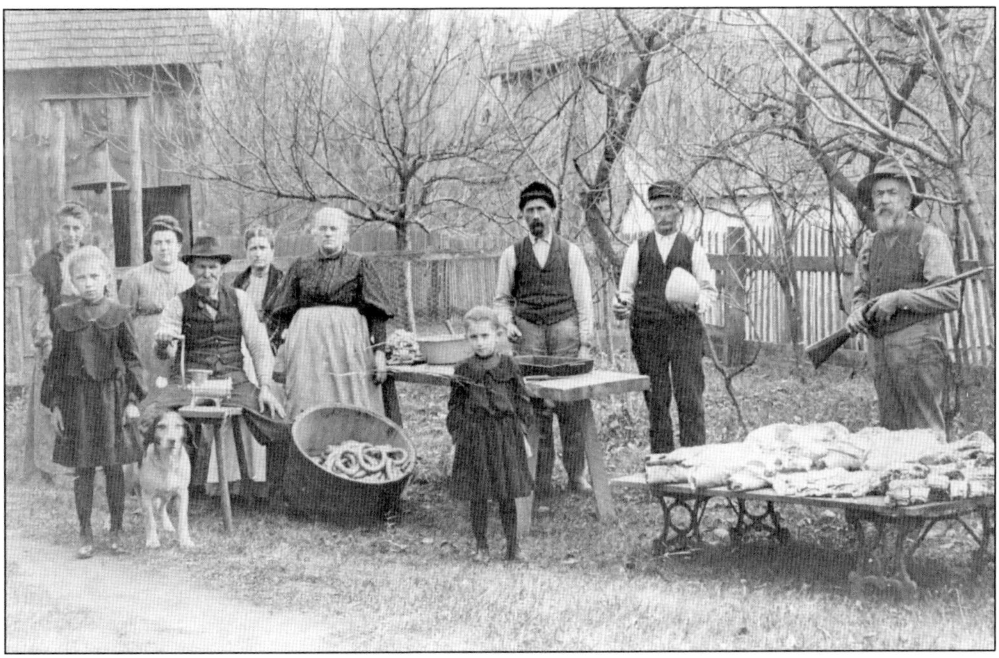

A butchering at a farm on Cannon Road near Cowan was recorded by a photographer staying at the Great Western Hotel in Vicksburg in 1902. Another butchering, at the Zimmerman home near Cowan, is seen here. Posing below are, from left to right, (first row) Grace Zimmerman Lohr, Fido (dog), Al Dieffenderfer, and Alma Zimmerman; (second row) Susan Zimmerman, Mrs. George Zimmerman, Mrs. Hemley, Mrs. Al Zimmerman, John Deitrich (butcher), Reuben Zimmerman, and John Hemley. (UCHS 89.5.20.13.)

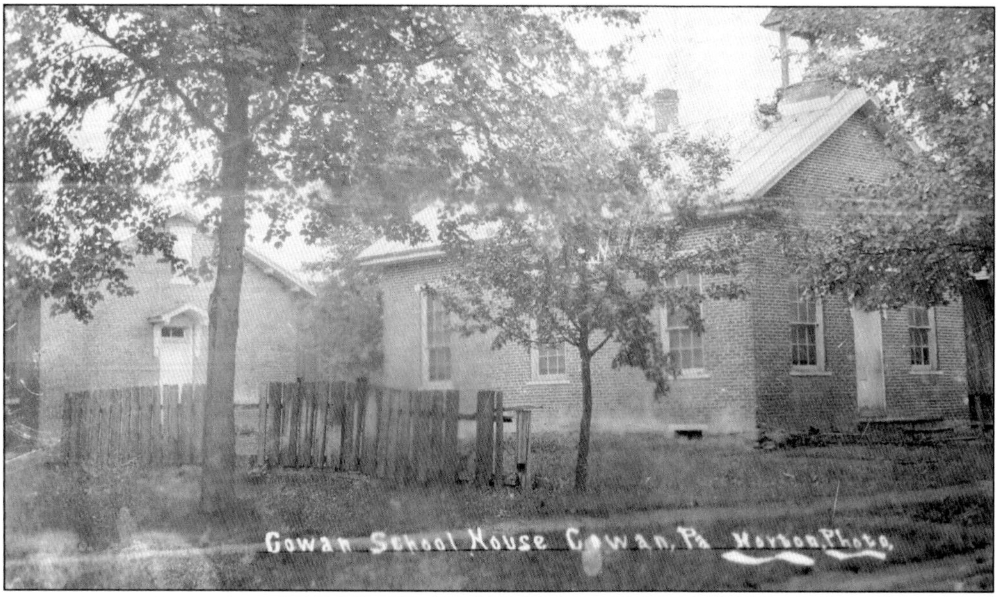

Cowan's second school was built of brick after the adoption of the Free Public School Law in 1837. It was located near the town's covered bridge over Buffalo Creek and just east of the community's first school, made of logs. Cowan's later primary and grammar schools were located on Church Road, just south of town, pictured above around 1907. In 1884, with more than 80 pupils enrolled, an assistant teacher was hired. Three years later, in 1887, the Grammar School was built in front of the Primary School, which had been erected in 1870. In the below photograph, students pose in 1909. By 1918, however, the Grammar School closed due to decreasing school population, and in 1953, the entire school property was sold to Trinity Lutheran Church. (UCHS 92.9.89.42-43.)

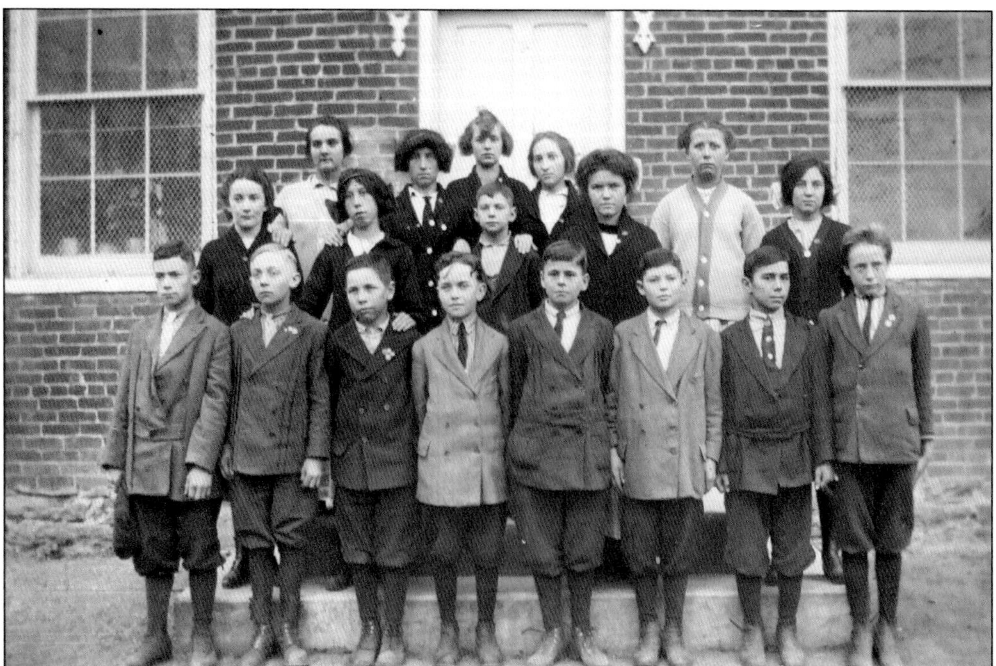

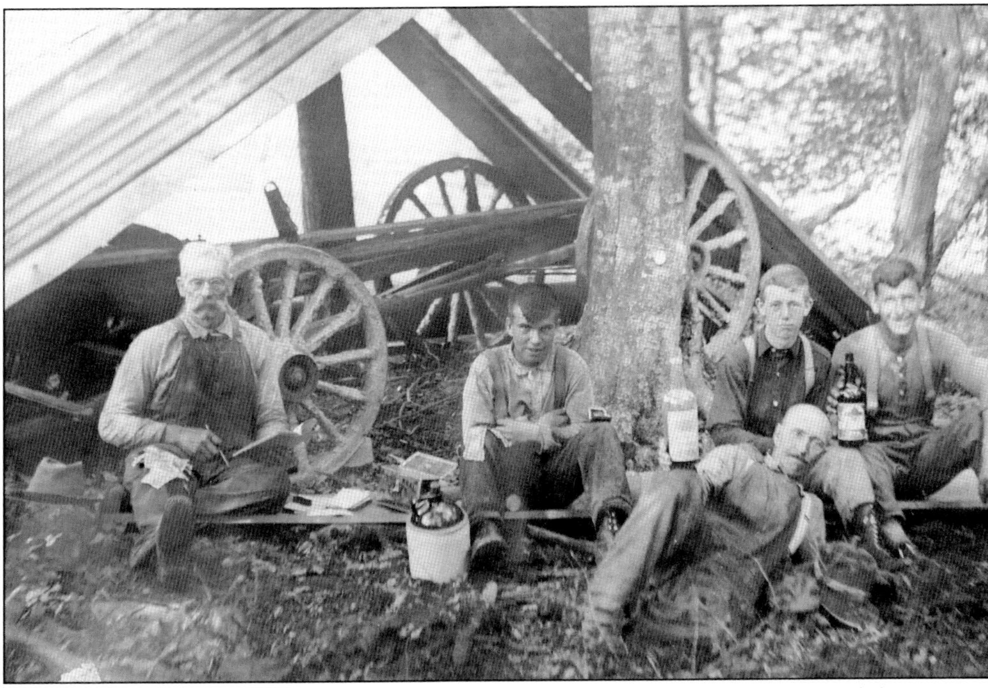

Joel Reish, holding an account book and pencil, and Cling Reish (second from right) are seated with others at the Reish Distillery on Rapid Run near Cowan. Joel was the grandson of the distillery's founder, Daniel Reish, a Berks County native. Joel and his brother James ran this distillery from 1873 to 1920, when Prohibition began. This portrait, issued after 1907, includes a pocket watch (hanging on a tree), a purse, and a dollar bill. Earlier Reish distillery locations were below northeast of the Forest Hill Cemetery on Rapid Run (post-1814 to 1865) and also at White Deer Mills along White Deer Creek (1866–1880). In 1878, Joel's father, Bennival, purchased Forest House, an inn and tavern at the foot of the Fourteen Mile Narrows. (Above, Billy Mattern; below, UCHS 2011.26.20.)

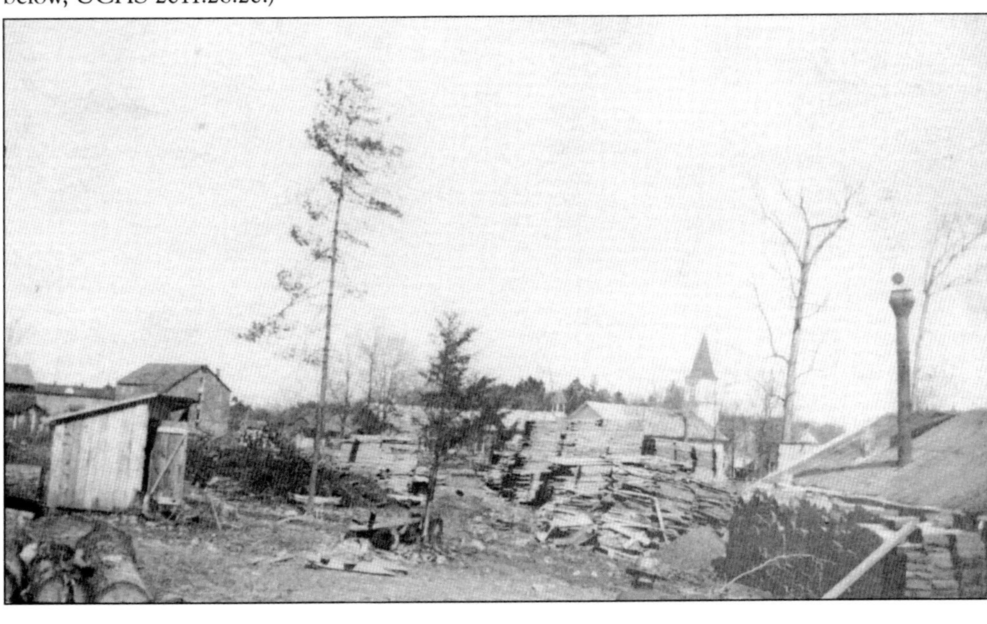

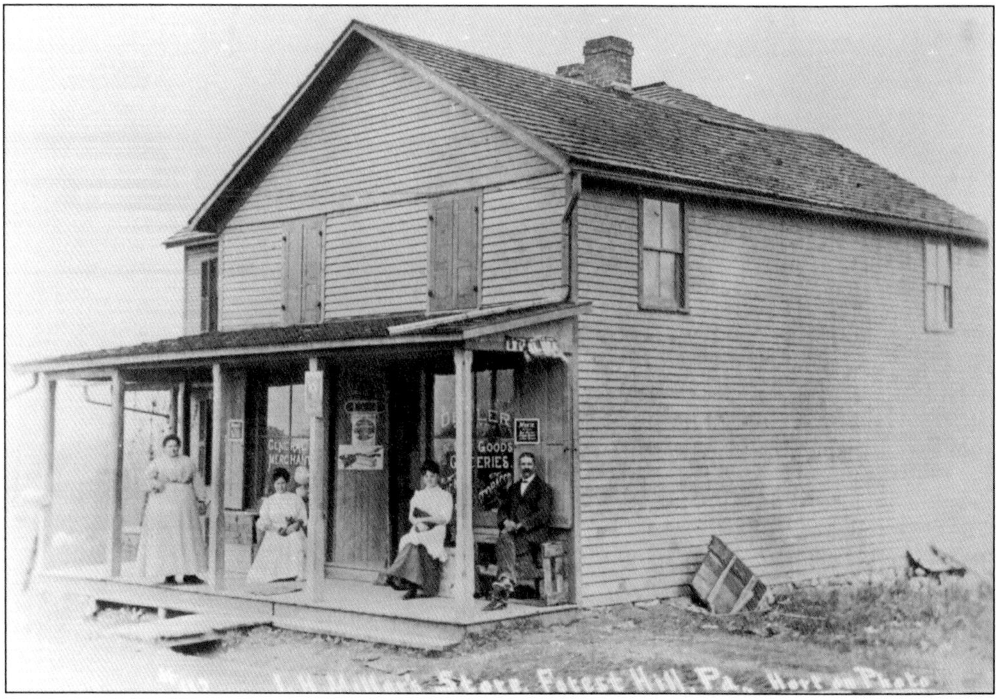

Dominated by the cooler woods of Jones, Notch, Buffalo, and Sand Mountains, communities like Red Bank, Rand, and Pleasant Grove existed in West Buffalo Township. Only Forest Hill, though, positioned at the east end of the Fourteen Mile Narrows, had a post office. Storekeeper Ammon Lutz became its first postmaster in 1850. He ran into financial difficulties and his store and saddlery were sold at a sheriff's sale in 1860 to John M. Benfer, who had sued Lutz. Lewis and Mary Yoder ran the store (above) around 1905–1922. The store was then owned by Jeremiah Cromley and, later, his son George. Jeremiah had been a clerk in the store under an earlier owner, George W. Himmelreich. A view of the modernized general store and an adjacent Atlantic gas station (below) was issued in a printed photo postcard. (UCHS 89.5.15.5 and 95.1.8.)

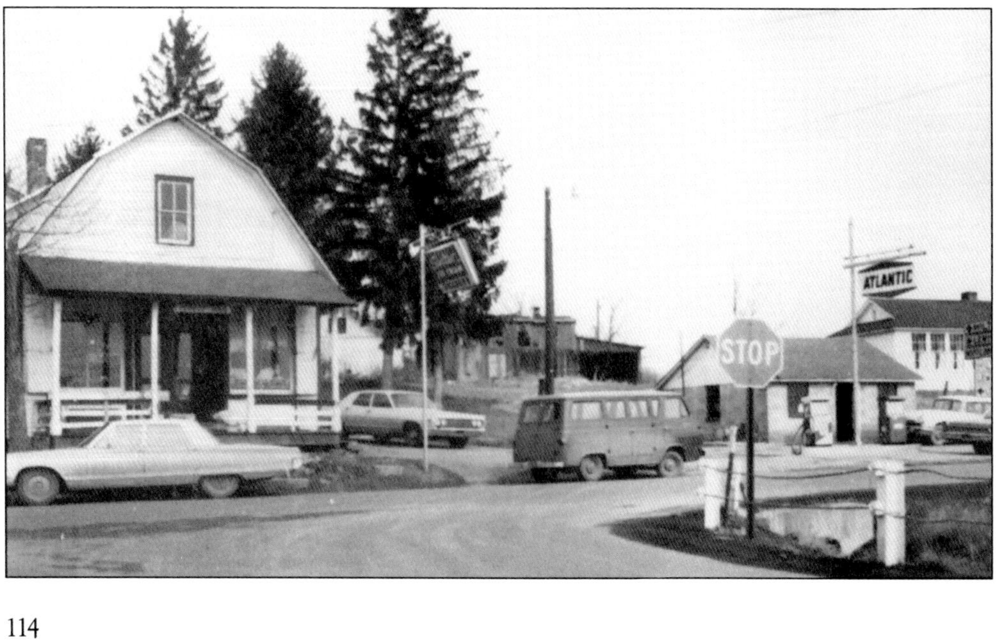

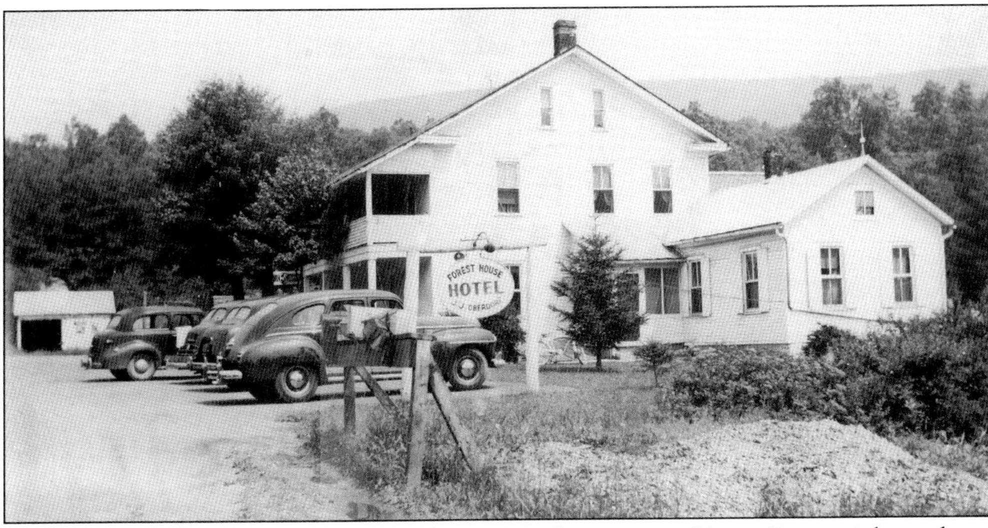

Forest House, one of the oldest continuously operating businesses in Union County, is located west of Forest Hill. It is featured in the late-1930s real-photo postcard above, complete with automobiles. It is also seen in an earlier cabinet photograph (below) with its inn-keeping family. Another, even later printed black-and-white photo card of Forest House includes a gas station beside it. Near Forest House, on the road going west to Brush Valley, formerly Route 95 and now Route 192, a marker stands, erected in 1922 by the Pennsylvania Historical and Museum Commission, the Union County Historical Society, and local Daughters of the American Revolution. It reminds all who stop of the settlers killed by Delaware Indians on May 16, 1780: John Foster Jr., George Etzweiler, James Chambers, and Samuel McLoughlin. The settlers were attacked and killed near French Jacob's gristmill. (UCHS 2011.2.12 and 2011.26.20.)

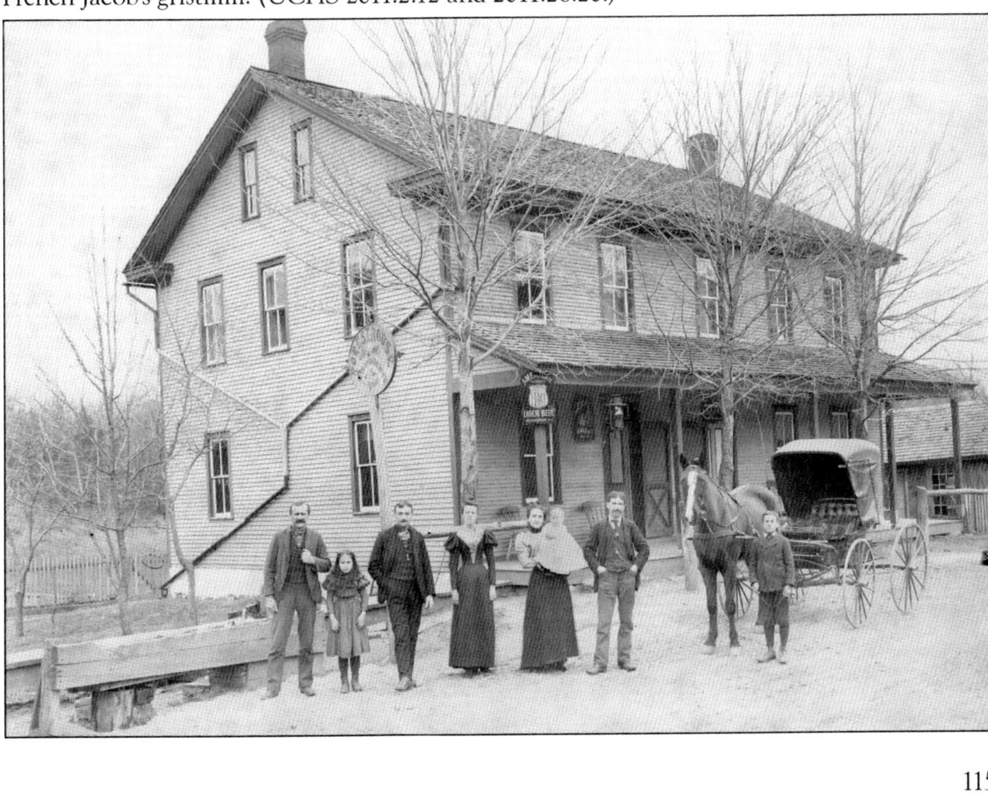

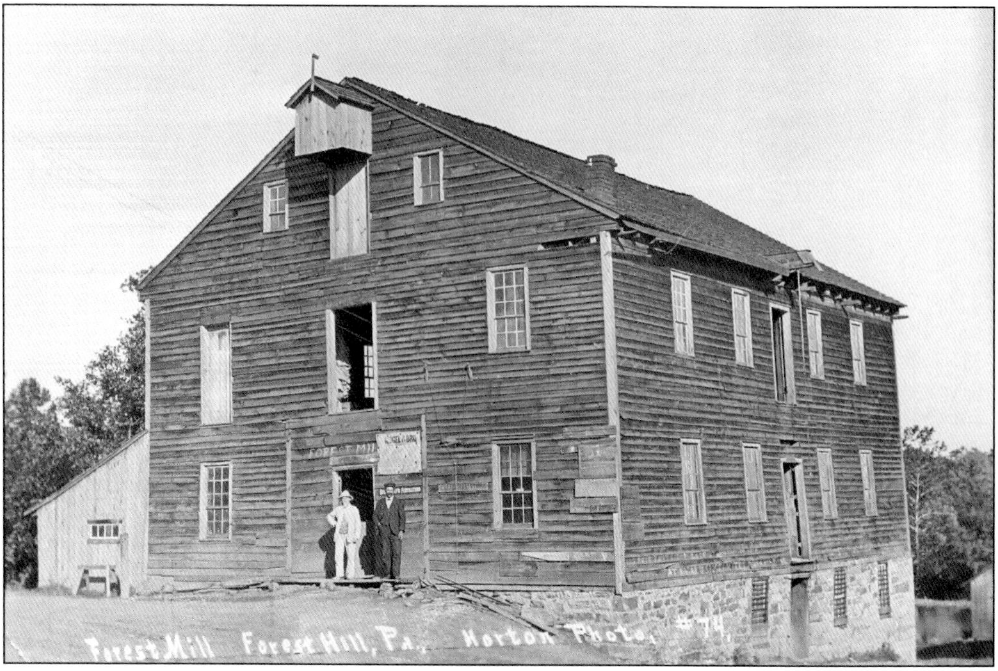

A Horton real-photo postcard (above) from between 1907 and 1911 illustrates the Forest Mill, which was the third mill built on the site of "French Jacob" Groshong's Mill, which was erected in 1792. The second mill at the site, built by Daniel Reish in 1820 and operated by his family for more than 60 years, processed rye for making flour as well as whiskey, for which they were known. The third mill was built by Charles Wolfe in 1886–1887. He added the new technology of roller mills, replacing the traditional millstones. In a forthcoming Union County Historical Society *Heritage* book, this mill, along with more than 40 in the county, will be documented along with their milling owners. The early real-photo postcard below shows Forest Hill's main street looking toward the northwest. (Above, UCHS 2011.2.24; below, Ron Nornhold.)

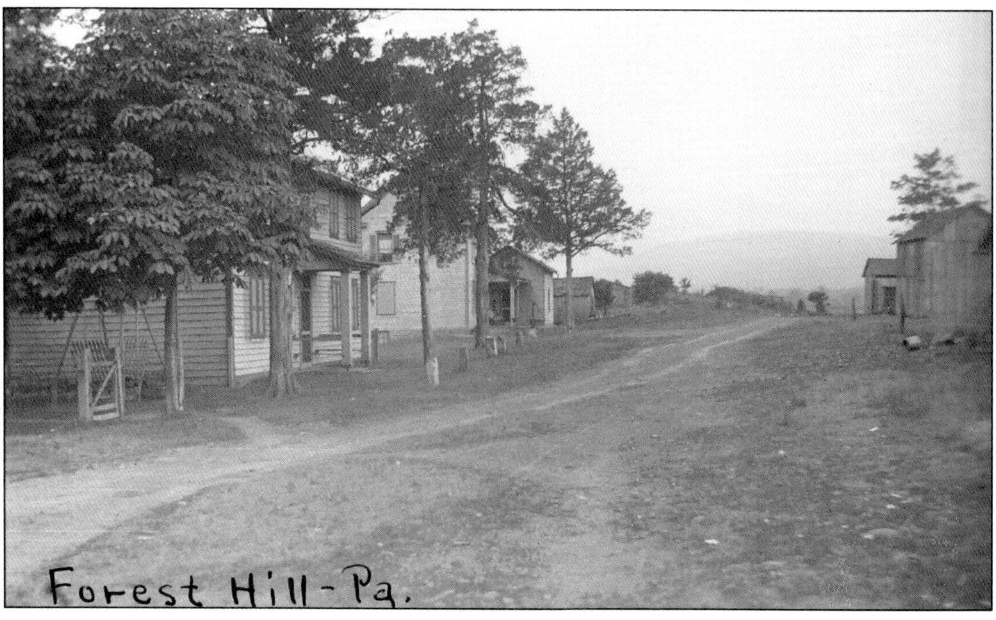

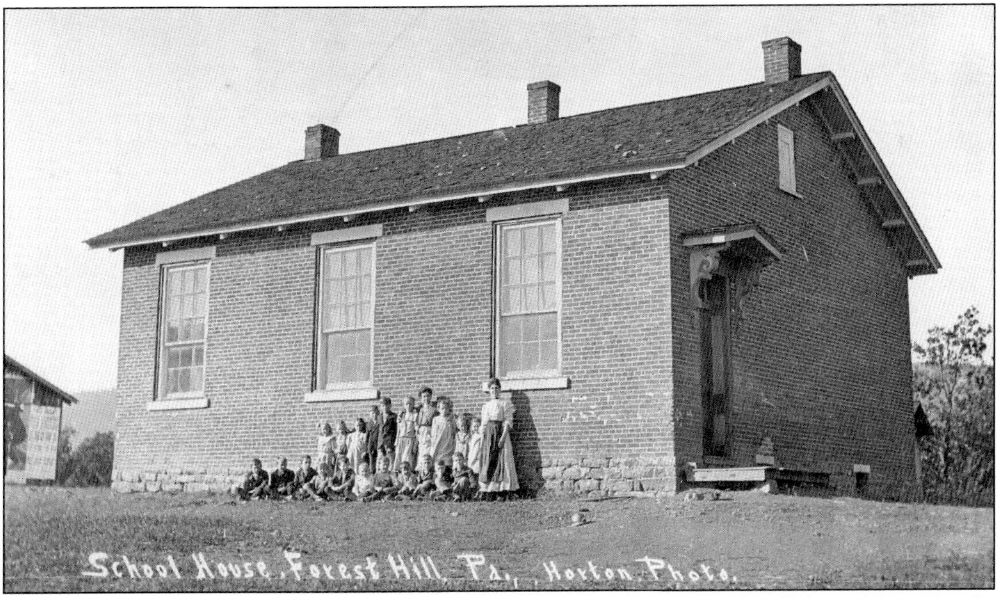

The first Forest Hill School, built prior to 1837 at the northeast corner of Buffalo and Gast Roads, was of log construction with wooden plank seats. It was replaced by a schoolhouse lined with boards on the inside and weather-boarded on the outside. A brick schoolhouse, built in 1886, is seen above in the real-photo postcard by Stephen Horton from between 1907 and 1911. More than 100 students were enrolled. The off-center front door placement on the gable end, as with another school in Rand, is quite unusual. The interior of the Forest Hill School (below) was issued as a cabinet photograph in 1902. In the 1920s, a tornado partially destroyed the brick school, which was then razed and replaced with a wood building. In 1953, the West Buffalo School District sold it to the neighboring church. (UCHS 86.1.2 and 82.2.28.)

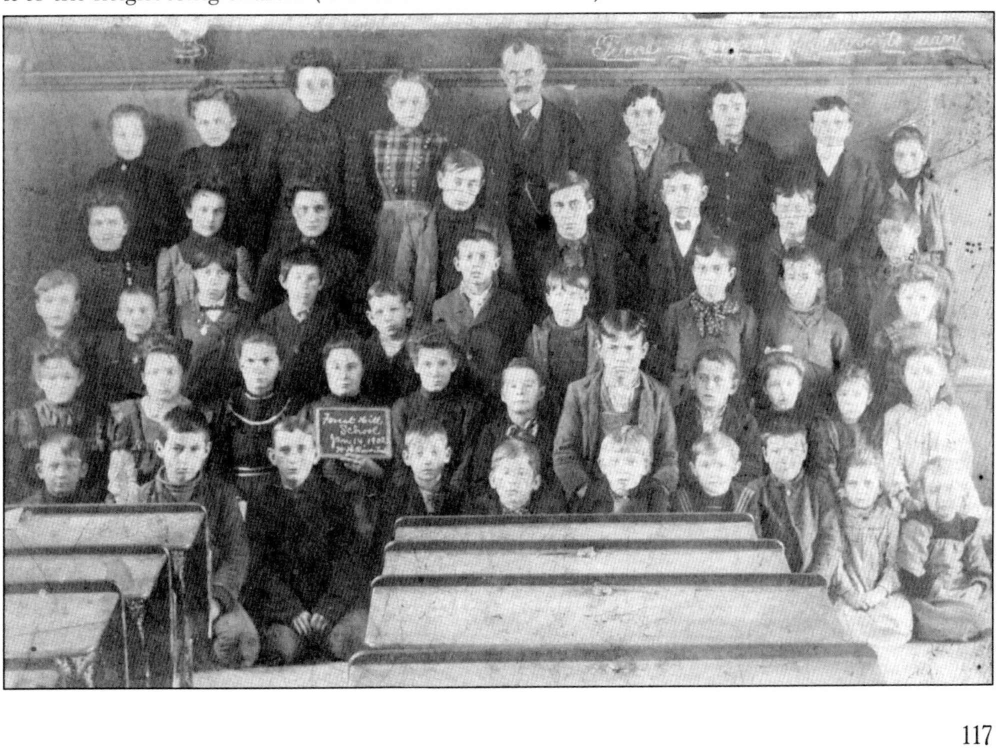

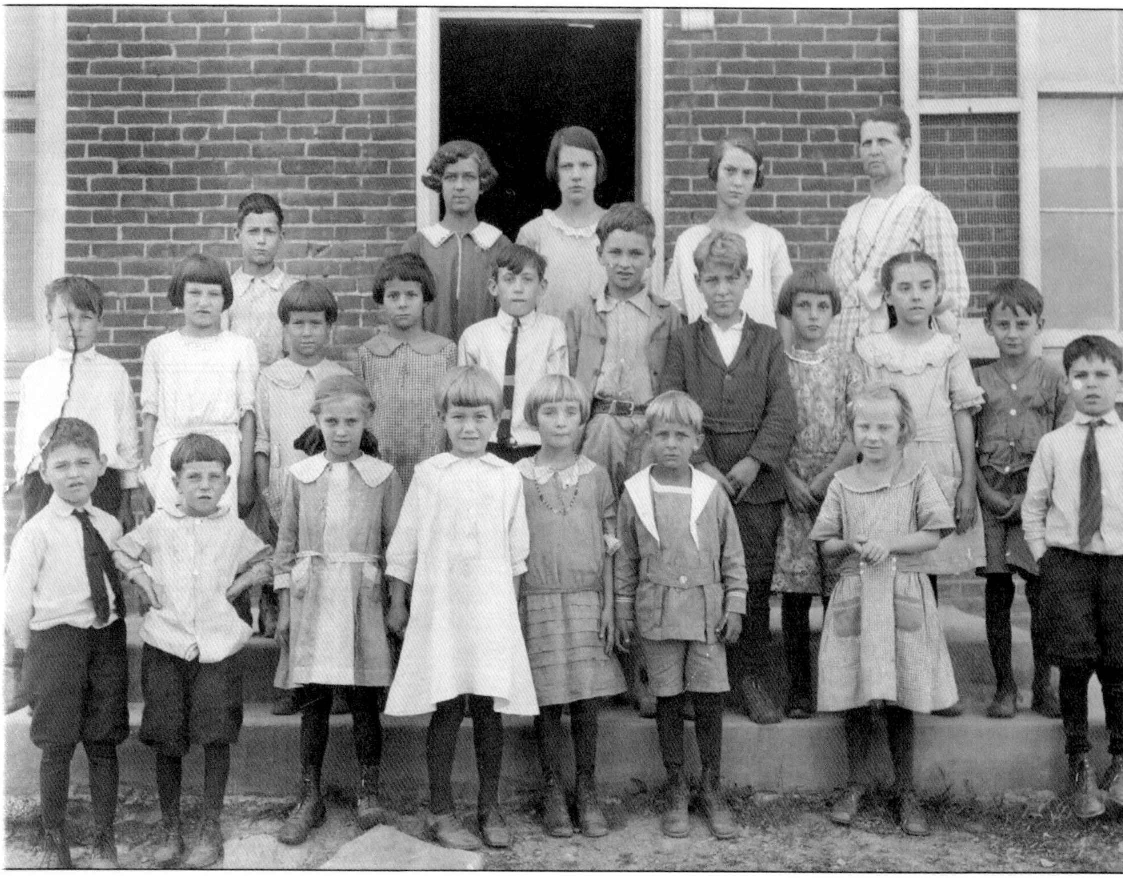

Children of the Kline, Prutzman, Herman, Wolfe, Roadermal, Schusey, Spotts, and Oberlin families are shown around 1917 at the Red Bank School. Initially, a wooden plank school was built on private land at the northwest corner of Forest Hill and Red Bank Roads. It was replaced in 1886 by a brick school (shown here) on land of the Edelmans a little farther east. The former wood school was moved beside the new school and served as its coal shed that was razed in the 1990s. The Red Bank School property had been sold by the school district to West Buffalo Township in 1953 for $1. Until a new township building was constructed on Johnstown Road in 1988, the old brick school was used to hold township meetings. The building and its school desks have been preserved by the township and are currently used by the Union County Historical Society and the Mifflinburg and Lewisburg School Districts for one-room school days for all fourth graders. (UCHS 2000.19.2.)

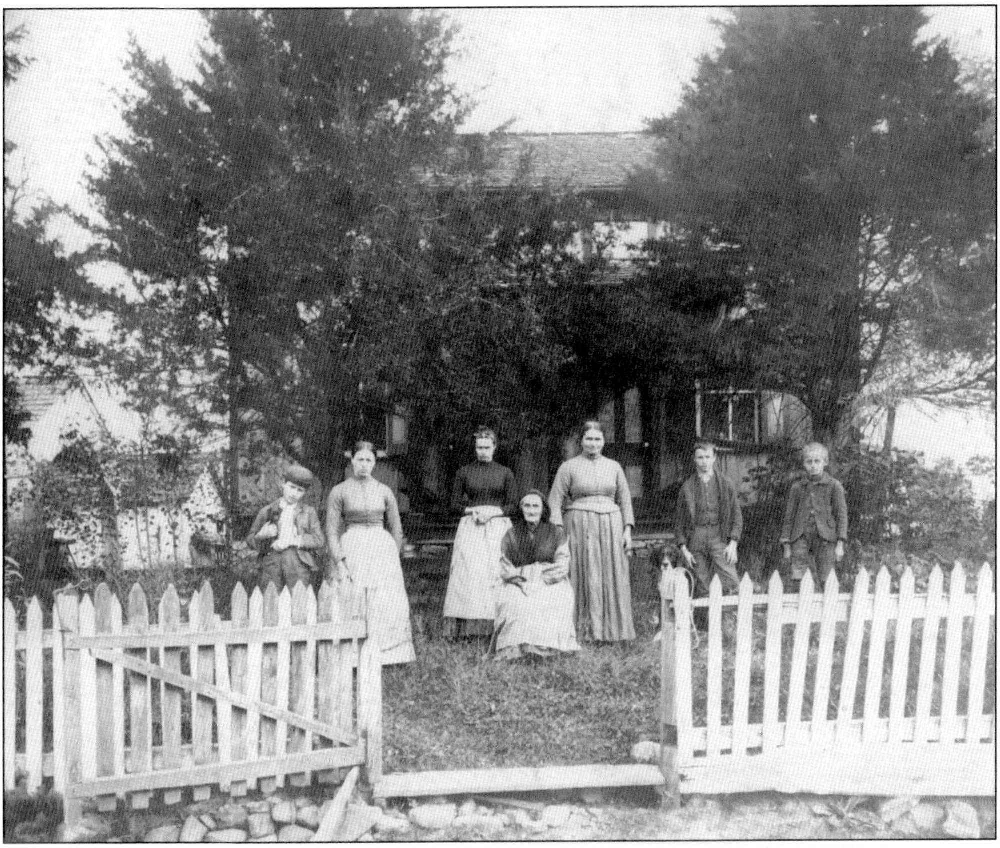

The Page homestead in Red Bank was photographed twice over a span of time. The large group cabinet photograph above is labeled "Grandnanny Jane Page seated with Robert R. and Margaret Page." The Page farm is seen around 1912 in the below photograph. Shown here are, from left to right, Robert R. Page, William K. Page, hired man John Snyder, Margaret L. Page, and Bessie Page. (Robert Page.)

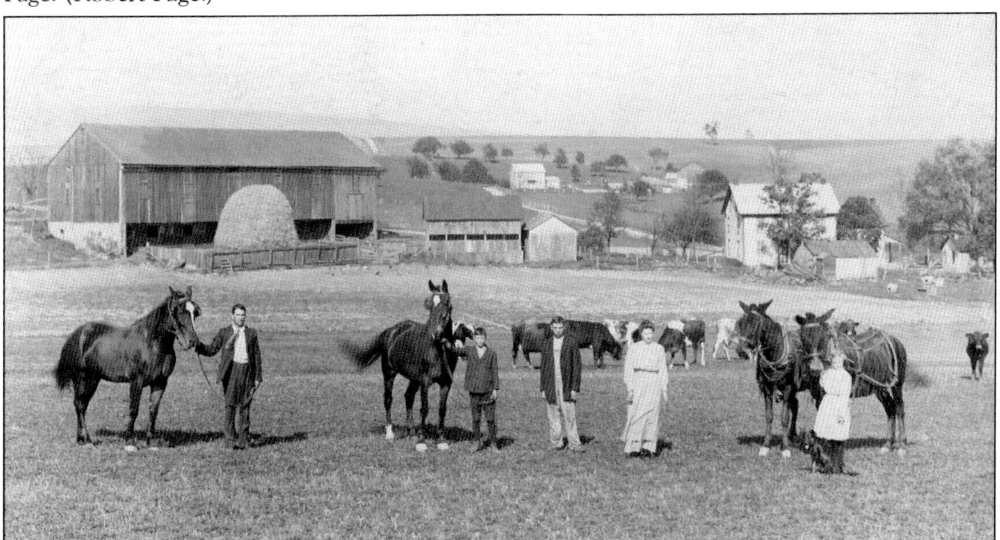

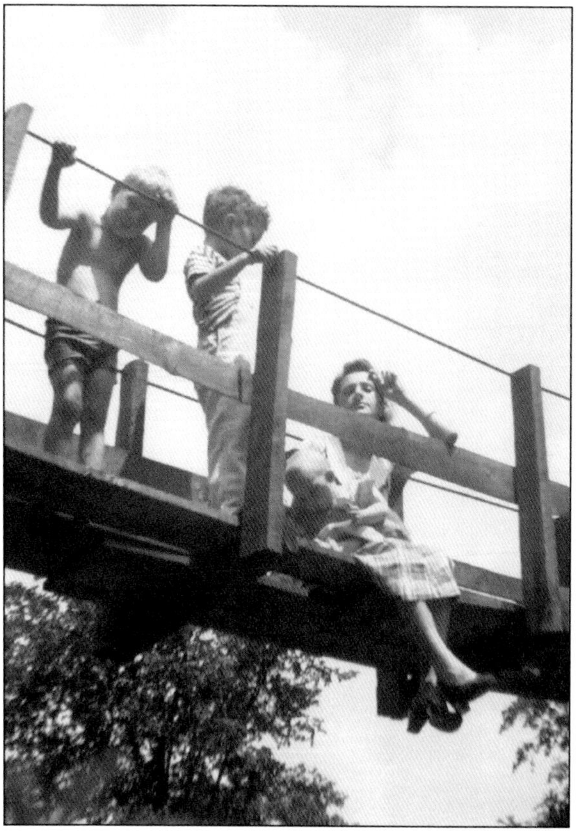

Near Red Bank, the Hoffman family enjoys the water of Buffalo Creek in 1949. Left, Gary Hoffman and an unidentified peer down from the swinging bridge while Gary's mother holds baby Eileen. Below, Gary's father, Merlyn, stands beside his 1933 Dodge while baby Eileen sits up on her blanket and Gary plays in the water. There are few swinging bridges like this in the county now, but one crosses Buffalo Creek near the base of Dale's Ridge in Kelly Township. (UCHS 95.38.1 and.4.)

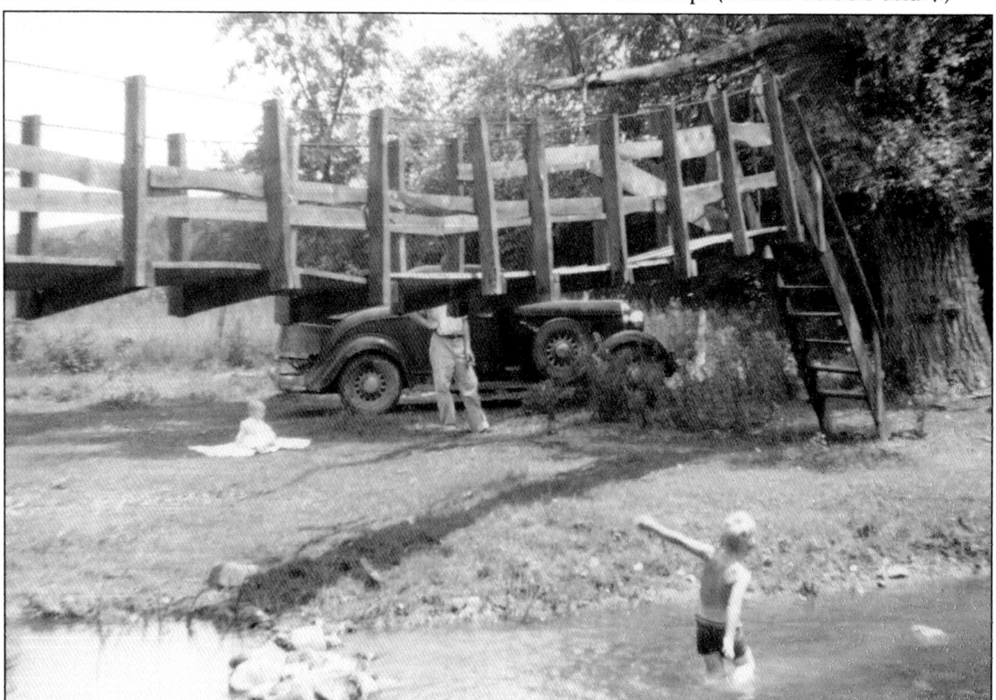

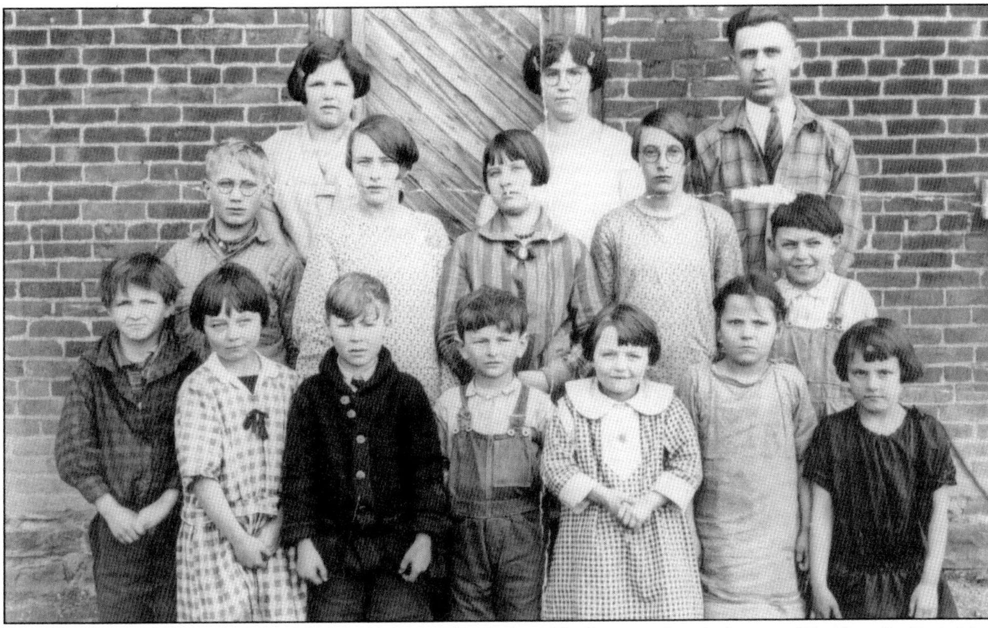

The 1884 Rand brick schoolhouse (also called Strickler) is on land donated by Jacob Strickler on Rand Road, just south of Dietrich Road. An earlier wood-plank structure was built in 1850 by neighbors. Shown in the above photograph from 1926 are, from left to right, (first row) Frederick Rathpon, Ruth Rathpon, Wilbur Kahler, Charles Neisweinder, Florence Campbell, Katherine Campbell, and Eleanor Valentine; (second row) Earl Haines, Lena Zimmerman, Ruth Shumbach, Ethel Zimmerman, and Earl Campbell; (third row) Laura Kaler, Maude Haines, and teacher Clark Mitch. The school closed in 1953. A stone marker in Rand, formerly called Hardscrabble, notes that the village had a general store/post office and that a train took sawn lumber from the local sawmill to the main rail line. The below photograph features the brick Louden School (also called Kauffman) in West Buffalo Township in 1913. It is located on the south side of Pleasant Grove Road, north of the intersection with Red Bank Road. (UCHS 94.28.1 and 2009.11.1.)

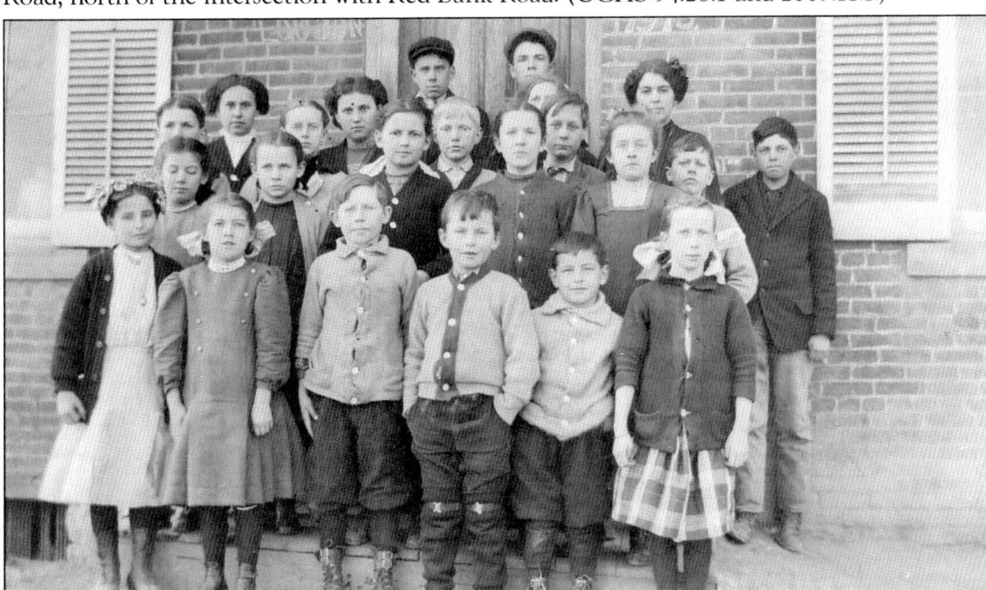

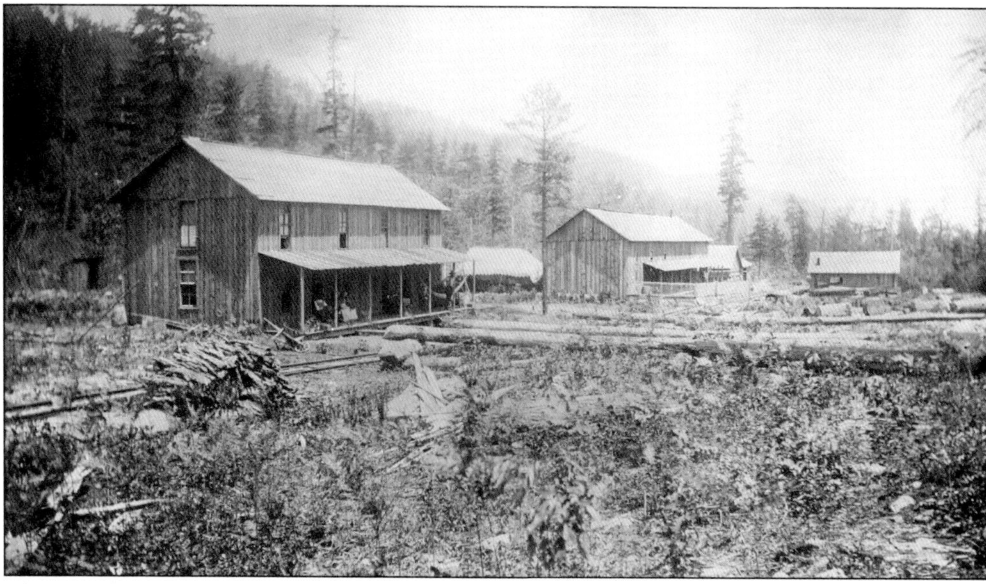

The Lewisburg & Buffalo Valley Rail Road (L&BV) was formed in 1897 and operated through mid-August 1906, when the track was torn up. The company did extensive tree-cutting for mine props and lumber in West Buffalo and Buffalo Townships, and had about 16 miles of track, some following Spruce Run in its western reaches. The wood was transported on narrow-gauge lines to Lewisburg. A sawmill was located in what became Linntown, but burned down in 1906. The L&BV operated several camps like the large one in the above photograph, with living and dining accommodations for as many as 100 men in one facility and stalls for the workhorses. Below, an excursion train pulls up to a camp. Passenger service ran up to Zimmerman's in the northwest corner of Union County, now named Sand Run Lodge. (UCHS 2010.21.180.)

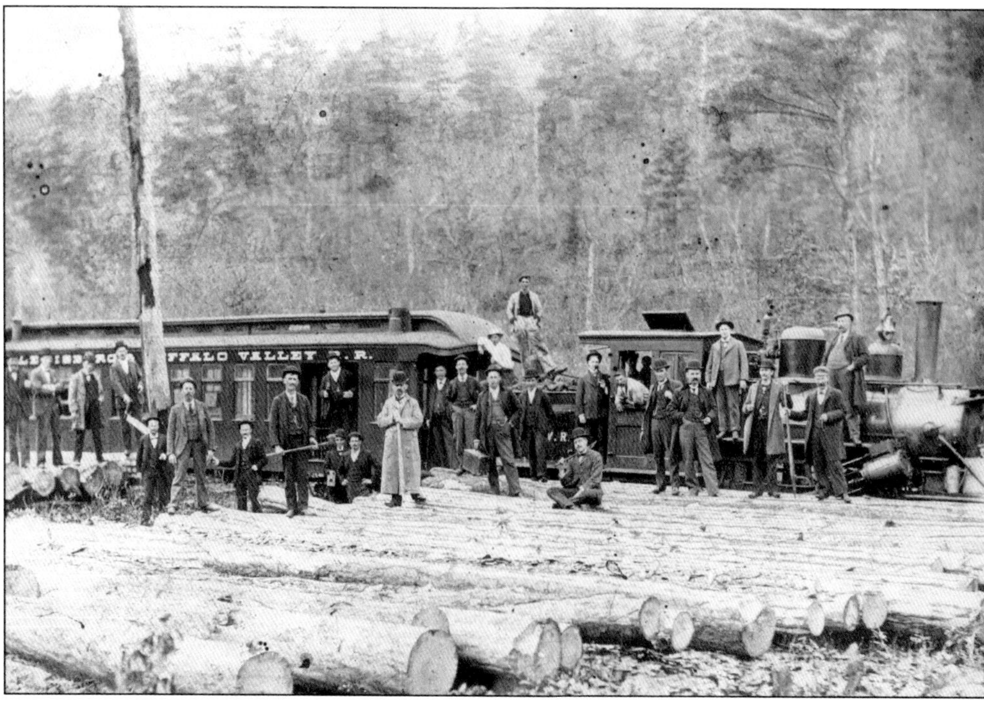

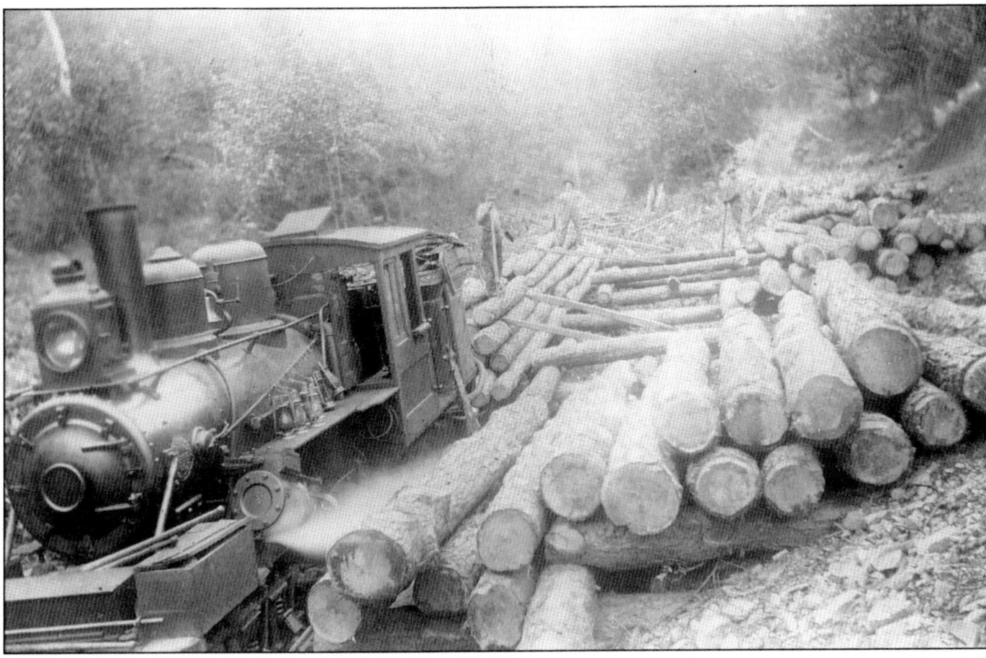

Monroe Kulp's Lewisburg & Buffalo Valley Rail Road did not use log loaders, but instead rolled the logs onto skid ways, and from the skid ways onto the train's bed, as seen above. Albert Moyer, Charles Cornelius, and William Hugton were the line's train engineers. The line was unusual in that its rail beds used rock ballast (below). Monroe Kulp had five different locomotives over time: a Shay, a Dunkirk, and three Climax engines. (UCHS 2010.21.180.)

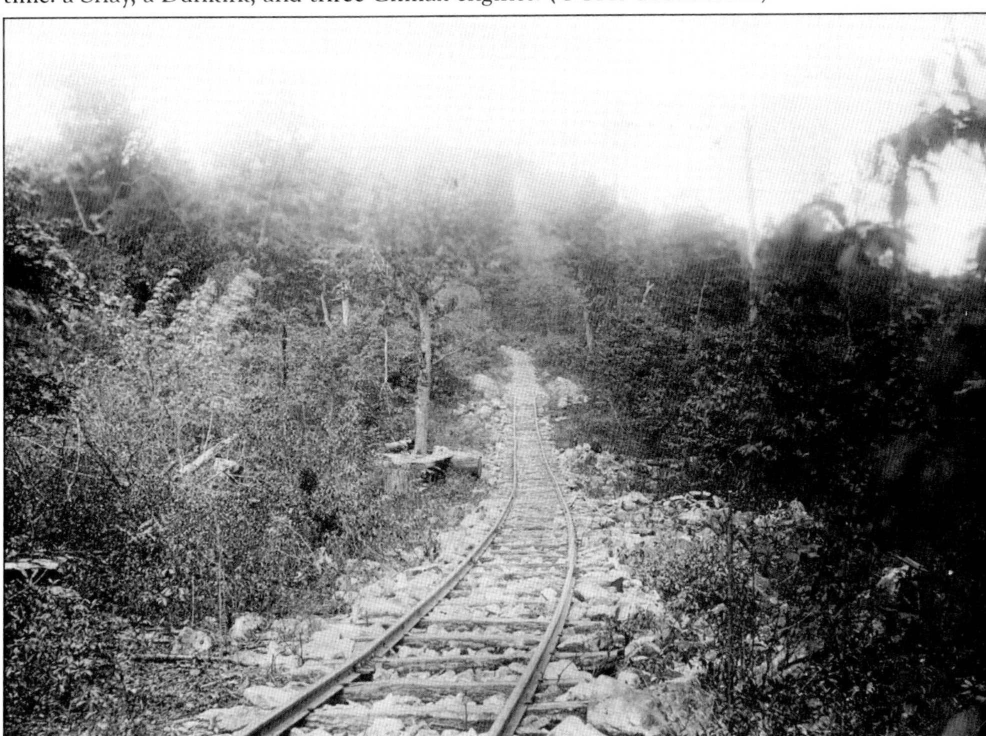

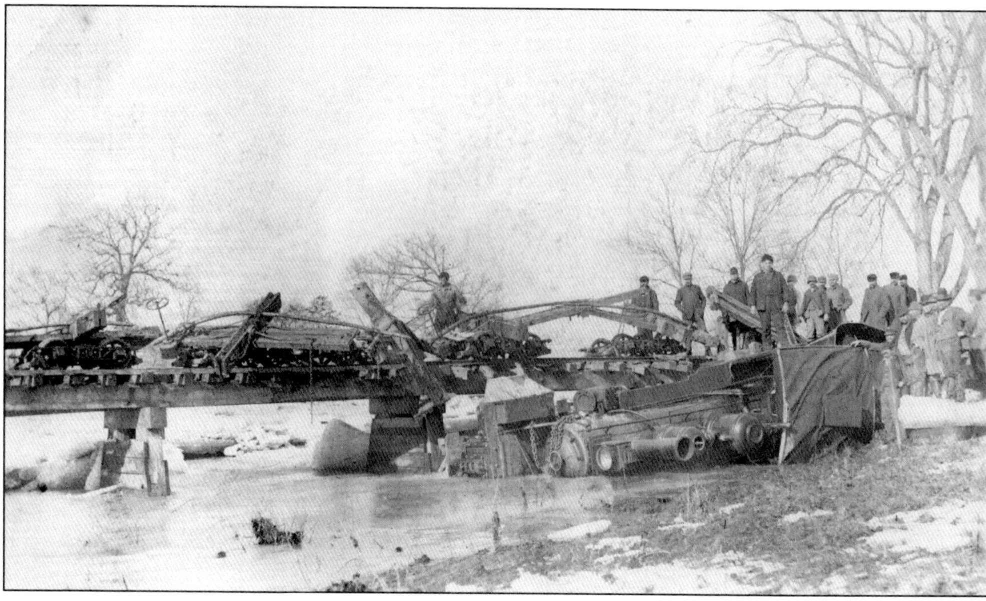

Accidents occurred on the L&BV line. Above, locomotive No. 7 and four cars derailed into Buffalo Creek near the Clingman farm in February 1899. No one was seriously injured, but it took time to right the 30-ton locomotive. In 1903, Charles and Jack Cornelius, Oscar Zimmerman, and George Dorman were in another accident west of Lewisburg when their train went out of control on wet rails for 18 miles. Choice and large diameter trees were transported from northwestern Union County sites, as was smaller prop timber, as seen in the below photograph. (UCHS 2010.21.180.)

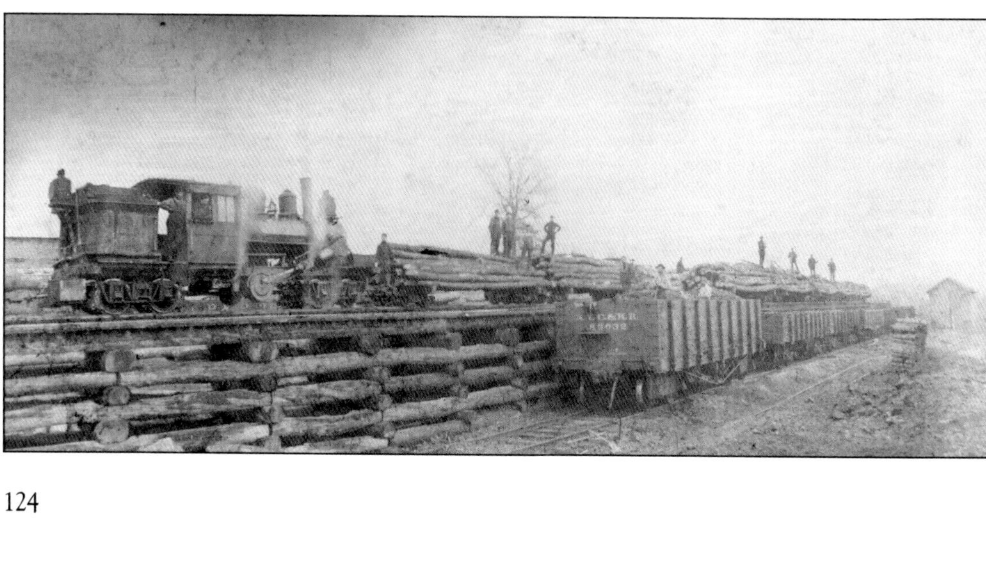

Tomorrow's New Berlin and Buffalo Valley

This region of Union County is defined by the classic town-and-country setting: thousands of forested and working farm acres provide the backdrop for the occasional rural village. It is the heart of our agricultural and small-town heritage in the county. Undeveloped land accounts for 90 percent of the county, with 60 percent of that forested and 30 percent developed for agriculture. It is true that many of the original settlements are a shadow of their vibrant past selves, bearing only memories of general stores, gristmills, shops, and schools. However, New Berlin and Buffalo, Limestone, and West Buffalo Townships have enjoyed a robust 24-percent population increase over the past two decades. This trend will continue, as projections show future population rising by nearly 70 percent to more than 15,000 residents by the year 2050.

In addition to the expected population gains, agriculture, forestry, outdoor recreation, and other resource-dependent endeavors will continue to drive the economy and dominate the landscape as they have for centuries. This trend will be complemented by an increase in cottage industries and homegrown businesses, primarily owned and operated by Plain Sect families, while some small manufacturing will remain viable. Tourism could increase due to the Buffalo Valley Rail Trail passing through Vicksburg and from the appeal of established nearby attractions such as R.B. Winter State Park and Bald Eagle State Forest. Given infrastructure limitations and location, New Berlin and the hamlets of Vicksburg, Mazeppa, White Springs, and Forest Hill will continue to serve as bedroom communities for larger employment and activity centers in the Susquehanna Valley.

Proximity to metropolitan areas will continue to attract visitors and new residents drawn by the allure of small-town Americana and rural living. How and where anticipated population growth and new development occur, and how finite land resources are allocated among more people and competing needs, is not a new concern, but perhaps will become the larger challenge. The manner in which the broader community responds will have a lasting impact on how future generations live, work, and celebrate in the Buffalo Valley and Union County for the next 200 years.

—Shawn McLaughlin
Director of Union County Planning

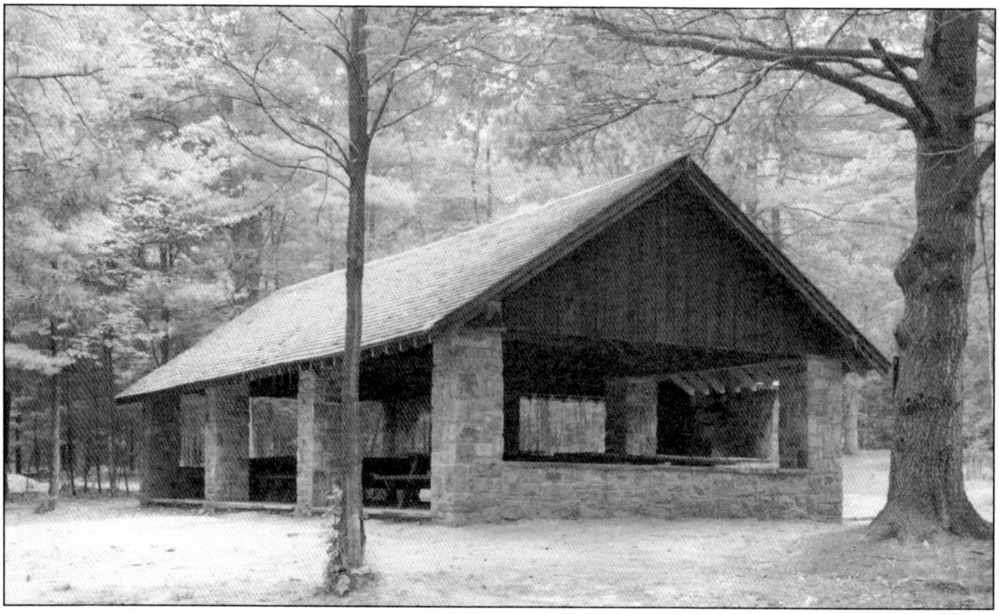

From 1933 to 1942, the Civilian Conservation Corps produced lasting recreational opportunities for generations with its extensive reforestation efforts, bridge and trail building, road maintenance, and construction of masonry structures such as the dam and pavilion (above). The water sources of the man-made lake are underground artesian springs and Half Way and Rapid Runs. Raymond B. Winter, the district forest ranger for whom the park is named, supervised a bounty of acreage bought for as little as $1 an acre. It is a favorite destination in all seasons for snow and ice sports, spring hikes, summer swimming, picnics, and camping. The Fourteen Mile Narrows extends to Livonia in Centre County at the eastern edge of Brush Valley. Another real-photo postcard (below) captures the tranquility that has attracted beachgoers, campers, and fishermen for 80 years. (UCHS 82.5.1 and 82.2.35.)

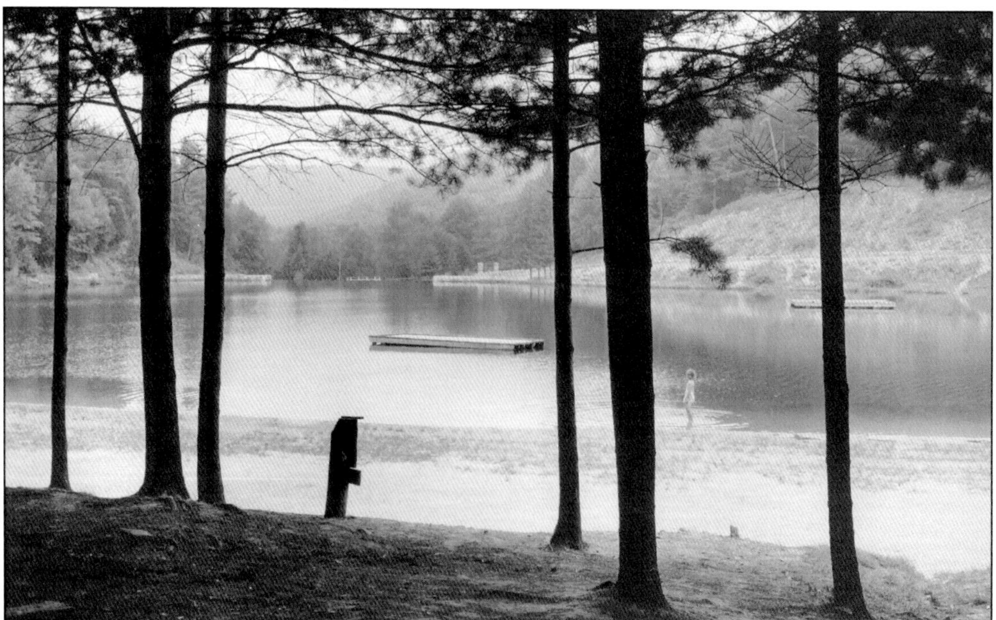

Bibliography

A *Bicentennial History: New Berlin, PA: 1792–1992*. New Berlin, PA: New Berlin Heritage Association, 1992.

Beers, D.G. *Atlas of Union & Snyder Counties, Pennsylvania*. Philadelphia: Pomeroy & Beers, 1868.

Blake, Jody and Jeannette Lasansky. *Rural Delivery: Real Photo Postcards from Central Pennsylvania: 1905–1935*. Lewisburg, PA: Oral Traditions Project of the Union County Historical Society, 1985.

Frey, S.G. "The History of Cowan," *The Lewisburg Journal* 1897, reissued as typescript. Lewisburg, PA: Union County Historical Society, circa 1990.

Horning, Alice, Adin Zimmerman, Eli Reiff, and Luke Weaver. *History of the Groffdale Mennonites in Union County*. Morgantown, PA: Masthof Press, 2004.

Lincoln, Richard Van Boskirk. *History of Union County including the Townships of Hartley, Lewis and West Buffalo and the Borough of Hartleton* (originally published in *The Mifflinburg Telegraph* 1899–1900), reprinted as Union County *Heritage*. Lewisburg, PA: Union County Historical Society, 1994.

———. *History of Union County including New Berlin and the Townships of Limestone and Buffalo* (originally published in *The Mifflinburg Telegraph* 1899–1900), reprinted as Union County *Heritage*. Lewisburg, PA: Union County Historical Society, 1996.

Linn, John Blair. *The Annals of Buffalo Valley, Pennsylvania, 1755–1855*. Harrisburg, PA: Lane S. Hart, 1877.

Lontz, Mary Belle. *History of the Schools of Union County*. Milton, PA: 1984.

Snyder, Charles M. *Union Count Pennsylvania/A Celebration of History*, Lewisburg, PA: Union County Historical Society, revised and reprinted 2000.

Consistent with our mission to preserve history on a local level, this book was printed in South Carolina on American-made paper and manufactured entirely in the United States. Products carrying the accredited Forest Stewardship Council (FSC) label are printed on 100 percent FSC-certified paper.

MADE IN THE USA